The Badgers
of Summercombe

by Ewan Clarkson

The Badgers
of Summercombe

EWAN CLARKSON

A Sunrise Book

E. P. DUTTON | NEW YORK

LIBRARY OF CONGRESS CATALOGING IN PUBLICATION DATA

Clarkson, Ewan.
  The badgers of Summercombe.

  "A Sunrise book."
  I. Title.
PZ4.C6123Bad3   [PR6053.L36]   823'.9'14   76-41219

ISBN: 0-87690-230-1

Published simultaneously in Canada by Clarke, Irwin & Company Limited, Toronto and Vancouver

10 9 8 7 6 5 4 3 2 1

First Edition

To June. For Andrew.

Contents

vii

Contents

1. The Hollow Hill

It was raining again. Tobar lay just inside the entrance of the hole beneath the tree, listening to the drip of moisture from the leafless branches, sniffing the warm, damp wind that swept in from the Atlantic Ocean, and brought with it dense gray clouds that condensed into countless shimmering droplets, to silver the turf and stain the old yellow limestone rocks. Somewhere a blackbird sang a throaty serenade to this, the false promise of spring, for although the days were lengthening, and the sun, when it shone, held a soft warmth, winter could still return, locking the land in frost, and blanketing the fields with drifting snow.

Now, as daylight faded almost imperceptibly into the gathering gloom of dusk, the blackbird settled to roost in the elder thicket, and Tobar emerged into the open, his nose still questing the air and his ears alert for any hint of impending danger. Once satisfied that all was well, he set off at a brisk trot, down through the wood and into the valley.

Five hundred years before the birth of Christ, a band of savage and warlike people had come north out of the marshlands of Somerset, carrying weapons and implements of iron, and driving before them flocks of sheep, goats, and scrawny cattle. They were looking for land, well-drained, fertile land on which they could graze their herds, grow their meager crops, and where, if necessary, they could defend themselves against attack.

They came at last to this valley, hidden in a fold of the hills. Here the slopes were gentle and sun-warmed, sheltered from the cold winds that blew from the east and north, and the floor of the valley was wide and flat, a series of ancient meadows created by the labors of generations of beaver. Above the valley towered a hill, a weather-worn outcrop of limestone rock, and here on the plateau, close by a spring, they built their fort, a sturdy structure of timber and stone, surrounded by a wall and ditch.

Below, on the wooded slopes of the hill, where the rocks lay so close to the surface that their craggy heads were exposed, was another stronghold, a labyrinth of tunnels and passages dug deep into the hollow of the hillside. This fort was old before the coming of men, so old that its origins are lost in the unwritten annals of prehistoric time.

The Iron men are gone now, and their passing was so long ago that of their existence there is now barely a trace. Sheep graze where the fortifications once stood, and flowering grasses shiver in the breeze that blows eternally across the summit of the hill. Yet in the stronghold under the earth, life remains the same, for while down through the ages mankind has repeatedly changed his lifestyle, hoping each time that the new way would prove more successful than the last, the badgers of Summercombe have kept to the old ways, the ways that have served them well, that serve them still.

The European badgers are a proud and ancient race. There were badgers in Britain before the ice age, before primitive man crossed the marshy plains that are now the North Sea. A badger watched as the Bronze men hauled the mighty stones across the plains for the building of Stonehenge. A badger hid in a thicket as the Roman legions marched west to Bath and Bristol. A badger shied away from the campfires lit by the army of the luckless Duke of Monmouth, on the eve of his futile bid for the English crown. Throughout the blood-soaked annals of English history the badger has remained, living alongside man, yet secretly, apart, and though now driven back into the last tattered remnants of wilderness, he still survives.

On this moist February evening, Tobar foraged alone, for two days previously his mate, Mela, had retired to a small secluded chamber in an isolated corner of their underground home. Here, on a bed of dried fern and shriveled oak leaves, she had given birth to her cubs, and as yet Tobar had not been permitted to share the joys of parenthood with her. This was a familiar pattern in Tobar's life, for he was old, and had seen many litters raised by his mate.

He was old, and he was lean, for the long months of winter had taken their toll, and March, the hungry month, was yet to come. He still weighed over thirty pounds, and his yard-long body, built for strength rather than speed, was in no way weakened by the ordeal of winter. His gait was strong and purposeful, yet there was a curious rhythm to the pattern of his movement, for after every few strides, there came a check, a slight pause, as he stopped momentarily to listen.

In many ways Tobar resembled his American namesake. Both species have sturdy limbs, massively armed with strong black claws, and superbly adapted for digging. Both are shy and retiring, nocturnal in habit, but stubborn and fierce when roused. They share the same breeding pattern and diet, but the European badger is more catholic in his choice of food. In consequence, his premolar teeth are flattened, and he has four fewer than the American.

The European badger is slightly larger than his cousin, and his coat is grayer and coarser. He prefers to live in wooded hillsides, rather than open plains and prairies. His most distinctive feature, however, is his face. The American badger has a small, almost doglike face, with dark blotches on each cheek, and a thin stripe of white down the center of his forehead. The European badger's head is full and rounded, with wide cheeks and a high-domed forehead, tapering to a long, narrow snout, ending in a rounded boot button of a nose. The background color of his face and head is white, but starting about an inch from the tip of his nose, and running backward over the eyes and ears, are two broad black stripes, broken only by a white tuft at the tip of each ear.

Halfway down the hillside the woodland ended abruptly, to give way to arable land, a network of small fields, each bounded by thick hedgerows planted on top of a long earth mound, and bordered by a ditch, originally designed to drain the surplus water away from the fields. Many of these ditches had now fallen into disuse, and lay choked with leaves, weeds, fallen branches, and other debris.

These ditches were a favorite hunting ground for Tobar and his kind. He shuffled slowly along, his questing snout finding an earthworm here and there, an odd acorn overlooked by the pigeons the previous autumn, and now and again, in the mound beside the ditch, the sweet bulbs of wild hyacinth, already putting forth their green shoots. These Tobar dug from the moist earth with his powerful forelegs, crunching them with noisy gusto before moving on in search of fresh delicacies.

His way across the fields led him down the length of the valley, and parallel with the wood that cloaked the hill for more than a mile, until at last he came to the sunken track that ran at right angles to his path. Ahead lay the gaunt gray dwelling known as Bidewell Farm, standing like a sentinel guarding the entrance to the valley. Away to the left the track led to a tiny cottage, nestling close to the hillside on the verge of the wood. To the right it snaked uphill, leading to the road in the valley beyond. Tobar turned right, and wandered up the hill.

The rain had ceased now, but dense clouds still overhung the hills, and the light of the moon was veiled, so that even the startling striped mask of Tobar's face was barely visible in the shadowless pit of the night. Yet his progress up the track was so noisy, as he scratched and snuffled along, that a hunting owl, perched high in the bare branches of an ash tree, watched him as he passed underneath, and deciding that there wasn't room for two night hunters on the track, flew to a haystack three fields away.

The rain that had fallen during the day still flowed in a muddy rivulet beside the track, and here Tobar found more earthworms, washed out of the bank and now drowning in the cold water. He picked out each one, for earthworms were one of his favorite foods, and when conditions were right, they formed a large part of his diet. These victims of the rain were something of a bonus, although Tobar knew from experience that they were often to be found along the track in wet weather. His main objective, however, lay some distance away, beyond the crest of the hill and across the road.

The road itself was at once an attraction and a danger to wildlife. Once it had carried little traffic other than that belonging to the local people, and was largely deserted at night. Then a new multi-laned highway was built a few miles to the north, and what had once been a quiet country lane became an access road to the highway, and traffic flowed in an almost unceasing stream for twenty-four hours a day.

Small game, such as rabbits and voles, were frequently killed by passing vehicles, and their corpses lay smeared across the tarmac, attracting the attention of scavenging magpies, rooks, and crows. Hedgehogs were also drawn to the feast, and since their reaction to danger was to curl up in a tight, prickly ball, they, too, fell victim to the automobile. Tobar himself was not averse to a little scavenging, but tonight his destination was a field that bordered the other side of the road.

The previous year the farmer had planted potatoes in this field, harvesting the crop in late autumn. Tobar had visited the field one night when the crop was half gathered, and had developed a liking for the sweet white tubers. Now, although the crop had been lifted, and the field prepared for resowing, many potatoes still remained, some lying on the surface and washed clean by the rain, and others buried a few inches deep in the soil.

Tobar hesitated a long while before he crossed the road. The roar of the traffic bewildered him, and the glare of headlights, to eyes little accustomed to anything brighter than the dim light of the woodlands, was painful in the extreme. Nevertheless, he persisted, loitering on the verge of the road and waiting for a lull in the traffic. When it came he hurried across, and within seconds he had found and eaten his first potato.

An hour passed, and at the end of it Tobar was replete. By now the volume of traffic had lessened somewhat, and Tobar slipped through the hedge at a bend in the road. A heavy truck was climbing the hill. Tobar could hear the deep roar of its engine in the distance, but as yet it seemed a long way away. He did not know, as he set off across the road, that a fast sports car was coming down the hill.

It accelerated around the bend as he reached the center of the road, seeming to leap toward him as if to pin him to the ground with the twin beams of its headlights. Instinctively he turned away from the glare, and began running down the road, straight into the path of the oncoming truck. For a brief moment the world seemed ablaze with blinding light, and filled with the thunderous clamor of the diesel engine. Then he felt a heavy blow across his back, and there was nothing but a dark, empty void. The truck driver, dazzled by the lights of the other vehicle, had not seen the badger pass between his front wheels. He felt a slight jar as his rear wheel struck something, and then forgot it as the truck roared on into the night.

Tobar regained consciousness almost immediately, and made a desperate effort to stand, to regain the sanctuary of the field. He was unable to rise. His back was broken, his hindlegs trailing and useless. Slowly he hauled himself forward by his forelegs, his claws slipping and scrabbling on the smooth tarmac. He was bleeding from a dozen internal injuries, and though he felt no pain, his strength was ebbing fast. He reached the hedge, and gasping for breath, hauled himself through, to roll into the ditch beyond.

It was his last act. At the moment of his death the clouds parted, and a single star shone down. For an instant in time it sparkled, reflected in Tobar's eye, but then the star moved in the heavens, and its light was gone. Hidden in the undergrowth, the body of Tobar began to settle back into the earth from which it came, and all was one with the night and the silent stars.

2. The Heir to Summercombe

Deep in the darkness of the hill, Mela the sow badger groomed her solitary cub. Originally she had given birth to three, but one had failed to draw breath, and another had a heart deformity, so that its awakening brain was deprived of vital oxygen. On the second night of its life it slipped into a coma from which there was no awakening. The third cub, Borun, proved to be a fat and lusty infant, and since from the beginning he was assured of a more than ample supply of nourishment, he showed promise of becoming an exceptionally robust boar.

As soon as the bodies of the other cubs had grown cold, Mela had eaten them, clearing away their remains in the same fastidious manner she had disposed of the afterbirths. It may be that she felt no grief, or sense of loss, and perhaps without their soft, squirming embrace, without the sound of their infant voices to invoke mother love, they were of no interest to her. Instead, she concentrated on the living.

Borun was about four and a half inches long when he was born, and weighed three ounces. His short fur was a dirty white, and as yet the prominent black stripes of his face were but faintly etched, in mere suggestion of a design. He was blind and toothless, and totally dependent on his mother.

About an hour before dawn, Mela left him snug in his deep bed of fern, and slipped out of the nursery. Her sojourn outside was brief. She visited first the latrine, a series of small open pits screened by elder thickets, in a part of the woodland the badgers had set aside for this purpose. Then she moved off through the wood, following a wide, well-worn track that led to where a small spring bubbled out from beneath a limestone outcrop. Here she drank deep, and then, as if in sudden fear that her cub might be in danger, she hurried back to her nest.

Time passed. She slept a little, fed Borun, and meticulously groomed him, washing his plump, wriggling body with long strokes of her smooth, pink tongue. As the hours drifted by she began to grow increasingly uneasy, for she felt sure that her mate had not returned. She should have heard his purring call of greeting as he passed by the nesting chamber on his way to his own quarters. Even if she had been asleep she would have awakened to his call, and if he had returned while she had been at the spring they would have met, for the badgers' last act before retiring was to drink. Now the day was well advanced, and she was at a loss to understand his absence. Although the nest chamber had two exits, each discreetly hidden in the undergrowth, it did not connect in any way with the main network of tunnels that were mined into the hill. Shortly before dusk fell, Mela again left the nursery.

The evening was fine, but a cold wind from the north sent ragged black clouds racing over the crest of the hill, and the upper branches of the trees sighed and groaned. Mela stood in an amphitheater of bare, trodden earth. Above her were the dark openings of her citadel. The badgers made no attempt to disguise the whereabouts of their earth, or set, as it was called. Seven holes were visible, three at the base of trees, and one led deep under a rock. The others were mere holes in the sloping ground, and while some were quite small, so that it did not seem possible that a badger could squeeze down them, others were so large that it would be quite possible for a grown man to crawl inside. At the entrance to each hole a great mound of earth bore testimony to the mining activities that had taken place inside the hill. Over the years the badgers had excavated hundreds of tons of earth and small stones, and indeed the arena in which Mela stood was paved with the yellow sandy subsoil, some of it dug out centuries ago.

Mela went straight to an entrance beneath a great oak tree, where she and Tobar had last shared quarters before the birth of her cubs. Immediately inside the entrance the tunnel turned right, passing between the oak's roots, which now moved slightly as the wind swayed the tree. She was in darkness now, but she moved with the assurance of one long familiar with the layout of the tunnel, now dipping down, now squeezing flat to pass beneath a mighty rock whose base formed the roof of the tunnel. Thus she came to the sleeping chamber, but the bedding was cold, and the scent of her mate was stale on the crushed bracken fern.

She moved on, to a point where the tunnel forked, and emerged into the open from beneath the rock. Systematically she explored the whole set. It took her a long time, and at the end of her search she remained disquieted.

Meantime she was aware of other, more urgent needs. She was both hungry and thirsty, and it was now quite dark. First, however, she went to check on her cub.

Borun was lost to the world in warm, milky slumber. Mela withdrew silently, without waking him. Outside the wind was rising still, blowing almost to a full gale, but the woods and valley were sheltered from its main force. Stray gusts of wind tugged at the tops of the tallest trees, and ruffled the hair on Mela's back as she moved out of the woods and into the fields. The wind, and the light of the moon as it shone fitfully through the scudding clouds, had a curious effect on the badger's appearance. One moment she looked dark, almost black, and then the next minute she appeared to be as white as her newborn cub.

The explanation lay in the coloring of her hair. Each long hair on her back and flanks was white at the tip, for about a third of its length. The middle third was dark brown, almost black, but the lower third, to the root, was again white. So, as the wind disarranged the even lay of her hair, she seemed to change color, and from time to time she merged so successfully with the shadows of the night that she was completely invisible.

Almost at once she was lucky in her foraging. A mole, burrowing among the grass roots in search of earthworms, came so close to the surface that it made the ground heave. Instantly Mela pounced, tearing at the turf to expose the tunnel and thrusting her long snout into the cold, damp earth. Next moment the luckless mole was seized from behind and dragged out into the open.

Mela devoured her victim completely, skin, fur, and bones, even the tough, spadelike forefeet. Then she moved on, not daring to linger lest she should leave her cub unprotected for too long, although there was little danger from other predators. Stoats and weasels had too much respect for the size and strength of their cousin the badger, and even a fox was unlikely to venture into the set as long as her scent was fresh around the entrance. The chief danger to Borun was that of chilling, for he was not yet old enough or active enough to keep himself warm.

She snatched a few mouthfuls of grass, and behind the bark of a rotting tree stump she discovered a small colony of hibernating snails. Then she dug a quantity of wild hyacinth bulbs from the hedge bank. In doing so she found several earthworms and the fat white grub of a cockchafer beetle. Her hunger satisfied, she hurried back to the set. The cloud had thickened, and flurries of snow were beginning to fall.

Borun woke as she entered the nest chamber and burrowed blindly to her side, thrusting his nose at her flank and kneading her with eager paws. Relaxing, she let him feed, and fell into a half doze, while outside the snow continued to fall, drifting in the strong northerly wind.

It snowed all night, and for most of the following day, but by nightfall the blizzard had passed. The wind died, and the moon shone over a white and silent world. Mela emerged briefly, but finding she was still alone, returned to the warmth and shelter of the nursery. At times like these there was nothing to do but sleep, and conserve energy. Like all her kind she had an infinite capacity for slumber, and although the reserves of fat she had accumulated the previous autumn were now dwindling, she could readily draw upon them for a few days without suffering any inconvenience. A few mouthfuls of snow, snatched up on one of her infrequent visits to the latrine, were sufficient to quench her thirst.

For three days and nights the frost held. In the bright moonlight the rabbits emerged from their burrows, to flounder through the snow and gnaw the bark of young hazel shoots. Some died, caught in the jaws of the lean red foxes that lay in ambush among the snowdrifts.

Beneath the snow, through a maze of tunnels and passageways that formed an intricate network between the stems and roots of the rough herbage, weasels harried the mice and voles, while the white owl floated in vain over the fields, and was eventually forced to compete with the farmyard cats around the rickyards, where the rats and mice robbed the farmer of his grain.

Then the wind rose again, this time from the south, blowing wet and warm and bringing rain to wash the snow away. The thaw brought relief to the disconsolate flocks of fieldfares and lapwings, but for two days life was a torment of shivering, sodden misery to the small creatures of the grasslands, who woke to find their homes and highways flooded with icy water. Then the sun shone, the blackbird sang his territorial song for all concerned to hear, and the tide of spring flowed once more.

Each year the pattern was the same, for the land lay on the western border of a huge continental land mass. High pressure over the continent brought fine weather and clear skies to Britain, hot in summer, cold in winter, but these high-pressure systems were continually in conflict with depressions and troughs of low pressure from out in the Atlantic, and the tide of victory ebbed and flowed. So, as the earth tilted on its axis, and the hours of daylight slowly lengthened, each living thing, moss and fern and grass and gnarled old oak, waited its time, and when the temperature rose sufficiently high, responded in growth. Each time the temperature dropped, growth ceased, but the advance of spring, though slow and hesitant, was sure, until at last it swelled forward on a running tide that could not be stemmed.

Snug in the confines of the set, Borun continued to thrive. His eyes opened on the eleventh day, and at a month old he was exploring the confines of the nursery. His mother left him on most evenings, but never for long periods, and usually while he slept. As he grew older and stronger he spent hours playing and wrestling with her, tugging and pulling at her hair and trying to nip her with his baby teeth. Mela bore the torment with good humor, seeming to realize instinctively that the exercise was vital for his development and growth.

He got his first glimpse of the outside world on a fine warm evening in the middle of April. For some days he had shown signs of restlessness, of an eagerness to explore, and on several occasions he had left the nursery and crept hesitantly along the tunnel to the point where it forked. Each time his nerve had then failed him, and he had scuttled back to the safety of the nest. On this night his mother left him as usual, only to return after about ten minutes and nose him gently out of the chamber and along the tunnel. So he emerged, to sniff the sweet-scented air of spring and to sit trembling with mingled fear and excitement, secure between the stout forelegs of his mother.

Mela was equally nervous and apprehensive, and after about ten minutes she drove him underground, but the next night he stayed out longer, and made several short exploratory dashes around the mouth of the set, returning panting to his mother's side. Each night he grew a little bolder, a little more venturesome, while she stayed at the mouth of the set, growling a warning only if in her opinion he strayed too far.

She seemed to have wholly forgotten about her mate, and indeed she had long since ceased to look for him, but from time to time half-forgotten memories of him returned, and she found herself waiting to hear the pad of his feet on the path or the purring call of his greeting at the mouth of the set.

Once, as she was crossing the dew-drenched valley in the gray light of an April dawn, she heard the distinctive pad of feet that heralded the approach of another badger, and she stopped still, waiting as he came into view from behind a hawthorn thicket. She whickered a call of greeting, for she was sure that it was Tobar. Then she realized her error. The badger was a stranger, and he stood aloof, disinterested, respecting her sex and her right to be present, but offering no friendship. After a moment she moved on, and the young boar, a bachelor, returned to his own set, which he had dug in an old rabbit warren on the other side of the valley to the wood.

3. Woodland Childhood

In the weeks that followed, as spring matured into full-leafed summer, Borun grew in strength, stature, and wisdom. Each evening as the sun set and the last light of day lingered beneath the trees, he emerged from the stuffy confines of the set, a small, snub-nosed replica of his mother, to breathe air fragrant with the perfume of green growth. The sharp smell of moss, the spicy aroma of sun-warmed earth, the pungency of crushed fern, blended with a thousand other scents, stimulated and intoxicated him, and the pent-up energy within him exploded in a wild capering romp, a headlong gallop around the arena, up and down the worn paths, in and out of the bushes, until at last he collapsed at his mother's side.

During this outburst Mela was content to relax, to scratch

and groom herself, and enjoy the luxury of lying stretched out, limbs asprawl, in the cool evening air. Then, when the first wave of exuberance had passed, and Borun had sobered down a little, the serious business of his education could begin.

She led him along the ancient badger highways that criss-crossed the wooded hillside, taught him to use the latrine, and showed him the spring that bubbled out from beneath the limestone outcrop. He learned how to dig for wild hyacinth bulbs, and how to locate the fat white cockchafer grubs that lay hidden among the grass roots. She encouraged him to rip the bark from rotten tree stumps in search of beetles and woodlice, and showed him where the bank voles built their nests.

Each night he learned something new: how to de-slime a slug by rolling it on the ground with his forepaws, and how to catch earthworms as they lay outstretched on the short, sheep-bitten turf of the pastures, stalking them as they glinted in the starlight and snapping them up before they had time to withdraw into their burrows. Best of all, she taught him how to find young rabbits.

Rabbits swarmed everywhere in the valley, honeycombing the banks and hedgerows with their burrows, and robbing the farmer of his grass. Some years previously they had been virtually wiped out by a virus disease called myxomatosis, artificially introduced into Britain from the continent, but a few individuals remained immune, and from these survivors the rabbits began once again to populate the land. Since in favorable conditions rabbit does could produce a litter of five or six young every month from January to June, their numbers were soon restored. Five rabbits together consumed as much grass as one sheep, so they were not popular with the farmers on whose land they lived.

Before the arrival of her litter, each doe rabbit dug a short, blind burrow on the edge of the warren, scooping out a nest chamber at the end of the tunnel and lining it with fur plucked from her own breast. Here she could raise her young in secrecy, and if she left the burrow for any reason, she would block the entrance against the danger of a marauding weasel or stoat.

Many of these nest chambers lay close to the surface of the soil. Mela taught Borun to listen for the muffled squeaking of the young, and to sniff out the strong scent that rose up through the turf. Whenever they located such a nest, Mela dug down, tearing away the turf with her powerful claws, and scratching away the soil until she broke through into the nest chamber. Then, as the terrified mother fled, the helpless infants were snatched from the warmth of their nest and devoured on the spot. Borun always grew intensely excited on these rabbiting expeditions, so keenly did he appreciate the flavor of milk-fed rabbit, and tried hard to help with the digging. He was as yet more of a hindrance than a help, but his small forearms grew stronger as the weeks passed.

The badgers were true opportunity feeders, ready to sample anything that came within reach of their questing snouts. From time to time they came upon birds' nests containing eggs or young, and these they ate, as they did the fledglings that were unlucky enough to fall from the nest. They also ate snakes and frogs when they were to be found, and this caused Borun to make a tactical error, when one night he caught a toad between his jaws. The secretions from the toad's warty skin burned his gums and tongue, and caused him to shake his head in anger and irritation. The toad crawled safely away, and thereafter Borun was careful to avoid them.

On another occasion Borun made a more serious mistake, when he happened on a nest of leverets. Hares were scarce in the valley, and Borun did not know that while a mother rabbit might flee in terror, an angry mother hare was made of sterner stuff. As Borun ran at the leverets, he was knocked sideways by a resounding blow across the ear. Even as he tried to recover he was kicked again and again, and if his mother had not come to his rescue by distracting the hare and drawing her attention away from him, he might have suffered serious injury. Much chastened, he fled, and the hare abandoned her wild, leaping attack and returned to her young.

By preying on the rabbit population, and by cleansing the fields of the voracious cockchafer grubs that ate the grass roots and sometimes swarmed in such numbers that they threatened to destroy the pastures, the badgers were unwittingly helping the farmers whose fields they roamed. Yet because they went about their affairs in secret, and at night, their efforts went largely unnoticed. More evident was the occasional damage they inflicted, as when they wrecked a hedge bank in pursuit of rabbits, and so allowed stock to stray into adjacent fields.

Equally tactless was their habit of flattening growing cereal crops. Both Mela and Borun savored the sweet milky grains of young wheat and oats, and Borun could never resist romping and rolling through the stalks. His high spirits sometimes infected Mela, so that she played with him, and between them, in a very short space of time, they could flatten quite a large area. The loss to the farmer was not serious, but it was irritating, and gave the badgers a bad name, one that was not wholly justified.

For much of the time, however, the badgers limited their foraging to the wood. From a distance the wood looked like a cloak, flung carelessly asprawl the shoulder of the hill, extending for about a mile, and in places it was perhaps a quarter mile deep, a tiny fragment of the vast deciduous forests that had spread across southern England following the retreat of the last ice age.

It had survived for two reasons—the slopes of the hill were too precipitous and rock strewn to make it worth while attempting to clear the land for pasture, and until comparatively recent times, woodland was an important asset to any estate. Wood was needed for a multitude of purposes, from faggots for kitchen stoves to charcoal for blast furnaces, from floorboards to rafters for house and barn. Timber was needed for farm wagons and fence stakes, doors and window frames, handles for tools, chairs, tables, and beds. The newborn child was laid in a cradle of carved wood, and the old made their last journey to the grave in a rough-hewn coffin of oak or elm.

For many centuries most of this wood had to be found on or near the estate, so that although the woodland had survived the attentions of man, it had not escaped unharmed, and the marks of his handling were still to be traced.

At one time the woods had been as carefully managed as any other growing crop. Certain species of tree, such as oak and ash, were highly prized for their straight-grained, strong timber and good burning properties. Groves of hazelwood were cropped in the winter, and the smooth, straight rods were split and made into hurdles, portable sections of fencing to give shelter to the sheep at lambing time. Dead or decayed wood was cleared away, and scrub cut down to give light and air to the more valuable trees. In the autumn herds of pigs were allowed to graze through the woodlands, to grow fat on the acorns that fell from the oaks, and to fertilize the ground with their droppings.

Then came a period of abuse, with whole stands of trees cropped and sold as a commercial enterprise, until finally the woods were allowed to fall into disuse and neglect. Yet centuries would have to pass before the woods could return to their natural state. The hazel trees grew all awry, planted so close together that in competing for light they outgrew their root systems and fell, one against the other. From the boles of felled ash trees new growth pushed forth, so that throughout the woodland each massive base supported five, six, or seven tall trunks, each thicker than a man, and towering like gray-green spires to the sky.

Beneath the trees lay a jungle of twisted bramble and briar, from which sprang the climbing tendrils of honeysuckle and ivy, reaching out to the trees for support in their upward quest for light. Below the badger sets, in the soil spilled out over centuries of excavation, thickets of elder and nettle flourished so thickly as to inhibit any other form of growth.

The rich, moist leafmold of the woodland floor supported a host of flowering plants. First to flower were the tiny wood anemones, spilled like drops of congealed moonlight around the trunks of the trees. Then came the violets, in massed banks of purple, flanked by the green of their leaves. Primroses shone like pale yellow stars.

In May, as the cuckoo called and the swifts flew screaming over the meadows, the sunlit glades glowed with the blue haze of the wild hyacinths, their bell-shaped blossoms giving off a perfume so strong as to mask all others. In high summer the tangle of growth, of bracken fern and briar, was so tall that only the rosebay willow herb could tower above it, but the woods were sweet with the scent of the climbing honeysuckle and dog rose.

Unwanted and ignored by man, the woodland was in effect a focal point for the absorption of inspired energy. The damp leafmold, the yeasts and bacteria and fungi, the flowers and plants, the bees, wasps, and other insects, the mice and voles, the squirrels and birds and bats, all were so conjoined and interwoven as to become as one, and in the warm, heady stillness of a summer night this energy could be felt, as a soft, low vibration that was the pulse of the living earth.

The badgers were part of the pattern of woodland life, and while it might be said that the woodland was their domain, they were stewards rather than landlords, servants rather than masters. They were suffered, and their survival was guaranteed, only for so long as their energies were concentrated on creation rather than destruction.

If at times it seemed that the badgers were dedicated to a

lifetime of demolition, as when they wrecked a rotting tree stump in search of grubs or beetles, when they dug up wild hyacinths before they had a chance to flower, or when they tore open a vole's nest, spilling out the naked young and munching them up like soft-centered candies, then this was illusion. Such behavior, wanton and wasteful though it might appear, aided and assisted in the recycling of the elements of life, so that life, in all its myriad forms and bewildering complexity, could be reborn, fresh and new, over and over again.

By the middle of June, when Borun was four months old, he knew every inch of the woodlands, and had met all his neighbors, including the old dog fox that slept all day on a redolent bed of fern in a hollow ash stump at the top of the wood. If the wind was in the right direction Borun could smell the soft-footed old hermit coming long before he heard him. The badgers always gave him a wide berth, not because they were afraid of him but because, through no fault of his own, he offended their fastidious senses.

Occasionally the badgers ventured right across the wood, to where a small cottage stood at the end of a rutted track, in a small walled clearing amid the trees. Mela always seemed unduly nervous as they approached the clearing, and when Borun wanted to explore closer she drove him back. Many years ago Mela had been chased from the cottage by a pack of terrier dogs, and though the cottage had now changed hands, and the terriers long since departed, she had not forgotten the terror of that flight through the darkened wood.

The new owner of the cottage did have a pet though, and Borun met him on a hot windless night toward the end of June, as he padded quietly past the dwelling. The meeting was sudden. Borun rounded a bend in the path, and there, not a yard away, its back toward him, sat a half-grown, pure white tomcat. It was crouched, ready to spring on something about to emerge from the undergrowth, and for a moment the cat was unaware of the badger's approach. Then he turned, arched his back, and spat, and when Borun, in the short-sighted manner of his kind, took a couple of paces forward, the cat sprang into a tree and glared down at him. Borun was intrigued and puzzled, and would have liked to linger, but within seconds his mother was behind him, nervous as ever, and hustling him down the path. Borun cast a lingering look back, and the cat, which had settled itself comfortably on a branch, paws folded beneath it, yawned, and blinked compla-cently.

Mela led Borun out of the wood and down the hill, cross-ing several fields until they came to a narrow sunken track that ran the length of the valley, and gave access to the pas-tures that lay on either side. High banks, clothed with rank herbage, bordered the track, and Borun forgot the cat as he foraged for the fat black beetles that lumbered awkwardly among the plant stems.

A rattle of stones startled him, and he turned to see his mother attacking the top of the earth bank. She was clearly in a high state of excitement. The coarse hair on her back stood out at right angles, making her appear twice as large as nor-mal, and as she dug she gave vent to a series of high-pitched grunts and squeals. A small flock of sheep stood bunched together at the far end of the field, watching, half fearful, half curious, as she sent showers of earth and large stones thudding down onto the track. Borun clambered up to join her, but she ignored him, and since he could see nothing that could justify the expenditure of such energy he grew bored, and wandered away.

The bank had been built almost a century ago, of stones loosely piled together, packed with soil, and thatched with turf. Thus secured, it had withstood the ravages of wind and rain for season after season, but it could not long withstand a determined assault by a badger. When Borun returned the bank was down, the lane partly blocked by rocks and soil, and Mela had uncovered her prize.

It was a large ball made from some papery, brown substance, and several black and yellow insects buzzed around it in sleepy, stupefied fashion. Mela broke open the ball, to reveal row after row of fat white grubs, and once Borun had tasted them, he understood why Mela had gone to so much trouble to unearth them, for to a badger there is no greater delicacy on earth than a wasps' nest.

The badgers finished their feast, and after lingering awhile to root about among the scattered fragments of the nest for any grub that might have been overlooked, they moved off into the night. An hour later the sheep, led by an old ewe, filed out of the field through the gap dug by Mela, and made off down the lane.

4. The Runaways

For Mr. Fletcher, of Bidewell Farm, the day started as on
any other morning. Quite unaware that he had suffered any
loss, he went about his routine tasks, milking his small herd
of Friesian cows, tending to his pigs, and feeding the suckler
calves that bawled their impatience from the old stable he had
converted into a rearing pen. So it was not until after breakfast that he took his stick and walked up the lane that led to
the valley.

Two miles away in the opposite direction, old Miss Ponsonby paused in the act of dressing to glance out her bedroom
window. What she saw caused her to utter a shriek of dismay
and hurry downstairs to the kitchen. Seizing a broom, she
charged out the back door and into the vegetable garden,

24

where a small flock of sheep were browsing contentedly on her lettuces. She was an agile and energetic old lady, and the sheep, panicking under the fury of her onslaught, scurried bleating out onto the road. Miss Ponsonby firmly latched the gate, and then, since she was not yet properly attired to appear in public, she hastened back indoors. She had just gained the sanctuary of her kitchen when she heard the high-pitched hornet whine of young Tommy Thornbeare's motorbike coming down the lane, and she heaved a sigh of relief that he had not arrived on the scene a few seconds earlier.

Tommy Thornbeare's great love in life was his shiny new Japanese two-stroke. He had twice failed to pass his driving test, but he was convinced that his lack of success was due to prejudice on the part of the examiners, and was in no way a reflection of his driving skill, which he rated high. Now, as he flung the machine into a bend, he saw himself crouched low over the handlebars, leading the field in some motorcycle Grand Prix. The next instant he found himself floundering in a sea of wool.

The sheep were all over the road, galloping at breakneck speed, but Tommy was going faster. Miraculously, he passed through the flock without causing a single casualty, although all the while he was skidding and lurching and fighting for control of his machine. There remained one old ewe out in front, and it seemed to Tommy that his front wheel was drawn to her like a magnet. The wheel butted her none too gently from behind, and with an indignant bleat, the ewe darted off at a tangent. Tommy went straight on, over the handlebars of his bike, and through the hedge, where he lay paralyzed with shock and fright, as the bleating of the sheep faded in the distance.

At first Tommy was convinced that every bone in his body was broken, so he was surprised, and even a little disappointed, to discover that he was in fact unhurt. Nor was his machine damaged, but his bright red crash helmet was scratched, and his yellow plastic jacket was torn beyond repair. Thoroughly out of humor, he remounted his machine and rode off, this time at a more sedate pace, determined to find the owner of the sheep and sue him for damages.

The owner was at that moment staring with horror at the empty field where his sheep should be. The flock which was missing was a very special one, one which he had recently spent a great deal of money to acquire. They belonged to an ancient breed known as the Ryeland, very hardy and resistant to disease, producing high-quality meat and yielding heavy fleeces of soft fine wool. With them he hoped not only to make a handsome profit, but to gain prestige by exhibiting them at the various agricultural shows. Now he had lost them.

At first he thought he had been the victim of sheep rustlers, for a gang had been known to operate in the district, but then he found the gap in the hedge. For a moment or two his feeling was one of relief, that the sheep were not stolen, but strayed, but then he found the remains of the wasps' nest, and his anger grew as he recognized the identity of the culprit. Hurrying back to the farm, he flung open the door. "The Ryelands have gone," he shouted.

Mrs. Fletcher appeared from the kitchen, drying her hands on her apron. "Gone? What do you mean, gone?" she queried.

"Strayed, of course. Broken out of the field and gone. Heaven knows where they are now, or how I'll get them back again."

Mrs. Fletcher sniffed. She had never entirely approved of her husband's lifelong obsession with sheep. They brought more plague than profit, in her opinion, and buying this latest lot of Ryeland ewes had seemed to her an act of extreme folly. "You want to spend more time with your fences if you want to keep fancy sheep," she remarked tartly. "I've said before that they are a disgrace to the farm."

Fletcher's eyes bulged and his neck reddened. He was a

big blond man with shambling limbs and powerful, work-worn hands, normally placid and easygoing, but at times like this rage made him inarticulate. He found his tongue at last. "It was a badger, you stupid woman. A badger dug out a wasps' nest and broke down the bank. I'll have him directly. In fact, if anything has happened to those ewes I'll kill every badger in the county."

Mrs. Fletcher was in no way cowed by his anger. "Perhaps you'd be better employed looking for your sheep, than standing there bellowing," she remarked. "Take the dog and be off. I've got my own work to do."

Still grumbling, Fletcher turned on his heel, but at that moment the telephone rang. Mrs. Fletcher picked up the receiver, and then called to her husband. "It's for you. Seems Mrs. Applecross has found your sheep."

In two strides Fletcher was at the telephone. "Where are they?" he snapped.

"Why, in Major Fuller's orchard," replied Mrs. Applecross. "I was just looking out across the valley . . ."

She was left talking to herself. Fletcher was racing for his Land Rover, and shouting instructions to Mrs. Fletcher to call Major Fuller and ask him to hold the sheep. As he drove away he was wishing that his flock had chosen somewhere else to stray. Major Fuller was a magistrate, and a stickler for law and order. He was also of uncertain temperament, and he was quite likely to impound the sheep until Fletcher could prove ownership, and then charge him for their keep.

He need not have worried. Major Fuller, less red in the face and peppery than usual, met him at the gate. "Sorry, Fletcher," he barked. "Lost 'em. My dog drove them off just before your wife phoned. They'll be right down in the village by now."

Fletcher groaned and crashed the Land Rover into gear. The day was not working out at all well. He finally ran his sheep to ground in the churchyard, where they were grazing placidly among the tombstones, and stubbornly resisting the somewhat half-hearted efforts of the verger to drive them out. The flock was by now thoroughly unsettled, and reluctant to move in the heat of the day, so Fletcher had to abandon his Land Rover and walk in front of the flock, all the way back to the farm, while his dog brought them on from behind. On the way he had a painful interview with Miss Ponsonby, who had been lying in wait for him, and then he met the village constable, who told him with some relish about the adventures of young Tommy Thornbeare.

It was a depressed and weary man who finally penned his sheep securely in a field close by the farmhouse. Although, legally, he could not be held responsible for the damage caused by his straying flock, he still had to live with his neighbors, and he had managed to upset quite a few. Somehow he would have to make amends. At the back of his mind, too, was the fear that while they were free the sheep might well have eaten something that would upset them. He reflected grimly that if they had eaten as much fresh greenstuff as Miss Ponsonby had claimed, they would all be down with colic by now.

Meanwhile, he still had to collect his Land Rover from where he had abandoned it, and there was work on the farm which could not be left for the morrow.

It took him the greater part of the following day to repair the damage done by Mela to the earth bank. After a day of hard labor and smoldering resentment under the hot sun, he took a walk round his fields, noting several places where the badgers had pushed through the hedge and slid down the earth bank. His Ryeland ewes were secure in their field, and seemed to have suffered no ill effects from their outing. All the same, a long hot summer lay ahead, and there were bound to be many more wasps' nests in the banks. Fletcher felt he could not risk further disaster. The next day was market day, and he took time to visit the ironmongers in the town.

5. Fletcher's Revenge

The weather continued hot and dry, with little or no dew at night. Instead, a warm breeze drifted over the land, keeping the night air warm, so that the moisture that had transpired from the earth during the day was carried high into the sky, instead of condensing on the ground. The pastures were arid and brown, and the earthworms lay deep in their burrows, each tightly coiled in a ball to conserve moisture.

Borun and Mela now emerged from the set in full daylight, to forage through the leafy stillness of the wood. All bird song had now ceased, save for the monotonous call of the wood pigeons and the occasional raucous scream of a jay. In spite of the drought, and the hard-baked earth, that made digging a laborious and often futile task, the badgers continued to feed well. Nests of young rabbits were still plentiful, and formed a major part of the badgers' diet at this time. In addition, there were cockchafers, fat brown beetles that droned through the air in clumsy, laborious flight, and pitched on the ground with an audible thump that never failed to attract the badgers' attention. The cockchafers laid their eggs in pasture, where the larvae remained for three years, eating the grass roots. From time to time the cockchafers occurred in such numbers as to destroy whole fields, but the badgers helped to keep them in check, eating adults and larvae with equal gusto.

Always there were mice and voles. Left to themselves, the voles alone would destroy the world. Although each weighed less than an ounce, a vole could eat its own weight in dry matter in ten days, and there could be as many as five hundred voles to the acre in neglected grassland. Such a heavy population, if it remained constant, would eat the equivalent of half a ton of hay in a year, but if the population was allowed to grow unchecked it would multiply tenfold in six months, and long before the end of the year would have consumed more than ten tons of vegetable matter, more than the most fertile acre could produce.

It was now high summer, and the vole population was at its peak. Every female was pregnant, and each was raising a litter of five or six young. In three weeks' time she would have weaned that litter, and be giving birth again, while the survivors of her first brood, if any, would be fast approaching maturity. Fortunately, few voles lived longer than six months, and not one in a thousand survived for more than a year.

The remainder got eaten, devoured by foxes, cats, stoats, weasels, hawks, crows, owls, herons, and jays. Grass snakes and adders took them from their nests, birds harried them by day and night, and even the fat old toad took an occasional infant if it ventured too close. It was as though some supreme intelligence had taken the cellulose and undigestible carbohydrate of the field and processed it through some vast factory, turning out the vole as a prepackaged survival ration, not too big or too small, containing all the essential ingredients, blood, bone, fur, and meat, in an easily available form. The very name vole is Old English for field, and this was what the voles were, a living, moving, hot-blooded field on which the predators could graze. As a final touch of genius, it was ordained that the supply would be available for twenty-four hours a day, for the vole divided each day into two-hour periods of activity, with short rests in between.

With such a surfeit of food, Borun developed rapidly. He was now almost half grown, and quite able to forage for himself, but badgers are sociable animals, and Borun still felt the need for companionship and security. So mother and son continued to keep each other company on the nightly forage, returning together to the set in the cool milky light of the dawn.

Gradually, however, a change was coming over Mela. She felt irritable and frustrated, frequently impatient of Borun and intolerant of his demands to share whatever food she found. Quarrels were frequent, and on occasions Borun got sharply nipped for importuning too persistently.

Mela did not understand what was happening to her. She could not know that the radiation of the sun, the moon, and the stars, the tilting of the earth on its axis, its position in the planetary system, all were conspiring with the chemistry of her glands to send hormones coursing through her system. Mela, in short, needed a mate, for now was the honeymoon season of the badgers. Normally Tobar would have been around, but he had never returned, and the young boar across the valley had taken a mate of his own.

The fine spell ended at last, with low cloud obscuring the moon and a thin drizzle soaking gently into the dry earth. The earthworms, sensing the presence of moisture, climbed up their burrows to emerge into the night, and Borun and Mela fed well, for once without quarreling over the spoils.

Maybe it was her pleasure over the feast of earthworms, or maybe it was the pent-up desires still smoldering within her that made Mela careless. She ran down the hill, pushed through a gap in the hedge, and started to slide down the bank. Next moment she was held tight, by the constricting wire of a snare, set none too expertly by Fletcher a week ago, gripping her tightly around the waist. She hung head down, screaming with rage and pain, while Borun whimpered anxiously behind her.

The noose had been set too wide, or it would have caught her around the neck, strangling her as she fell. As it was, she was still alive, but trapped. She managed to claw herself around, and pull herself back onto the hedge bank, where she began to bite and tug at the roots and branches around her. She dug and fought and tore until her pads were broken and her claws torn, her gums bleeding and raw, but to no avail. The farmer had fastened the snare to the root of a gnarled old hawthorn, thicker than a man's arm, and so tough and strong that it would have held a bear.

Toward dawn she ceased to struggle, and lay exhausted, her coat matted with mud and sticky earth, mixed with blood and saliva. Borun had tried to help even to the point of trying to bite through the wire, but it had been twisted from many fine strands, and foiled every attempt to cut it. Now as he approached her she screamed and snapped at him, half mad with fear, and so at last he went and crouched down some distance away, afraid of her in her rage. Still he lingered, long into the gray daylight, while Mela lay amid the wreckage of the hedge, demolished in her struggles.

Footsteps, and a man's cough, alerted Borun. They drew nearer. His frayed nerves failed him, and he bolted. As he reached the sanctuary of the woods he was deafened by the blast of a shotgun.

Borun remained in the set throughout the day, and for most of the following night, emerging just before dawn and creeping fearfully, almost unwillingly, to the site where he had left his mother the morning before. The bank had been repaired, and the gap plugged with a bush of thorn, but Mela's body still lay in the ditch where Fletcher had thrown it. Borun approached cautiously, the hairs on his spine stiff and erect. He called, a low, hesitant greeting, but there was no response. Then he drew nearer, and sniffed around her corpse. Recognizing the smell of death, he turned away, and finally made his way slowly back into the woods. Ever after, he avoided going near the place.

Gradually, in the days that followed, he began to forget about her, but often, in the evenings after the sun had gone down, in the lingering afterlight of summer, he would wander disconsolately about the set, pausing at each entrance in turn, listening, but hearing nothing but the silence of the hollow hill. At length he would turn away, padding doggedly down the worn trail to start another lonely night's foraging.

6. Vandal

Over the years the cottage seemed to have settled cozily into the side of the hill, so that now the thatch, made rotten by the moss that grew thick upon it, merged with the green canopy of the trees, and the weather-worn stone of the walls exactly matched the hue of the yellow sandy soil. Climbing tendrils of ivy, which had sent their suckerlike roots deep into the crevices between the stones, further obscured the outline of the cottage, so that from across the valley it was barely visible, except when a thin gray column of smoke rose from the chimney.

All day the sun had shone down on the garden, warming the rich, moist soil so that the serried ranks of vegetables, the peas and carrots and cabbages, the green-leaved lettuces, and the golden bulbs of the onions seemed to swell visibly by the hour. Now the sun was westering. As it passed behind the cottage, just before it slid beneath the crest of the hill, its rays penetrated a small casement window, and a beam of soft rosy light fell upon the sleeping form of a white cat, curled at the foot of the bed.

In response to the sun's caress, an ear twitched. The cat raised his head, opened his eyes, and yawned. Then he lay still as his senses alerted him to the pattern of his surroundings.

Almost at once he realized that something was wrong. There should have been the rich smell of cooking, but only the stale smells of yesterday lingered on the air. There should have been a scattering of tiny sounds, all significant, all related to the time of day. There was nothing, only the ticking of the clock in the living room, the faint creaking of timbers as the house cooled after the heat of the day, and an intermittent rustling in the roof as the bats beneath the thatch began to wake from their daytime sleep.

For a short while the cat, whose name was Vandal, remained on the bed, hoping at least to hear his favorite sounds, the rattle of a saucer and the rhythmic scrape of a can-opener cutting its way around the lid of a can, sure signs that a meal was ready. Vandal waited in vain, and eventually he slid off the bed, stretched, and made his cautious way downstairs.

The living room and the kitchen were deserted. The ashes of the fire were cold in the hearth, and the breakfast table lay uncleared. There was a thick package wedged in the letter slot in the front door, but nothing else. Vandal turned, and went back upstairs, to pause and scratch at the closed door on the landing. In the past this act had always evoked a response, though not always friendly. This evening it brought nothing.

Vandal returned to the kitchen. The situation was not en-

tirely novel to him. In the past he had been left alone on several occasions, but each time there had been food left out for
him, and milk in a saucer under the table. This time there
were only the stale, sour remains of his breakfast, which after
sniffing tentatively for a while he rejected, performing a rit-
ual burial act with his paw on the tiled floor surrounding the
plate.

Then he left the house. The kitchen door was closed and
locked, but there was an ingenious device known as a cat-
flap fixed in the lower panel of the door, through which he
could come and go at will. Outside the air was cool and
fresh, and heavy with the scent of elder flower and honeysuckle, but the fragrant beauty of the summer evening was
wasted on Vandal. He moved away uphill, past the chickens
bunched together in their pen, past the rabbit that stamped
nervously in her hutch, over the loose stone wall, and into
the wood. Blackbirds chinked angrily from the safety of their
roosts in the elder thickets. A wood pigeon flew out with a
clatter of noisy wings, making Vandal flatten his ears and
spit in futile rage. He came at last to the badger track that ran
athwart the hill, and followed it, pausing every now and then
to listen, until he came at last to the edge of the wood, and
the hedge that bordered the field.

Rabbits had emerged from their burrows, and begun to
feed on the short, sheep-cropped turf of the field. In the afterlight their gray forms were clearly visible against the green
of the grass. Vandal's teeth chattered in anticipation as the
rich gamy scent reached him, and belly flat to the ground, he
stole down the hedgerow to the shelter of a bramble patch.

The bramble patch, a seemingly impenetrable thicket of
hawthorn, blackthorn, and wild briar rose, tightly interwoven
with the heavily barbed growth of the brambles, was in fact
honeycombed with tunnels cut by the rabbits themselves, and
it was through this maze that the cat made his way, until at
last he lay in ambush, hidden by the overgrowth, but with a

clear view of the field, and of several young rabbits that were feeding upwind, and steadily moving nearer the thicket. Vandal, the events of the past few hours obliterated from his mind, waited for the moment to spring.

Three young rabbits were now within range. Though little more than a quarter grown, one would provide an ample meal. The cat took a quick glance around. The nearest full-grown rabbits were several yards away. There would be no danger of a humiliating and painful attack from an angry buck or protective doe.

Vandal's gaze returned to his prey. One young female detached herself from the group and hopped his way. Saliva filled his mouth as he sprang. The soft furry form squirmed beneath him as his teeth met in her neck. He felt the vertebrae part and the blood from her severed arteries flow into his mouth, heard vaguely the angry stamp of warning as the other rabbits bobbed away with flashing white tails, and then he was dragging his quarry back into the bramble thicket.

He fed then, starting at the head and crunching his way through bone, skin, fur, and sinew as well as the soft, succulent flesh, savoring the liver and heart but rejecting the stomach and entrails, until all else that remained were the hind-legs. Then he paused, satiated, and washed his feet as the fleas from the dead rabbit burrowed to safety in the short fur on his head. Replete and lazy, he sprawled out on the litter of dried grass and leaves beside the remains of his feast, and dozed off as the moon rose high in the sky and the rabbits re-emerged, to feed on the dew-drenched grass. This time they gave the bramble thicket a wide berth.

When next the cat woke, the moon was still high in the sky, but now it was riding to the west, and already the eastern sky was silvered with the first light of dawn. The rabbits had deserted the field, and the air was chill. The cat stretched, making the time-honored obeisance of his kind, sniffed at the remains of the rabbit, and made a half-hearted attempt to finish them, but the flesh was cold and stiff, so he turned away, back toward the wood. Next morning a flesh fly found the remains of the rabbit, and laid her eggs on the meat. Her labors were in vain, for the following evening a foraging hedgehog found the carrion, and ate it with relish, eggs and all.

The cat made its way slowly back through the wood, turning aside once to drink the brackish water that had accumulated in the center of an ash stump. A few laps sufficed, not because the taste was alien to him, but because he required little in the way of moisture to quench his thirst. Dawn was breaking as he slipped through the cat-flap, to find the house as still and silent as he had left it. He curled up in his favorite place on the bed in the spare room, and though he roused himself several times during the day, no sound came to disturb the peace of the cottage.

That evening the sun woke him as usual, and again the alien silence greeted him as before, with one difference. The ticking of the clock had ceased. This time he did not bother scratching at the closed bedroom door, nor did he search for food. Instead he went straight out, and sat for a while watching the chickens, which, having heard the rattle of the cat-flap, had crowded in eager anticipation around the door of the hen run. All day they had scratched without reward at the bare earth of the run, seeking for some overlooked scrap of food. Now with empty crops they crooned hopefully, gazing with bright eyes toward the house.

Vandal lingered, enjoying the familiarity of their presence. He was just over half grown, and at an age when he still desired company, had not yet fully acquired the self-sufficiency and assurance that marked his kind. In his memory lurked half-forgotten images, the warm, silken flank that was his mother, the rough tongues and squirming bodies that were his litter brothers and sisters. Overlaid on these mind pictures were more recent recollections, of an ample lap clad in rough tweed, a billowing satin bosom, and an endearing voice that used to croon to him as he lay, full fed and half asleep, in front of the flickering light and warmth of the fire.

Without the reassurance of such a presence, he felt insecure, uneasy. So he sat on, in the company of the fowls, until darkness fell, and one by one the hens went to roost in the fusty darkness of their coop. Then, reluctantly, he moved away in search of his supper.

He leapt onto the wall and dropped down into a clearing among the fern, and at once the mystery of the night surrounded and captivated him, so that he forgot his earlier unease. The air was filled with soft, furtive sounds, a rustle in the dry leaves, a flurry of movement in the honeysuckle vines, a crashing far off, and once a thin, high scream that ended in a choking gasp. He moved cautiously but confidently along the badger track, a predator with little to fear, alone in a world in which he was superbly equipped to survive.

He killed quickly and fed. This time his prey was a short-tailed vole, sweet and succulent, but not bulky enough to induce in him the lethargy that followed gorging to capacity. So he moved on, and surprised yet another vole as she scurried toward her nest of dried grass. This time he played with his victim, tossing her in the air and allowing her to crawl a few feet toward sanctuary before clawing her back and patting her, soft-footed, around, until at last she died of fear and shock. When at last he was convinced that she would run no more, Vandal ate her, leaving only her stomach, which he cut neatly out with his teeth. Then, aroused by the squeaking that emanated from the nearby nest, he clawed out and ate the pink hairless young of the vole.

So the night passed, but with the coming of the dawn Vandal was once more drawn toward the comfort and safety of the cottage. He retraced his steps in the direction of the house, and had almost reached the wall when, rounding a bend in the path, he came face to face with Borun the badger cub.

The cat froze, and so did the badger. They stood in the moonlight, immobile, each waiting for the other to move first. For perhaps half a minute neither animal flinched, and then Borun sank down on one haunch, and scratched himself vigorously with his hindclaws. Even to Vandal it was clear that this gesture could in no way appear aggressive. In token of acknowledgment he licked the inside of his forepaw, and then groomed his chest. Then he sat down and waited for the badger's next move.

Borun nodded his head several times, peering at the cat with myopic eyes, and then advanced. As he drew nearer Vandal's nerve slowly began to crack, until at last he stood up, ready to flee or attack. Then Borun moved to one side, and slowly, as Vandal circled to keep facing him, the cub passed him by, and rejoining the track, trundled slowly out of view. Five minutes later the cat was back in the bedroom of the cottage, where, after a prolonged and vigorous grooming session, he fell asleep. From time to time his body twitched, as he dreamed about badgers, and the voles that scurried and squeaked in the silver-splashed shadows of the moonlit wood.

He woke suddenly, to the sound of vehicles being driven slowly up the track that led to the cottage. He heard the slamming of car doors, footsteps, and a hubbub of alien voices, and then he fled, out of the cottage and into the sanctuary of the woodshed, where he crouched behind a pile of logs. He waited a long while, and although he was tempted to creep out and make acquaintance with these humans, fear held him back.

Outside the front door of the cottage, the village policeman stood talking to the doctor, as attendants bore a white-shrouded burden to the waiting ambulance. "It was the postman who reported it. He didn't call yesterday, but this morning he noticed that a package he'd delivered the day before was still wedged in the letter slot. Seems the old girl got up as usual, fed the cat and had breakfast, and then felt unwell and went back to bed.''

The doctor nodded absently. He was late for his surgery and anxious to be away. ''There's a brother, I believe?''

''That's right,'' nodded the policeman. ''He lives down in the village. I'll call round and see him directly. Someone will have to come and see to the hens and so forth. I expect the cat's about somewhere too.''

''I expect he's taken to the woods by now,'' said the doctor. ''At least there's plenty of food about for him. The rabbits seem to have come back thicker than ever since the myxomatosis.''

One by one the vehicles departed, and once again the silence of the summer day hung heavily over the deserted cottage. Gradually the stuffy heat of the woodshed grew unbearable to Vandal, and at last he crept out. This time, however, he did not return to the bedroom, but sought the leafy green shade of the woods. So he did not hear the arrival of the old man who fed the hens and the rabbit. Nor did he know that on the tiled floor of the kitchen were a saucer of fresh milk and a plate of cat food.

7. Strange Company

The long summer day was well advanced when Vandal next woke. For a while he lay still, couched on a bed of dried leaves that filled the hollow of an old ash stump, listening as the sounds of the day gave way to those of the night. Somewhere the distant drone of a tractor coughed and died, and a dog barked briefly in the silence. The thin, dry bleat of a half-grown lamb scraped across the evening air, and as if in answer a crow called, once, twice, as he winged his solitary way across the wood. Then an owl cried, the low, wavering voice echoing down the aisles of darkness.

In response the woodland came alive with movement. Bats began to flicker black-winged between the tree trunks, and from the undergrowth came the busy sound of small teeth, a brief patter of feet, a scuffle, and a muffled squeak as two mice fought a lilliputian duel, their tiny tempers white hot with rage. The nightjar detached himself from his roost on the bare branch of an oak and flew off to circle the cattle that grazed in the meadow, hawking for the flies that swarmed around the beasts. The woodcock in the fern opened her eyes and flopped away, ghostlike among the trees, to probe for worms in the marshland at the bottom of the valley.

Vandal slipped from his perch and padded off through the shadows. A dormouse shredding bark from the honeysuckle vine for her nest saw him as he passed beneath her, and whisked her tail as she fled upward into the high branches. A bank vole caught his scent and froze in the shelter of a fallen branch as he passed by. A young rabbit feeding in a clearing among the fern was not so alert. Vandal sprang, and there was a brief flurry of movement, a flash of white fur, and the next moment Vandal was dragging his limp prey into the shelter of the bushes.

Half an hour later the cat lay sprawled beside the remains of his feast, his flanks heaving and distended. Vandal was rather more than comfortably full, and disinclined to action of any kind, so for the next hour he stayed where he was, licking the blood from his paws in a rather desultory fashion, until his supper had settled somewhat. Then he got up, to prowl aimlessly through the wood.

He was not disposed to hunt further that night, and thoughts of his comfortable couch on the bed in the cottage lured him to return. Yet he could not forget his unease at the empty silence of the house, and the sudden invasion of his privacy by so many strangers. It was as though the whereabouts of his sanctuary had suddenly been betrayed to aliens, and once exposed, its safety could no longer be depended upon. Nor could he expect any affection or companionship on his return, for somehow he knew that his mistress had left the cottage. So he wandered on, and eventually emerged onto the badger track at the exact moment that Borun joined it, fifty yards away.

So the two animals met again, for the third time in their lives. For a long while each stood stock still, waiting for the other to make the first move. Both animals were certain that they had nothing to fear from each other, both were young and immature, and each nursed in his heart a feeling of loss, of loneliness, and a desire for companionship. Slowly, infinitely slowly, Vandal crept nearer and nearer to Borun, who remained rooted to the spot. At last they touched noses.

There followed a tentative inquiry into each other's person, the pair circling around and sniffing each other carefully. Borun had little scent, for like all badgers he was scrupulously clean in his person and living quarters. Vandal, for his part, smelled strongly of rabbit, which may have puzzled Borun, but almost certainly endeared Vandal to him. Satisfied, Borun set off down the track, with Vandal dancing along behind him.

During that first night Vandal watched, intrigued, as Borun wrecked a rotten tree stump, ripping off the bark and scooping up the beetles and other insects that tumbled in all directions. He grew disinterested when Borun dug for roots and bulbs among the bracken fern, but brightened up when the badger found a vole's nest, pouncing on the fleeing mother while Borun demolished the young voles. Vandal killed the mother, but he was not interested in food, and willingly allowed Borun to take possession of his prize.

By dawn, they had invented a curious game of tag, in which Borun first rushed at Vandal, who sat as still as a statue until the very last moment, and then sprang high into the air, so that Borun shot headlong under him. Then Vandal chased Borun, cuffing him with his paws, but making sure his claws were never unsheathed. Borun, long used to far heavier blows than Vandal could deal, nevertheless squealed in pretended terror and turned somersaults in his efforts to avoid them.

The game ended with the coming of daylight. The two made their way to the spring and quenched their thirst, and then as of habit Borun returned to the set. Vandal hesitated outside the entrance for a moment, and then, as Borun's rather portly rump disappeared into the darkness, he followed. The bed of fern and leaves was crisp and comfortable, and Borun's warm flank was soft and reassuring. As the tractor in the valley grumbled into life for yet another day, as the nightjar returned to his roost on the oak branch, and the sun climbed high in the sky, the strange companions slept.

Gradually, in the days that followed, the pair worked out a scheme of coexistence that suited them both. Although Vandal easily adapted to nocturnal life, he preferred to hunt and kill alone, early in the evening before the sun had set and the countryside had become soaked with dew. His hunger satisfied, Vandal was content to accompany Borun on his foraging, and lend assistance when necessary. Often, when Borun emerged from the set, there would be a portion of rabbit, still warm, waiting for him, and this was most acceptable to the badger cub, who was still at times inexpert and bungling in his attempts to find food.

For much of the time Vandal also preferred to sleep alone. Catlike, he chose to change his sleeping quarters regularly, to bask in the sun of early morning and late evening, but to seek shade during the noonday heat. So he had a succession of sleeping places near the set, each chosen in relation to the position of the sun and the direction of the wind. Only when it rained did he join Borun in the set, and as the summer wore on this happened less and less. The water level in the lakes and reservoirs dropped, the ground cracked, and the once green pastures turned a golden brown.

Early on an August morning, as the sun shone again from a cloudless sky, and the wind rustled through the acres of ripe wheat, Vandal was roused from a half slumber by a distant high-pitched bark. The yapping was persistent, rising and falling on the breeze, but drawing nearer. Fully awake now, Vandal listened, folding his paws beneath him, but poised for instant action if need be.

A terrier had escaped just after dawn from the farm where it was kept to control the rats that swarmed around the rickyards. Once before it had escaped, by scratching and biting until it had chewed a hole through the bottom of the shed door. The farmer had nailed a wooden patch over the hole, and forgotten it, but the terrier had not. Every night, after it had been locked in the shed, it went to work on the patch, and every day the hot sun and the lack of rain aided the terrier in its efforts. The timber dried out, the nails loosened in their holes, and the patch warped until finally it fell free.

The terrier had one idea in mind, and that was to run wild among the hordes of rabbits that swarmed amid the hedgerows, and as he hunted and killed, and missed, and chased again, he slowly went silly with excitement, barking hysterically the while, and running from warren to warren, until at last he entered the wood.

Vandal lingered a split second too long. He saw the black and white form of the terrier coming up the badger trail, and slid from his bed of fern, making for the shelter of the set. The terrier spotted him, and with a joyous yelp, dived in pursuit. Vandal reached the mouth of the set with the terrier in close pursuit.

It was hard on his heels as he ran down the tunnel, to the airy main chamber under the oak tree, where Borun now slept. The badger woke to hear the sounds of pursuit, the scrabble of claws, and the snuffling bark of the dog. Next moment Vandal burst into the chamber, a split second before the terrier, and as the cat turned to face his adversary the dog leapt at him, aiming for the throat, but seizing him at the side of the neck, just below his ear. As Vandal screamed Borun leapt to attack, and with a sudden lurch of fear the terrier felt the badger's teeth sink into his foreleg.

In the darkness the noise and confusion were bewildering to all three contestants. The terrier yelled as Borun's teeth grated on bone, and Borun released his hold, leaping for the terrier's throat. He caught the dog instead behind the ears, holding it by the scruff of the neck and effectively preventing it from biting any more. The dog struggled frantically, shaking Borun around the chamber, and forgetting about Vandal, who had broken free when the terrier opened its jaws to yell.

Few dogs have ever been forced to endure the unbridled fury of an enraged tomcat, and those who have are reluctant to suffer the experience ever again. The terrier was within seconds of such a punishment, and there could be no reprieve. Vandal sprang at the dog, biting and slashing with razor-sharp teeth, all the while clinging to the dog's back with claws that gored deep. Finally he brought the powerful muscles of his hindlegs into action, raking the soft flanks of the terrier with the terrible back-raking kick that could disembowel a rabbit.

Between them, the companions might well have succeeded in killing the terrier, had it not, with one last effort, managed to reach the exit from the chamber, forcing its way into the tunnel and brushing the pair off. It crawled painfully back to the farm, where Fletcher, who had been prepared to give it a beating for straying away, could only look at it in wonder and dismay. He told his friends about it, in the public bar of the inn that evening. "Little old dog looked as though he'd been through a threshing machine. He's cut and tore and scratched, and I can't see how badly for caked blood. One drink of milk he's had, and laid like a dead thing ever since. What manner of beast could do that to him I can't imagine."

Nor, for that matter, could anyone else. The two assailants were little the worse for wear after their adventure. Borun had a few scratches, dealt him in error by Vandal in the height of the melee, and Vandal had a nasty tear in the side of his neck. Carefully, they administered first aid to each other, each licking those injuries the other couldn't reach, and their wounds healed without complication. The terrier recovered in time, but he never went near the wood again.

8. Polly and Her Guests

As soon as Polly saw the cottage she knew she had found the place she had been looking for. It was September, and the garden was derelict and weed strewn, but in her mind's eye she saw it well tended and trim, with serried rows of vegetables flourishing in the plump soil. There was a lawn, with a gnarled old damson tree. In the spring bulbs would force their green spears above the grass, first snowdrops, then crocuses, purple and yellow and white, and then daffodils, nodding in the wind and flaunting their golden trumpets in the thin March sun. There were apple trees, a peach tree, and a neglected raspberry patch, and behind the cottage a range of stone outbuildings, including a woodshed still stacked with dry logs. All it lacked was the greenhouse, and that was easily remedied.

Inside, she pottered around, visualizing the firelight winking on her few pieces of silver and the furniture she had garnered so carefully over the years. Up in the bedroom she admired the white walls and the sagging oak-beamed ceiling, and peered out of the tiny casement window below the thatch, gazing into the shadowy woods. "Chintz," she said. "I can go chintz mad."

"I beg your pardon," said the agent, an apprehensive young man in his early twenties.

Polly flushed. She had not realized that she had spoken aloud. She had even forgotten that the estate agent was with her. There and then she made up her mind. She would buy Summercombe Cottage, and as she came to her decision the years fell away, years of dusty, chalk-impregnated classrooms, with their hordes of unruly, shrieking children, years of marking papers, and endless academic argument in the smoke-laden atmosphere of shabby staff rooms. At last she was free, and there was no one in the world to dictate to her.

The agent was delighted, for none knew better than he the defects of Summercombe Cottage, isolated, drafty, and damp, and riddled with woodworm. Her solicitor thought her quite mad, and said so in no uncertain terms. "You are preparing to invest almost all your life savings into a property which needs considerable improvement and repair, a property which will prove almost unsalable if, after a few months there, you find you can't bear the loneliness. You really ought to reconsider, Miss Shaw."

But Polly was adamant. She sat in her chair, a plump, defiant little figure, her dark hair gathered in a bun at the nape of her neck, and her chin quivered with determination as she resisted all efforts to dissuade her. So it came about that in a remarkably short space of time, at dusk on an autumn day, she struck a match and lit the first fire in her new home. As the yellow flames licked hungrily at the dry sticks, the scent of wood smoke evoked memories of summers long ago, when she had been a captain of Girl Guides, and gangling girls now grown to be mothers with children of their own. She poured herself some coffee and sat down amid the packing cases and cartons that littered the floor, while outside the last light faded from the hills. There was no hurry to unpack. She had only herself to please, and there was all winter ahead. At least the cottage had electricity. On impulse she jumped from her chair and rushed around turning on all the lights. Then she went out into the garden.

The stars shone white in the cold air above the sheltering shoulders of the hills, and the dark and brooding trees seemed to crowd around the cottage and hold it out to her, a glowing casket of light, as if to say, "This is our most precious possession. Take it and cherish it."

Alone in the darkness, she felt the presence of the earth as a living, sentient being, and at that moment she felt more at one with the valley and the hills and the silent trees than she did with her fellow men. It was a feeling that was to grow, in the weeks that followed, as by day she labored in the garden, and by night sat at her sewing machine, or wielded a paintbrush in the darker, more cobwebby corners of the cottage.

One of her first acts was to hang a bird table from the bough of the damson tree. She found an old slab of elm wood, nearly two inches thick, and screwed hooks into each of the four corners. Then she hung chains from the bough of the tree and hooked the slab to them, carefully adjusting the height until the table was level. From the table she hung hoppers for peanuts and sunflower seeds, lumps of fat and suet, a large marrow bone, and pieces of bacon rind. Her first task each morning was to replenish the table, and then she could sit and enjoy her own breakfast, as the birds arrived to take theirs.

She was astonished at the variety of the visitors. Blackbirds and thrushes hopped about on the grass beneath the tree. Chaffinches and greenfinches, hedge sparrows and linnets jostled and pushed each other on the table, and were themselves chivied by a solitary robin. Tits came: blue tits, great tits, a cole tit, and a pair of willow tits, in such a confusion of color and design that Polly had to buy a bird book in order to identify them all. Nuthatches were regular visitors, and occasionally a woodpecker arrived, his vermilion cap nodding as he surveyed what was on offer.

Polly was also amazed at the amount of food consumed. Whoever coined the phrase "an appetite like a bird's," has never met this lot, she thought, as she prepared yet another bowl of scraps.

Late one evening she sat beside the window. The curtains remained undrawn, and the window was open, for the weather had remained dry, and the nights unseasonably warm. A book lay on her lap. She sat thinking over what she had just read, for one of her self-imposed tasks on retirement was a study of comparative religions. In recent years she had found herself increasingly at odds with the simple faith in which she had been raised, and which she had taught to generations of children. Now she wondered if the fault lay in herself or in the creed by which she had tried to live, and she was determined to find out. Already she had discovered the immensity of her task, but she persevered, hoping the work would get easier as she progressed.

A muffled squeaking in the garden roused her from her reveries, and she peered cautiously out of the window, hardly daring to breathe lest she frightened whatever it was away. Out of the shadows, and into the pool of light beneath the damson tree, came a family of hedgehogs, looking like animated pincushions as they waddled across the turf on short, bandy legs. They fell upon the remains of the bird food on the lawn with squeals of delight, and foraged busily around, moving surprisingly fast for such ungainly-looking creatures.

Polly watched entranced, until finally they trundled off into the night. Later she lay in bed wondering what she could do to encourage them to stay. Hedgehogs, she had read somewhere, were most beneficial to gardeners, eating all manner of insect pests. Even if they weren't, she thought, they were worth fostering for their entertainment value. She had to go into town the following day, so she would see what she could find.

The town was hot and noisy and smelly after the peace of Summercombe wood, and the people seemed more surly and ill mannered than ever. Polly was glad when she could load her week's provisions into the back of her old Morris, and drive back up into the valley. At the farm she stopped to collect her milk, and to ask if, for the next few days at least, she could have an extra pint.

"Expecting company then, Miss Shaw?" Mrs. Fletcher's curiosity about her nearest heighbor did not get enough nourishment to satisfy it.

"Why, no," began Polly, and then hesitated. She had been about to say she wanted to put a bowl of milk out for some hedgehogs, and then decided not to. She was considered eccentric enough in the village without giving cause for further gossip. "I, I get very thirsty working in the garden, and milk is very nourishing."

Fattening too, thought Mrs. Fletcher, eyeing Polly's plump, rounded figure with a certain amount of envy. She was as thin as a beanpole, as her husband was tactless enough to remind her. Aloud she said, "You can take an extra pint now if you wish."

Polly accepted gladly, and hastened away before the farmer's wife could question her further. Ridiculous, she thought, a woman of my age afraid of answering a straight question, guilty of a silly lie. I must be turning into a recluse.

Yet her sense of relief when she reached the sanctuary of her cottage was almost overwhelming, and it worried her.

"What comes of being alone too much, I suppose," she murmured to herself. "Now I'm even talking to myself. Perhaps I ought to invite a friend or two for the odd weekend?" Even as the thought phrased itself, she knew the idea had no appeal.

She dumped the carton of groceries on the kitchen floor, and rummaged around until she found the packet of cat food she had bought. It was a garishly colored package with a picture of a fat, complacent cat licking its lips. Polly read the instructions carefully. FIT KIT came in five different flavors, liver, fish, beef, chicken, and rabbit. It was a complete cat food, containing all necessary proteins, carbohydrates and fats, minerals, vitamins, and trace elements, and could be fed wet or dry. Polly opened the packet. Rather cleverly, she thought, she had chosen the rabbit flavor.

It looked revolting. She emptied the food into two bowls, poured the extra pint of milk over them, and then carried them out into the garden, setting them down under the damson tree. Then she returned to the house, to prepare something that looked a little more appetizing for herself, before assuming her vigil beside the window.

They came soon after dark, having remembered from the previous night that there were some very interesting tidbits to be found beneath the tree. It occurred to Polly that she had been overgenerous with the cat food, but even so she was astounded at the amount the hedgehogs were able to consume. They ate and ate, but it was not mere gluttony that drove them to excess. Soon the frosts would come, and the bitter winds of winter, and when that time came the hedgehogs would seek some refuge that was sheltered and dry. There, buried beneath dried grass and leaves, they would fall asleep. Their body temperature would fall, their heartbeats slow, and their breathing almost cease, as they sank deeper and deeper into a coma that would last until the warm days of spring.

In readiness for that time, the hedgehogs were now accumulating a thick layer of fat, enough fuel to drive the fires of life, to keep their metabolic processes just ticking through the long winter months. The young hedgehogs in particular had to reach a certain body weight if they were to survive. So through September and October they ate and ate and ate.

Even so, they did not quite manage to empty the bowls before they moved off, and Polly left the remains of the food on the lawn, in case the hedgehogs returned later in the night. She went to bed feeing very pleased with the success of her experiment, and fell asleep wondering if the manufacturers of FIT KIT ever imagined that their product would be used for feeding hedgehogs. Her last conscious thought was a fervent hope that it would not upset their stomachs.

At that moment, Borun and Vandal entered the garden.

9. The Intruders

For both animals, the task of finding food had of late grown more difficult. The rabbits had virtually ceased to breed for the season, and those litters that had survived the first few weeks of existence had grown lean and fast and wary. The prolonged drought had not helped. The earthworms had hidden themselves away until the coming of the rains, and the ground was baked harder than stone. Worse, for Borun, was the fact that the acorn crop had failed, and so instead of being able to stuff himself on the hard, bitter fruit, he had to be content with the few that the wood pigeons missed.

Like the hedgehogs, Borun needed at this time to accumulate a layer of fat, against the time of the hard weather, when instead of foraging he would pass the long nights drowsing in the warmth and security of the set. For Vandal the problem was not so serious, although normally he would have put on some weight at this time of year. Both he and Borun, moreover, were still growing, and the demands of muscle and bone had to be met. Though far from starving, their appetites were keen, and so they had taken to roving farther afield. On this night, greatly daring, they had come to explore the garden of the cottage.

They found the food the hedgehogs had left almost immediately, and Vandal, who had not tasted cat food or milk for a long while, soon cleared one bowl. Borun, slightly more suspicious, sniffed the food carefully, but after a few tentative licks he found it to his liking. He polished the bowl, turned it over in the hope of finding more underneath, and then, disappointed, began scavenging under the damson tree for the scraps that had fallen from the bird table.

The taste of the cat food revived old memories for Vandal, and Borun looked up from his foraging to see the cat sneaking away round the corner of the house. Borun followed, to find Vandal sniffing at the back door.

The cat-flap was still there. Vandal pushed cautiously, and it opened. He stood for a moment, his head just inside the kitchen, listening and waiting in case anything stirred. All was still, and he slid through into the house, the flap closing behind him. After a second's hesitation, Borun followed him, and for a long time the pair stood motionless, eager to explore further, yet poised for instant flight.

Polly had never been a tidy housekeeper, and since she had come to live alone she had grown more and more heedless of convention. The groceries she had bought that day still stood in their carton on the kitchen floor, and Borun, ever curious, was eager to discover what treasure this strange square tree stump might contain.

It came apart easily enough, and Borun's strong claws were soon ripping through cardboard and paper and plastic.

A flour bag broke first, but after a few licks Borun turned his attention elsewhere. Cornflakes were much nicer. Borun crunched happily for a while, until he found the sugar. This was better than all the wasps' nests in Somerset, and Borun licked and scrunched, all the time burrowing deeper into the carton.

Vandal watched disinterestedly, even when Borun unearthed another packet of FIT KIT. What Vandal craved was a long cool drink of milk. He remembered that in the past, all he had had to do was to rub himself against the door of the refrigerator and mew, and his mistress would open the door, take out the milk, and pour it into a bowl. Automatically, Vandal went through the routine, not once, but several times.

Nothing happened. No one came, and Borun was still head and shoulders inside the carton, oblivious to everything but the sugar. Indeed, he might have stayed there all night, had he not broken into a packet of detergent. He came out backward as if he had been shot from a gun, snorting and sneezing. When he had recovered somewhat he saw Vandal scratching and rubbing against the refrigerator door.

Unfortunately for Polly, the door of the refrigerator was of the kind that is held by a magnetic catch, and it presented no problem to Borun. Three rashers of bacon, some cheese, and an egg disappeared inside the badger, while Vandal pushed and mewed, still impatient for his milk.

It stood on a shelf in a jug. As Borun stood up on his hindlegs and thrust his greedy little snout further into the refrigerator he dislodged the shelf. The jug slid forward, and Vandal got his milk, rather more than he required, all over his head and shoulders.

The crash of the falling jug woke Polly. She lay for a moment, cold fear clutching her heart. Then she pulled herself together, and got out of bed. If there were intruders in the house, it was better she faced them standing, than abed at their mercy. With any luck, they would not realize she was alone in the house, and if she gave them plenty of warning, they might flee.

Noisily she opened the bedroom door, stood for a moment on the landing, and then began to clump heavily downstairs. Outside the living room she stopped and listened, but no sound except the ticking of the clock came to her ears, so at last, screwing up all her courage, she stepped inside and turned on the light.

All seemed to be in order. Her handbag was just where she had left it on the table, and the silver candlesticks were on the mantelpiece as usual. Perhaps it had all been a dream. By now, however, she was thoroughly awake, and she decided to make a hot drink to take back to bed.

Her first reaction when she saw the kitchen was one of horror and disgust. The shambles that was once a cardboard carton held a revolting mixture of flour, sugar, cornflakes, and cat food, all mixed with detergent. The floor was strewn with torn scraps of paper and cardboard, and covered with floury footprints. The refrigerator door was open, its contents warming in a pool of milk.

Then Polly spotted the milky paw marks leading to the cat-flap, and she realized what must have happened, although she was unsure about the exact identity of her nocturnal visitors. It wasn't hedgehogs, she was sure, and while some of the prints looked like those of a cat, others were larger. Certainly no cat could wreak such havoc as this, yet whatever it was had to be small enough to get through the flap. Suddenly a mental image of Mrs. Fletcher came to her. "Expecting company then, Miss Shaw?" Standing there in the ruins of her kitchen, she began to laugh.

She went back upstairs and dressed, then set to work to clean up the kitchen. Ruefully she reflected that she would have to make another journey to town to replace those provisions that had been ruined, but first of all she meant to catch up on a few hours' lost sleep. Her last act before retiring was to nail a stout batten of wood across the cat-flap, and so prevent any further nocturnal visitations.

It was close on noon when next she woke, and consequently bedtime found her wide awake. Once again she had put out food for the hedgehogs, and they had been and gone. Still she sat on, hoping to discover the identity of the invaders of the previous night. She waited in vain. The moon rose and journeyed across the sky, the fire died in the hearth, and the room fell chill. At last, stiff and weary, she went to bed. Her sleep was undisturbed.

Vandal in fact had hunted alone that night, for Borun was feeling distinctly unwell, and reluctant to leave the set. By dusk of the following day, however, Borun had recovered from the effects of his overeating, and was once again eager for food. Together the pair set off, by tacit consent heading for the cottage, in hopes of finding more food under the damson tree.

The rattling of the bowls alerted Polly, and she peeped cautiously out the window. She saw Vandal at once, and at first thought he must have come up the track from the farm. Then she remembered Mrs. Fletcher telling her about a white kitten that was missing after the previous owner of the cottage had died, and wondered if it could be the same one that was now feeding on the lawn.

Borun had his back to the window, and at first she did not notice his gray form. Then suddenly he turned, and Polly caught her breath in surprise and delight. As she watched, Vandal disappeared around the side of the house, and she heard the rattle of the cat-flap. Suddenly, all was explained, and Polly now knew who the miscreant was who had all but wrecked her kitchen.

Vandal's attempts to gain entry to the kitchen failed, and he rejoined Borun on the lawn. Only when they were quite certain that not a single crumb of food remained uneaten did the pair move off into the night, leaving Polly alone at the window.

They came every night after that, and Polly made sure that there were adequate supplies of food available. On the third night she put the food out as usual, and then, dressed in warm dark clothing, she sat down at the foot of the damson tree.

Half an hour passed, and then she saw the white figure of the cat materialize out of the darkness. Close behind him came the young badger, and both animals made straight for the feeding bowls on the grass. Then Vandal noticed her and froze, one paw raised, ready to flee at the slightest sign of danger, but reluctant to forgo his supper unless it was absolutely necessary.

Polly sat motionless, hardly daring to breathe, and at long last Vandal relaxed, crept forward, and began to feed. Reassured, Borun did likewise, and found that as well as the usual cat food and milk, there was a slice of bread and honey in his bowl. This find went a long way toward easing his nervousness, and he cleared his plate before helping Vandal to finish his meal.

Each night Polly positioned the bowls a little closer to her, and within a week the pair were feeding beside her feet. Soon they were taking scraps from her hand, though both shied away if she tried to touch them. It did not occur to her to question the wisdom of her actions. She was merely amusing herself, and gave no thought to the fact that she might be endangering the young badger's chances of survival by making it dependent on her for food.

She was almost tempted to open up the cat-flap, but reluctantly she decided against it, for she saw very clearly that there was no way of making her kitchen badger proof, and the thought of the pair romping around her house at night convinced her that her plan was not practical.

So the nightly visits continued, as winter drew nearer and darkness came earlier each evening. Polly no longer sat under the damson tree to await her guests, but simply took the bowls out to them when they arrived. The nights were now cold, and frequently it was raining. For Polly, the novelty of the situation had worn off, and the arrival of her visitors merely necessitated one more chore.

Then, one night, Borun disgraced himself. Inevitably, sooner or later, the hedgehogs were bound still to be feeding when Borun and Vandal appeared. Polly had thought about this, but knowing the hedgehogs' trick of rolling into a tight prickly ball when molested, she felt quite sure that they would be safe. She did not know that badgers have a way of dealing with hedgehogs.

So, when the encounter finally did occur, Polly watched unconcerned, and with a certain amount of detached amusement. Three of the hedgehogs scattered and ran, but the fourth, which had delayed flight a little too long, curled into a ball. Borun strolled over to it. Gingerly, he rolled it on to its back, and then, before Polly could do anything to stop him, he plunged his claws deep into the place where the head of the hedgehog met its tail, and pried the unfortunate beast open. He gave one quick bite, the hedgehog squealed and died, and Borun was already crunching its skull when Polly attacked him with a broom.

Borun gave a gruff bark of fear and fled, closely followed by Vandal, leaving Polly to mourn the death of the hedgehog, and reflect rather shakily on the strength of the dark forces she had been impertinent enough to try and tame.

There was no supper for anyone the next night, but it did not matter, for nobody came. The hedgehogs were too afraid of meeting the badger again, and Borun was understandably reluctant to face an angry woman armed with a broom. Next morning, however, Vandal surprised Polly by appearing in broad daylight sitting on the garden wall and watching her with yellow eyes. She brought him a bowl of milk and he lapped it, before disappearing back into the woods.

He appeared more frequently after that, often hanging around the garden for hours at a time, and then, one night, as a gale roared through the trees and howled in the chimney, he scratched at the door. When Polly opened it he came in, to sit on the rug in front of the fire, as if he had never been away.

The explanation was quite simple. Borun was spending more and more time asleep in the set, and as winter wore on, life in the woods was growing ever more uncomfortable for Vandal. No longer could he pass the long day snoozing in the sun, and the dark, stuffy confines of the set were not particularly agreeable to him. So he had returned from the wild, and though he still saw Borun from time to time, they were no longer such close companions. The partnership, such as it was, had served its purpose, and now it was ended.

At first Polly was inclined to regard her adoption by Vandal with amused indignation, but then she remembered that recently she had suffered a minor invasion of fieldmice, also seeking shelter from the weather. On two occasions she had been forced to set traps in the kitchen, and each time she had sat in an agony of suspense, waiting for the "snap" that announced the execution of the furry little trespasser. Then she had had to face the distasteful business of disposing of the corpse.

Vandal, she knew, would relieve her of both tasks, and his presence in the cottage might deter further invaders. So he stayed, readily accepting a bowl of milk when it was offered, and occasionally a dish of cat food, though on the whole he preferred to hunt and catch his own food. Fortunately, he was disinterested in the birds that came to the bird table, or he might soon have disgraced himself in Polly's eyes. Instead, she came to look forward to his company during the long winter evenings, and the soothing sound of his deep-throated purr, as he relaxed by the fire.

10. One Eye

One Eye the vixen came to Summercombe in the new year, when the January moon shone white over a valley bare of snow, but locked in the grip of a hard black frost. Here she was courted and won by the old dog fox that lived at the top of the wood, and for a fortnight the woods and hillsides echoed to the sound of their love calls. Each evening the vixen's scream, loud and haunting, told her need and desire, and always in answer came the triple bark of the dog fox. Ever and again the calls were repeated, until at last the two came together, to be united under the stars.

The courtship was torrid, but brief, and afterward the pair went their separate ways, the dog fox back to his old haunt in the wood, and the vixen to the shelter of a gorse thicket high on the hill. Here she slept by day, basking in the pale winter sunlight, or lying curled in a ball, her pads tucked close to her body, and her face and nose covered by the dense brush of her tail. Thus protected, she was impervious to the cold.

By night she hunted, leaving the shelter of the gorse thicket each dusk to stalk the rabbits that had already begun to breed again among the hedgerows, or to wait patiently beside a ditch, watching and listening for the telltale rustle and the bright dark eye of an emerging vole. She was quicker and more light-footed than a cat, and possessed of a cunning and patience that more than compensated for the loss of her eye.

It was now almost a year since the injury had occurred, late one afternoon when the world lay blanketed in deep snow. She had succeeded in stalking a heron, that wiliest of birds, as it stood in the shallow waters of a stream that flowed sluggishly between ice-rimmed banks.

As she sprang, the vixen's hindfoot slipped on the ice, and although she seized her prey, it was by the wing rather than the throat. In the struggle that followed, in a flurry of icy spray, the daggerlike beak of the heron caught her across the eye. A moment later the heron died, as the vixen's teeth closed on her throat, and in her savage joy the killer barely noticed her own injury. She ate as much of the heron as she could manage, and then buried the remains in a snowdrift, leaving one scaly foot exposed, as if in a last silent tribute to a world that had betrayed it. It was later found by a buzzard, who had not fed for three days, and would have died if it had spent one more night with an empty crop.

The vixen's injury seemed trifling, but gradually the scratched cornea turned opaque and white, leaving her blind on one side. In the weeks that followed, One Eye fared badly, as she learned to adjust to her impediment. Consequently she did not breed that year, and the unborn cubs she now carried in her womb were to be her first litter. So the days passed, and as the icy bonds of winter melted before the warm breath of spring, One Eye's flanks grew a little rounder and thicker, but if she was perhaps a little slower on her feet, it still meant no reprieve for the rabbits of Summercombe.

On a bright day in late March, as the daffodils in the churchyard shone yellow amid the gray of the headstones, and the sable rooks in the elms above solemnly discussed the mechanics of repairing their nests, a cheerful assembly gathered on the village green. Riders on horseback clattered in from all directions, some resplendent in hunting scarlet, others wearing nondescript habits and jodhpurs. Ruddy-faced farmers in weather-worn tweeds sat astride heavy hunters, and sallow-cheeked children nervously straddled fat ponies, each silently praying that he or she would not disgrace themselves by inadvertently breaking the unwritten but complex code of the hunting field. The master sat a little to one side, raising his hunting crop in salute to each newcomer, and talking quietly to his groom, all the while keeping one eye on the church clock.

The landlord of the village inn bustled about, chivying his wife and daughters, who bore trays laden with glasses of amber liquid, as they handed round the traditional stirrup cup. The rest of the villagers looked on, enjoying the spectacle of the North Somerset Foxhounds gathering in Summercombe. The church clock struck eleven, and the hounds moved off, flowing in a liver and white stream up the lane that led to Bidewell Farm. With a creaking of leather and jingling of harness the horses followed, while those who were to follow the hunt by foot or by car also moved away, each to seek the best vantage point for watching the chase. In a few moments the square was deserted, except for the landlord of the inn, and the bent, stooping figure of Bill Fernybrass. Bill was a fanatical gardener, and winner of all the prizes at the annual village flower show. Now he was reaping, with bucket and shovel, an eagerly awaited harvest of horse manure to spread beneath his roses.

One Eye, asleep in the gorse thicket, heard the clamor of the hounds as they poured through the valley, and watched as they spread out over the hillside opposite, to converge on a small clump of hawthorn bushes, that stood stark, black, and leafless amid a sea of rust-red bracken. After a few minutes they moved on, drawing each small corpse and thicket in turn, and gradually working their way along the hillside until they reached the head of the valley. Here they turned about, and made their way back toward the farm, following the floor of the valley, threading in and out of the hedges and ditches and checking every bramble patch and weed-strewed ruin. Finally, they turned about again, to cover the hill where One Eye lay.

Even then One Eye did not move, until, rising and falling on the breeze, she heard the clamor of the hounds' tongues as they sang their death song. Then she slipped away, climbing the hill until she reached the rocky ramparts of the old hill fort. Here, among the gray limestone rocks and the stunted, twisted thorn trees, she rested, waiting as the hounds found her scent in the gorse thicket, and followed the running line of her flight.

As the hounds crested the hill she moved again, and the russet gleam of her coat was spotted by a watcher standing on the site of the old fort. The man waved his hat and yelled to the hunt, who toiled behind the hounds on mud-spattered horses, and spurs dug into flanks as the riders urged their mounts forward. Hounds fanned out, foaming through the rocks and withered fern, and then came a renewal of their song as they converged once more upon her scent.

She led them downhill now, back into the valley and up toward its head. Twice she lost them, once when she dived into a drain which led through a hedge mound, and through which hounds could not follow. Here she gained some time, as hounds bayed in frustration at the entrance to the drain, until an older, wiser hound mounted the hedge bank and picked up her scent on the other side.

One Eye, crouched panting in a ditch, heard the music of the hounds ring out above the pounding of her heart, and ran once more. For a second time she managed to throw them off the scent, by zigzagging to and fro between the terrified members of a flock of sheep, and again she managed to snatch a few moments of much needed rest, before she was on her feet once more.

She was slower now. Her tongue lolled, and her one good eye was glazed as she gained the shelter of the wood, and the panting of her labored breath was clearly audible as she stood beneath the sheltering trees, listening again for the sounds of pursuit. Still the hounds came on, and she circled around, keeping just inside the wood, but following the hedge that divided the trees from the field. Just before she reached the highest point of the woodlands, she passed within a few feet of the old dog fox.

Now her strength was failing fast. She staggered as she ran, and once she fell, to lie on her side for a brief moment before plunging on. She wanted to regain the sanctuary of the fort, to try and lose the hounds among the welter of boulders and weather-worn limestone that littered the crown of the hill, but she knew she was not equal to the task. Instead, she turned downhill, following the worn badger track that wound through the undergrowth.

She reached the entrance to the badger set, and for a moment she paused, and in that instant of time she realized that the hounds were no longer following her, that the hideous belling cry that had haunted her throughout the afternoon was gradually growing fainter. It mattered little. She could run no further, and here was sanctuary of a sort. Gratefully, she slipped into the tunnel, and when she found a chamber, lined with old and musty bedding, she collapsed.

Ten minutes later and a mile away, after a screaming run that led hounds in a dead straight line across country, that left the horses far behind and unseated two riders, the old dog fox was torn to pieces by the hounds. It mattered nothing to him.

His old heart had burst, seconds before, and he was dead long before the first hound closed on him. He won fame, of a kind, in the annals of the hunt, as an old warrior who had provided one of the longest runs of the century. Only the whipper-in guessed the truth, and perhaps the master, but one was too cautious, and the other too wise, to spoil the beginnings of a legend.

11. The Squatters

Borun was not immediately aware of the presence of his uninvited guest. The refuge One Eye had chosen was the old nursery, a part of the set Borun rarely visited, and so it was not until dusk fell that the badger, emerging, found the atmosphere around the set redolent with the musky odor of fox. He tracked the scent to its source, and having confirmed his suspicions that he now had a new neighbor, he departed on the night's forage, grumbling to himself as he trotted down the track. There was nothing he could do about the situation, even if it had occurred to him to take action, which it did not. To the badger, foxes—like frost, and snow, and ache in the bones—were an inevitable fact of life.

For sixteen hours One Eye lay exhausted in the nursery

set. Then, as the gray dawn turned to silver over the misty landscape, she crawled from the set and made her way stiffly through the wood in search of water. She found it at the limestone spring, and having drunk her fill, limped painfully back to the set. Here she met Borun, and the two animals stared in hostility at each other before disappearing into their separate quarters. Time, and destiny, had caught up with One Eye, and now she could not leave the set, even if she had wanted to.

In the next four hours she gave birth to four cubs, all naked, blind, and helpless. In spite of the mental trauma their mother had suffered, and her physical ordeal of the previous day, the cubs were strong and lusty, and they all thrived. Within fourteen days their eyes were open, and at three weeks they made their first stumbling appearance at the mouth of the set, small, sooty, furred imps with bright eyes, short pointed noses, and big ears, wobbling about on rubbery legs and waving ridiculous little wisps of tails.

For a week or so the cubs played at the mouth of the set, romping like kittens under the watchful eye of their mother, and when Borun passed they sat very still and upright, affording Borun the respect a child might have for an elderly and crochety uncle. Then, as the cubs grew older, their mother began to wean them.

The woods and fields of the valley were alive with young birds and animals too silly and inexperienced to survive for long, and One Eye brought back to the set young rabbits and pheasant chicks, voles, mice and leverets, lapwing, partridge, and moorhen. Occasionally she even brought lizards and slow worms, and once a luckless green woodpecker, caught napping as he probed the turf of the woodland floor for grubs late one evening. Mice and voles she brought by the mouthful, appearing at the set with the tiny corpses packed sideways between her jaws, the tails hanging down on either side of her nuzzle like a drooping walrus moustache.

After a while she began to bring back her victims maimed, but not dead, and these she released for the cubs to chase and kill. She brought back more, far more, than either she or the cubs could eat. Gradually the arena around the set became littered with the remains of small corpses, many of which the cubs continued to use as playthings, the pelt of a rabbit, the wing of a moorhen, the leg and foot of a pheasant.

Now the sweet sickly scent of rotting flesh was added to the aroma of fox, and during the warm sunny days the air was loud with the buzzing of blowflies, come to lay their eggs on the rotting meat. Some of the flies even found their way into Borun's sleeping quarters, and roused him from his slumber. It was getting to be too much for him to bear.

The climax came one night in early June. For some days One Eye had realized that conditions in the nursery set were growing too cramped for herself and four lumping great cubs. The air was hot and stuffy, and what remained of the bedding was foul and verminous. A move was imperative, and so, taking advantage of Borun's absence, One Eye went on an exploration of the main set. She found Borun's sleeping chamber, freshly lined with grass and dry leaves, and knew at once that nothing could suit her needs better. Just before dawn she led her cubs down there, the last and smallest cub bringing up the rear and dragging his favorite plaything, the rabbit pelt, behind him. This he abandoned three feet inside the entrance to the tunnel.

Borun returned to find his entrance defiled and putrid with the stench of fox, and he did not need the evidence of the rabbit skin to tell him what had happened. One by one he inspected every entrance to the set, and in each case his nose told him the same story, that the entire set was contaminated by the presence of the foxes. It was too much. He could not endure the discomfort and the mess any longer. Abruptly he turned away from the set and padded off into the wood. For a moment his humped gray back was visible among the undergrowth, and then he was lost in the shadows of the trees.

He took the path uphill, and as the sun crested the horizon he entered the tangle of rock and twisted thorn that clung like old gray chain mail to the hillside below the Iron Age fort. Here he spent the day, curled in a tight ball at the foot of a gnarled old hawthorn tree, and apart from the steady rise and fall of his breathing, he was indistinguishable from the stones and boulders that littered the hill.

The shade of the tree had sheltered him from the heat of the noonday sun, but now its westering rays struck warm upon his flank, waking him and bringing him to remembrance of where he was. For a while he lay basking in the warmth and light, but as the sun sank below the shoulder of the hill he got up, scratched, and shook himself before setting off into what was for him unexplored territory.

He crossed the windswept plateau of the old fort, picking up an occasional beetle from the short, sheep-bitten turf, but all the while heading purposefully southeast, away from the valley of his birth. Soon he was in farmland again, wide fields planted with barley and root crops, and surrounded by carefully tended hedges and banks. A barn owl, drifting white and ghostlike over the land, swerved in startled surprise as Borun raised his black and white snout skyward, and a hunting stoat chattered angrily from the safety of the tangled hedge roots as he passed by.

Then he came to woodland again, a plantation of young spruce trees growing tall above the rotting stumps of what had once been giant old oaks, trees that had been felled so that the swifter-growing conifers could provide a cash crop for the farmer. Borun tried in vain to find a way into the plantation, but the area had been well and truly fenced off by the farmer, who was only too familiar with the sort of damage that rabbits and roe deer would cause once they gained entry. So Borun skirted around the plantation until he came to older, deciduous woodland, with a narrow rutted track, twisting between high banks, and still littered with the leaves of the previous autumn.

On top of the bank tall beech trees grew, their trunks silver in the moon that now shone down out of a starlit sky. Their tough old roots twisted and twined like great gray serpents over the eroded remains of the bank, while overhead the branches met in a graceful arc to form a canopy of leaves, black and metallic in the lunar light. The trees had stood there, season after season, surviving winter gales and summer drought, hail and rain and biting frost. They were at once a monument and a reminder that perhaps our forefathers were better conservationists than we give them credit for.

Some two hundred years ago a farsighted landowner had planted these beech trees, along with thousands of others, as part of a new and revolutionary system of farming known as a four-crop rotation. To this end he had divided his land into fields, surrounding each one with a hedge and a ditch, and the saplings he chose for his hedges were all beech. Once the saplings had taken firm root, the hedges were "laid." The saplings were cut halfway through, and laid over one against the other, and pegged down. The saplings did not die, but put forth fresh green growth, so that in a very short time they formed a stockproof barrier, and since the dead leaves hung on through the winter, they provided shelter from wind and rain.

At the same time, by allowing sections of hedge to sprout up, the farmer assured himself of a constant supply of firewood, that came in handy ten-foot lengths, and was exactly the right thickness for easy cutting and burning. After the firewood had been harvested, the fence was once more laid, and the cycle began anew.

Then came the industrial revolution, and a cheap and

seemingly inexhaustible supply of coal. Following that came a world war, and a shortage of manpower coincided with the invention of barbed wire, so that the beech hedgerow became an expensive anachronism. Except in a few districts, it disappeared from the country scene. Here, all that remained of the hedge was a twin avenue of tall trees, which for almost a century had escaped the power saw and the ax.

Rabbits swarmed among the beech roots, secure behind a tangled trelliswork that defied Borun's attempts to dig them out, but the deep litter of leafmold that lay in the track provided rich pickings in the way of worms and grubs. Borun dug and grunted happily, working his slow way down the track as the moon sailed her course across the sky.

As the short summer night came to an end, and the thin line of dawn brightened the northeastern sky, Borun came to a hole in the earth bank. It was little more than an overgrown rabbit burrow, scratched and dug and tunneled by generations of rabbits, but there was ample room for Borun, and he clambered inside. After a short distance underground, the tunnel widened out into a sizable chamber beneath a beech bole, and here Borun surprised a startled doe rabbit, who was too witless to flee. Borun grabbed her, and twenty minutes later, feeling uncomfortably full, settled to sleep.

Some hours later he awoke to instant alertness, roused by the deep-throated barking of a dog. He lay still, listening, and then came a scratching at the mouth of the tunnel, not three feet away. There came another bark, and then an excited, high-pitched whining, followed by a soft, snuffling sound. Suddenly the chamber was filled with the scent of dog, and Borun backed against the far wall, head down, hair bristling, and white teeth bared, ready to fight to the death if need be. Next moment he relaxed, as the dog suddenly moved away.

Outside in the lane the black Labrador raced after his master, in obedience to the gamekeeper's whistle. The man growled at him affectionately, "Who gave you leave to go off rabbiting, I'd like to know? Come in to heel."

Obediently the dog fell in behind the man, who walked on, his gun crooked comfortably over his arm. Again he spoke, more to himself than to the dog. "I see the pheasants have been feeding well in the lane. There's fresh leaves upturned that weren't disturbed yesterday."

12. The River

Borun passed an uneasy day in the hole under the beech tree. Long before sunset he was waiting at the mouth of the hole, anxious to be away from this place with its threat of danger from man and dog. He was in fact doubly fortunate, in that the retriever had warned him of his peril so soon after his arrival on the estate, and that the gamekeeper had so far failed to notice his presence. For Borun had unwittingly strayed onto a game preserve. The old deciduous woodland had been allowed to remain merely to act as cover for the pheasants that swarmed in the undergrowth.

In the autumn many of these birds would die, shot by syndicates of businessmen who were prepared to pay high fees for the privilege of hunting them, and so the pheasants represented a cash crop to the farmer, as valuable in its way as the cereals and root crops he grew. In consequence the woodlands were managed as efficiently as the rest of the farm. Borun's presence would not have gone unnoticed for long, and it would not have been tolerated, even though it posed little threat to the pheasant population.

The pheasants were flying to roost as Borun left his hideout, exploding out of the undergrowth with a clatter of wings and perching in the branches of the trees, their plump forms dark silhouettes against the night sky. Borun passed beneath them, following the course of a grassy ride that traversed the woodland, and soon he was out in open country again, crossing wide flat fertile fields which ended abruptly in an escarpment of low limestone cliffs. Below the cliffs a belt of thick woodland fell away to more open parkland, with tall trees casting deep pools of shadow in the bright moonlight. Beyond the park, shimmering like a silver snake, lay the broad sweep of the river.

The river was old and wide, meandering through fields and meadows, loitering on the last stage of its journey to the sea. A major artery of the land, it was fed by scores of tributaries, pouring their waters down out of the hills that lay to the east and south. Though cold and infertile at first, these waters contained one priceless asset, for they welled up out of the chalk, and they were rich in dissolved calcium.

Slowed down and sun warmed, the river maintained an immeasurable quantity and diversity of life, as the calcium provided a rich, alkaline medium in which vegetable and animal plankton flourished. This in turn supported vast armies of freshwater shrimps and insects, which contributed to the great size of the fish, the chub and trout, the perch and pike and roach. Eventually the calcium found its way to the teeth and bones of the water voles and otters, and to the eggshells of the coot and moorhen and mallard that nested on the banks. So a legacy laid down millions of years ago was returned once more to the living, for the chalk was formed out of the skeletons of other creatures, now long extinct, which once had swarmed in the sunlit shallow waters of a tropical sea.

Each winter, when the rains came, the volume of water cascading down out of the hills was too much for the river to carry away to the sea, and at least once or twice every year the river broke its banks, spreading its waters, laden with a heavy burden of silt, over the meadows on either side. This flooding enriched the pastures, and the grass grew lush and thick as the waters subsided in the spring, in turn supporting a wealth of life. Moles busily pursued the earthworms in the soft soil. Voles and mice squeaked and scurried through the grass roots, and in turn were harried by weasels and owls.

So Borun fed well that night, and the next, hiding by day in the dark recesses of a huge old hollow oak tree that had fallen one night in a winter gale ten years previously, and now lay in a corner of a field, conveniently out of the farmer's way, and overgrown with a thick tangle of bramble and briar rose.

He woke, late on the evening of the second day, to a strange hubbub and disturbance. Footsteps reverberated along the riverbank. Men called to each other on the still evening air. Somewhere in the distance, car doors were slamming. A transistor radio played tinny music, and a paraffin stove hissed as its flames blossomed like a blue rose around the base of a kettle.

Nervously, Borun peered out from the curtain of foliage that sheltered the entrance to his hideaway, unable to comprehend the sight that met his eyes. As far as he could see in the rapidly gathering dusk, men lined the river on both banks. Others were still arriving, each laden down with a mountain of gear, and carrying a bundle of fishing rods, the latecomers tramping past those who had already arrived, in search of a vacant space by the river. Meantime, those who had earlier staked their claims were busy assembling their rods, and setting up a variety of other items, such as large umbrellas, collapsible chairs, and beds. Here and there, some were even erecting tents.

Borun was witnessing what had now become an annual event in modern England, the opening night of the coarse fishing season. Nobody quite knew how many anglers there were. Some estimated the figure at three million, but this included the more solitary anglers for salmon and trout, and those who fished in the sea. Yet the greater proportion of anglers were the so-called coarse fishermen, who fished for freshwater species other than salmon and trout, and who angled purely for sport, returning their catch to the river at the end of each outing. The association that leased the fishing rights of this river had its headquarters in a city some twenty miles away, and the membership of the association numbered over ten thousand. Not every member turned out on the opening night, but the fishermen arrived in sufficient numbers to have a massive impact on their surroundings.

Borun waited for more than three hours, but the fishermen showed no signs of moving, so he slipped out of the hollow tree and made his way upstream, giving the riverbank a wide berth. After a journey of a mile or so, he realized that the serried ranks of anglers had come to an end. He had crossed the boundary of that stretch of river that the association leased, and he was now on land where the riparian owner kept the fishing for himself. So for the remainder of the night he foraged successfully and in peace, and because no suitable resting place offered itself, he returned at dawn to the hollow tree, noting, as he crept quietly into the bramble thicket, that the anglers were still there.

Many of the anglers returned to the city later in the morning, to sleep, or to yawn their way through a weary day at office or factory. Next evening other anglers came to the riverbank to take their place, and so it would continue throughout the summer, with numbers dwindling as the earlier novelty wore off, but always with someone in attendance by day or night. The anglers caught many fish, and some died as a result of handling, but most survived and lived to grow larger, and be caught another day.

The anglers had a profound effect on the country scene. The sheer weight of their numbers eroded the banks, and wore the grass bare, killing it so that when the winter floods came the grass no longer held the banks in place, and the floodwaters washed them away.

Many anglers used bread in large quantities, not only to bait their hooks, but as ground bait, throwing it into the stream to attract shoals of fish to the area around their hooks. Often surplus bread was left lying on the bank, or was thrown into the rushes bordering the stream, and while much of it was eaten by birds, the remainder attracted rats, who took up permanent residence by the stream.

Most of the anglers were considerate and thoughtful, at pains to preserve the beauty of a landscape they valued almost as much as the fishing itself, but a few were careless and untidy, leaving litter, always unsightly, and often dangerous. Small rodents squeezed their way into discarded bottles, only to starve when they found themselves unable to climb out up the slippery sides. Birds were trapped, snared by lengths of nylon monofilament line, which cut into their legs so tightly that even if they did not die, the victims escaped only at the cost of losing a limb. The majority of anglers were quick to condemn such practices, however, and most were agreed that much as they enjoyed the camaraderie of the riverbank, they would be only too happy to exchange it for solitude, and a stretch of the river to themselves. As things were, the very popularity of their sport was going a long way to destroying it.

Borun soon noticed that the anglers kept strictly to the riverbank, and deciding that they posed no threat to him, he came and went pretty much as he pleased, always being careful, however, to keep a safe distance away, and to enter and leave his hideout with extreme caution. All the same, he was observed by one or two keen-eyed anglers, who regarded his appearance as an added bonus to the fishing expedition, and were careful to leave him unmolested.

The month dragged on in sullen heat, as the brassy glare of the sun parched the earth, baking the muddy margins of the river so that they grew cracked and hard. By night a warm wind blew, so that no dew fell to freshen the dusty pastures. In the fields, sweating farmhands labored to bring in the hay, and gazing skyward, foretold the coming of the storm.

It broke late one afternoon. All day thunder had been muttering in the far-off hills, causing the pheasants in the copses to crow as if in answer. Already the waterfowl on the river had moved deep into the reedbeds for safety, warned of impending disaster by the slight, almost imperceptible rise in the level of the river, and the gathering of tiny twigs and grasses, washed down from far upstream, which together with flecks of foam presaged the coming of the flood. As the day wore on the sky darkened from sulfur yellow to deepest bronze, and then to black, to a darkness so extreme that birds flew prematurely to roost.

Then came the wind, blowing strong and chill, turning the leaves of the alders so that they showed their silvery undersides, and as that died away the first lightning bolt rent the skies. Hail fell, stripping the leaves from the trees and pounding young and tender growth into a slimy green pulp. Insects died in their thousands, as did any small bird or mammal that had not heeded the warning signs, or had been unlucky in its choice of shelter. As the hail ceased, and torrential rain took its place, the lightning and the thunder became a continuous bedlam of light and sound. Far away, on the coast thirty miles to the west, the tide began to rise.

It was the time of the new moon, and far out in the ocean

the waters had responded to the combined pull of the sun and the moon. Now they were rushing back landward, flooding into the estuaries and inlets, just in time to meet the storm water thundering down off the hills, swelling the waters of the river, and finding no outlet.

There was only one way they could go, and as the rain continued to fall, the river rose, inch by slow inch, until the first trickles spilled out over the banks and sent creeping, questing fingers of muddy water out into the meadow. The trickles grew into streams, the streams became torrents, and at last a swelling brown tide, foam-flecked and strewn with flotsam, sticks, and branches, old tree stumps, bottles, plastic containers of every shape and hue and size, twigs, grasses, and fragments of leaves, wisps of hay, and the decayed empty husk of a newborn calf, which had been washed into the river during an earlier flood, and which had hung drying in the branches of a riverside tree ever since.

Borun woke to an unpleasant feeling of cold and wetness, and leapt up to find water flowing into the hollow log. Earlier he had heard the tumult of the storm, and had curled tighter into a ball, covering his ears with his paws to drown the din. Now he was to regret his heedlessness. Grumbling to himself, he waded out into the open. In the dim light he saw a brown sea spreading in every direction, and noticed a ripple of movement by his feet. A short-tailed vole was swimming in search of safety. When it reached the rough bark of the log it scrambled up, shook itself, and began to groom its fur. For a moment Borun was tempted to snap the vole up, but self-preservation came first. He set off, splashing through the flood, which came almost to the level of his chin, and making for higher ground.

Several times he was forced to swim. He passed more small rodents, more unfortunate even than the vole on the log, swimming aimlessly around in small circles that could only end, when cold and fear and exhaustion had done their work, in death. For the vole on the log, life was to be endured for another four hours, until a hunting owl spotted the small form and sank its talons deep in the vole's heart.

Borun was in no such danger, but he was cold and wet and thoroughly out of temper by the time he reached dry land. He shook himself vigorously, and groomed as much of the moisture as possible out of his coat, before setting out across the sodden landscape. He still followed the course of the river upstream, but gave the water meadows a wide berth. The river was rich, and offered an easy living, but it was also treacherous.

In the event, the storm was over, the rain ceased, the tide turned, and the floodwaters began to recede. With the dawn, a watery sun embraced a steaming world with its warmth, and from an ash tree in a wayside thicket a blackbird sang a hymn of praise and gratitude for survival. Deep in the thicket Borun grunted, and slept.

13. The Romanies

The thicket in which Borun had taken refuge was comprised of a few tall and stately ash trees, protected by a dense undergrowth of blackthorn. It stood in the middle of a patch of wasteland that lay at the meeting of two roads. Beyond the wasteland was a small wood, where clumps of hazel grew beneath old and pollarded oaks, and beyond that flowed a stream, its waters still swollen and brown from the rainfall of the previous night. A rough track led across the wasteland, following the boundary of the wood, and screened from the road by the thorn thicket. Coarse grasses covered the rest of the land, yellowing in the sun as their flowers turned to seed.

The long day dragged on in silence under the sun. Once a

magpie flew into the thicket, to perch on the topmost branch of the tallest tree, and his raucous cry, as he spotted Borun asleep in the shade, ripped the air like rifle fire. Then he flew away and was lost to sight beyond the wood. The wasteland was still again, save for the drone of countless insects, each busy with its own mysterious lifestyle. No one came near, for the roads, dusty and forgotten, belonged to a bygone age. The countryside, burdened with the ripening wheat, lay quietly awaiting the bustle and noise of the harvest.

The afternoon was almost over when the travelers arrived at the wasteland. They came driving slowly down the road, a motley cavalcade, and one by one pulled onto the track beside the wood, parking their vehicles behind the dense screen of the thorn thicket. First came an expensive saloon car, towing a large black and white caravan that sported lace curtains at the windows, and shone with trimmings of chromium plate. Next came an open truck, half loaded with a miscellaneous collection of junk, scrap metal, rags, and wooden crates, and also towing a caravan, which, though smaller, was just as opulent as the first. Finally came a closed van, towing a third caravan, older and cheaper than the others, but still shining with bright green paint and polish.

The travelers were Romanies, whose ancestors had migrated out of India centuries ago, to travel west and spread out across the whole of Europe and, in spite of persistent persecution, to survive. This family, the older man and his wife, the two sons and their wives, together with four children, a goat, a crate of hens, and a pack of lean, hungry mongrel dogs, had been strawberry picking down in the south and were now moving slowly north to Gloucester, where soon there would be plums, apples, and hops to pick. They lived by casual labor, and on their travels they bought, and sometimes stole, scrap metal, collected rags, and sold clothes-pegs and artificial flowers. This wasteland had been from time immemorial one of their "atchin tans," or stopping places. Being isolated and lonely, it posed little danger to them from police or angry landowners.

Now the silence of the wasteland was shattered as the travelers clambered out of their vehicles, and with practiced ease set about preparing for their stay. The children were dispatched to collect firewood. The women began to prepare the evening meal, and the men unhitched the caravans and checked that they stood level. In a very short space of time a big black cooking pot hung over a crackling fire, the goat was tethered and grazing contentedly, and the hens were pecking busily around and under the caravans. The family gathered around the fire, the men swarthy and dark-skinned, with gaudy neckerchiefs knotted about their throats. The women were burned brown by the sun, their auburn hair coiled in plaited ropes around their heads, and the flames from the fire glinted hungrily on the gold that hung from their ears, necks, and wrists. The children were ragged and dirty, but happy and well fed. They joked and gossiped among themselves for a while, and then one of the sons remembered the dogs, still cooped up in the back of the van.

He strolled over and opened the door, and they poured out in a joyous yelping stream. There were five of them, an ill-assorted crew, but each chosen and kept for his particular qualities. There was a great gray brute, the result of a mating between a collie and a greyhound, who could run down a hare in fifty yards. There was an Alsatian crossed with a retriever, who could bring back a partridge chick to the hand alive, so soft was his mouth, but who, when left on guard, was better than any lock. There were two whippets, who, working together, kept the family supplied with as many rabbits as they could eat and sell, and a tiny rough brown terrier who had earned his owner many a pound by killing rats. Free at last from the stuffy confines of the van, they raced around for a while, chasing each other's tails and engaging in mock combat, until at last, as their first euphoria waned, they settled down to explore their surroundings.

All this time Borun had lain in the thorn thicket, wide awake and anxious, listening to the tumult of sound that echoed over the wasteland. Although tempted to flee, he nevertheless remained where he was, waiting for darkness, for he was in strange country, and he had no idea which direction to take in search of safety. The likelihood of his being discovered seemed at first remote, for the undergrowth in the thorn thicket was prickly and dense, and there was little chance of a human forcing a way in. Then he heard the clamor of the dogs, the sound he hated most in all the world, and his heart sank.

The terrier found him first, and the hysterical yapping of the little dog brought the others to the scene. Borun set his back to the base of the ash tree and waited, his white teeth bared in a snarl of rage and defiance, confident that he could deal with both the terrier and the whippets, should they attempt to close with him. When the bigger dogs arrived, however, he knew that he was outnumbered, and taking a desperate chance, he screamed with anger and charged at the terrier.

The little dog yelped in fear and leapt aside, leaving Borun free to bolt. As the larger dogs floundered around, hampered by the clinging undergrowth, Borun burst through the thicket and shot out into the clearing like a hairy gray cannonball, only to stop short at the sight of the Romany family, sitting in a half-circle around the fire, and staring in amazement at the sudden appearance of the badger.

Borun hesitated only briefly. Then, as one of the men leapt to his feet and snatched up a heavy log, the badger swerved and ran for the woods. Yet even before he had covered a few yards he knew that he would never reach his goal, for the gray dog had broken free of the thicket and raced around to cut off Borun's escape. There was only one way for him to go. In a last desperate attempt to find sanctuary, he jumped through the open door of one of the caravans, while the dog, knowing full well the terrible penalty that awaited him from his master if he attempted to follow, stood and howled outside.

The man with the log moved forward, confident now that Borun was at his mercy. He was halfway through the door of the caravan when the older man cried out, "Wait!"

The son turned, scowling, but obedient to the command. "What now, father? What's there to wait for, when there's a badger pelt worth a five-pound note there for the taking, and badger hams to smoke over our fire?"

The father made a gesture of impatience. "You'd make a poor bargain if you did not wait. Could you trade your badger pelt for, say, six bottles of good whiskey?" He moved closer, laying his hand on his son's shoulder and continuing in a low, confidential voice. "I know a man, not far from here, who would give not one, but four five-pound notes for this badger, but it must be delivered alive, and in good condition."

The son thought about this for a few moments, then, throwing down his log, he carefully closed the caravan door, and sitting down on the step, squinted up at his father. "All right then. Who's this fool of a man who would part with so much money for an old badger, and why? Besides, how do you propose to take the brute alive? It'll tear you to pieces if you go near."

"Patience, patience," said the old man. "The man lives not far from here. He runs a kind of zoo, a wildlife park he calls it, and he charges tourists who come to see the animals. I sold him a litter of fox cubs in the spring, when we passed through, and he told me then that if ever I found a live badger, he would buy it. This one is no cub, but it is only a youngster, and if he doesn't want it, well, then will be the time to knock it on the head. As to taking it live, watch, and you will learn."

He moved over to the truck, and from out of the pile of scrap metal he pulled a length of iron piping, about five feet long and half an inch in diameter. Then from under the seat in the driver's cab he took a length of strong, thin cord. One end of the cord he knotted tightly to an end of the piping, and then threaded the cord down the tube, so forming a noose, which he drew tight several times to ensure that it ran freely.

Next he went to the wood and cut a long hazel wand, and came back trimming the twigs and leaves from it with his pocketknife. "Get me that strong wooden crate off the back of the wagon," he commanded his sons, "and bring me a hammer and some nails to fasten down the lid."

When all was ready he took the hazel wand in his left hand, and the pipe in his right, the noose hanging in a wide loop. Then, after instructing his sons to open the caravan door, and to place the crate in front of it after he had entered, he stepped inside the caravan.

Borun, crouched in a tiny space between the caravan's stove and a bunk bed, heard the sound of the door opening, and turned to face fresh danger. The old Romany advanced toward him, very slowly, taking step after careful step, the hazel wand pointing toward Borun, the loop of cord hung over the wand.

Borun watched the wand, for this seemed to him to offer the greater threat. He did not notice the noose, or paid no heed to it if he did. When the wand was within six inches of his snout he snapped, seizing the hazel between his jaws and sinking his teeth into the wood. Being green and pliant, it did not sheer off, but merely splintered between his jaws, and Borun hung on grimly as the old man pulled firmly but smoothly on the wand. While Borun's neck was thus stretched, and his teeth fully occupied, the noose slid down the wand and settled softly over his head. Next moment the man had pulled it tight.

Borun's scream died in his throat as he felt himself swung into the air. Choking, clawing at his neck, twisting, squirming, he was carried along and swung out of the caravan door.

The box was open, and he was lowered into it. As his feet touched the wooden floor the lid was clapped on, and darkness descended, but mercifully the cord around his neck suddenly slackened, and once more he was able to breathe. For a few seconds he was deafened by the banging of the hammer as the lid was nailed down, and then he was left in peace.

With the badger successfully captured, the Romanies settled down to their evening meal, and when it was over they loaded the crate into the back of the van and set off back down the road they had traveled earlier in the afternoon. The journey was short, but to Borun it was a nightmare of noise, and the stuffy confines of the crate were made worse by the combined smells of petrol, exhaust fumes, and the hateful smell of dog. At first he tried to claw and bite his way out of the crate, but it was new and strongly made, and he could make no impression on the unyielding wood. At last, exhausted and half suffocated, he lay down, his claws torn and bleeding, but he was too terrified to sleep.

At last the van stopped, and the engine was cut. Alert again, Borun waited and listened, but all he could hear were voices, which were meaningless to him. They went on for what seemed an interminable while, now raised, now low and pleading. Then the van door was opened, the crate was lifted out and carried away, Borun inside standing straddle-legged in order to keep his balance. The box was set down, the nails in the lid were drawn, and Borun fell in a heap as the box was turned suddenly on its side. Then the lid was pulled to one side, and light flooded in, light and sweet fresh air.

14. The Prisoners

Borun was in no hurry to leave the box, however unpleasant it was, for outside, he knew, the men were waiting. He could smell them, and hear their heavy breathing, and so he crouched motionless in a corner of the crate, preferring to endure any discomfort rather than face the unknown dangers that lay outside.

He was not left in peace for long. A stiff-bristled broom was pushed into the crate, and Borun was prodded with it. Borun snapped and tore at the bristles, but they pricked his lips and gums, and no matter how many he cut through with his sharp teeth, there were still more to torment him. The broom was like a live thing that would not bleed or suffer,

91

and could not be vanquished. At last, Borun bolted from the crate.

Dazed and bewildered, Borun could see only that he was in a small enclosure, with smooth white walls and a concrete floor. He caught a brief glimpse of a pair of stoutly gaitered legs, guarded by the threatening broom, and then he spotted a pile of straw in a corner. He dived into it, burrowing down until he was lost to view, and the owner of the wildlife park, satisfied that he had a live badger in good condition, paid over the twenty pounds he had promised the Romanies. So the two men departed, well content with their evening's work.

The wildlife park, as it was called, had developed gradually over the years. At the end of the second world war a young army officer had bought a dilapidated mansion in the grounds of a small estate, with the intention of restoring the old house to its former grandeur. Purely as a temporary measure, he had moved into what had once been the head gardener's cottage, which stood in a walled garden, adjacent to the mansion. Now the old house was crumbling into ruin, and the officer, well past middle age, was still in the cottage.

At the end of the war building materials had been impossible to obtain, so to while away the time the young man had turned his attention to a small stream that flowed through the grounds, widening it and building several weirs. Then he fenced the water meadows into paddocks, and began to stock the stream with fish and wildfowl, ducks, geese, and swans. Gradually over the years he became more and more absorbed with his hobby, and as his interest grew, so his expenses became heavier, until one day, more to defray some of his costs than with any idea of making a profit, he opened his grounds to the public, advertising a riverside walk, and charging a modest entry fee.

The response took him totally by surprise, as thousands of visitors poured in on fine summer weekends. It was an age of affluence, and more and more people were acquiring cars, and the leisure to go touring. Bored and restless, they were eager for any diversion that came their way. So the riverside walk became a wildlife park. The rich brown loam of the kitchen gardens disappeared beneath lawns and gravel walks. The shrubberies were enclosed by aviaries, and the greenhouse became an aquarium and reptile house. The coach yard and stables became a children's corner, with Shetland ponies, goats, lambs and chickens, rabbits, cavies and doves all enjoying an indolent and more or less amicable existence. A restaurant was built, for the tourists arrived hungry and thirsty.

Gradually more exotic species made their appearance, and the green hills of England echoed to strange cries. A small herd of sea lions, never again to taste the salt spray of the Pacific Ocean, wallowed and splashed in the stream. An elderly lynx basked in the sun, and breathed air redolent of french fries and hamburgers instead of pine forests and muskeg swamps. A fish eagle from Africa brooded on the topmost branch of a dead pine stump, and ignored the blowflies that buzzed around the dried remains of a dead whiting lying on the floor of the cage. The animals were all well fed, and the cages clean and tidy, imaginatively designed to give the inmates the maximum of freedom and privacy, yet it seemed that an ineffable air of sadness hung over the grounds. Close by, the old mansion was settling slowly back into the earth. Plaster crumbled from the walls. Bats lived in the roof. A family of jackdaws nested in one of the chimneys, and a barn owl roosted in the tower.

Of late, the owner had conceived the idea of a section of the park devoted to mammals of the British Isles. To this end he had bought the fox cubs earlier in the spring, and he now had a badger. The arrival of Borun, however, had taken him by surprise, and since for the moment there was no suitable accommodation ready, Borun was temporarily housed in one

of a new range of pigsties, from which there seemed no possibility of escape. Here the owner left Borun to recover from
his ordeal, with a bowl of fresh water, and a dish of raw
meat, together with two thick slices of bread plastered with
honey.

Darkness fell, but Borun remained hidden in the straw
pile. For a long time he stayed awake, trembling with fear
and shock, but slowly his heart stopped hammering and his
limbs ceased their twitching, and he slept. He woke a little
before dawn and ventured out, feeling stiff and sore, but the
water revived him, and he licked the honey from the bread
before crawling back under the straw.

He slept but little during the following day, for the strange
scents and the variety of noises that came to him continued to
unnerve and bewilder him. Toward dusk he emerged again,
and began to explore his surroundings.

The sty was divided into two parts, a sleeping compartment with a raised concrete platform, windowless and roofed
over, and an outer yard, with walls four feet high, finished
with a smooth rendering of plaster. The gate was solidly
made of wood, clad with sheet steel and securely locked.
There seemed to be no possible avenue of escape, but Borun
persisted in his explorations, covering every inch of the enclosure, and from time to time standing on his hind legs and
reaching high up the walls, in the hope of finding some foothold. There was none.

Yet unknown to the owner, the laborer who had built the
pigsty had skimped the job. The specifications had called for
two inches of sand and cement laid over two inches of hard-
core, but in one corner of the sleeping compartment the covering was less than half an inch thick. The laborer had seen
that he was about to run out of material. It was almost time
for him to finish work, and he was too lazy to mix any more
sand and cement, so he had filled the corner with loose earth
and spread what mixture he had left thinly over it, confident
that no one would notice.

In drying, the unequal thickness had caused the sand and cement to crack, but in the darkness no one had detected the flaw. Borun found it, and began to scratch.

Soon he discovered he could get his claws under the slab, and in response to his tugging it began to rock. Gradually he raised it until he was able to bite at the edge, and at last he could get his strong snout beneath it. Three quick jerks and the slab broke in two halves, which Borun dragged away, exposing the soft loose earth beneath. Now he began to dig in earnest, loosening the earth still further and dragging it back by the armful. Before long he was lost to sight, and the floor of the pigsty was covered with fresh soil.

He came to the foundations of the walls, and dug down until he had passed beneath them. Then he began to dig upward, making rapid progress, for the ground outside the wall had recently been excavated for the laying of the foundations, and shoveled back after the building had been completed. From time to time he rested, and once he took time off to return to the enclosure and drink the water provided, but he took no food. There was still an hour of darkness left before the dawn when he broke free of his prison, and emerged into the open.

The night was warm and windy, the stars hidden by a veil of cloud. Borun wandered around, seeking some way out of the walled garden, but each path he followed ended against a brick wall, a fence of chicken wire, or a cage whose startled occupant peered at him through the darkness. A porcupine rattled its quills. A great horned owl snapped its beak and crouched low on its perch. A roosting peacock awoke to screaming, flapping flight, and the old lynx ceased his endless prowling to growl a throaty warning. Borun's nerves were almost at breaking point when at last, quite by chance, he found the main entrance, and walked out under the turnstile.

A long winding drive stretched away across parkland studded with ancient elms and oaks. Borun hurried across the short tussocky grass, anxious to get as far away as possible from the wildlife park before dawn, and also to find some cover in which to spend the hours of daylight. Yet he knew that he could not travel far. A great weariness was on him, and a ravenous hunger, which was hardly surprising, for he had eaten little or nothing for three nights and days.

The parkland ended abruptly beside a main road, and here Borun was in luck, for the corpse of a rabbit lay still warm in the verge, where it had crawled after being struck by a passing car. Borun picked up the rabbit and hurried across the road with it dangling from his jaws, settling down to a late supper as soon as he was safely hidden in the bushes.

It was breaking light by the time he had finished eating, and the clouds of night were dispersing before a chill breeze that heralded the rising of the sun. Below him the hillside fell away in rolling heathland, a thick carpet of dark heather, interspersed by clumps of gorse, spindly birch trees, and here and there a stand of pine. Beyond the heathland lay a river, and beyond that a ridge of hills ending in a steep limestone escarpment. Something about the hills and the escarpment struck a chord in Borun's memory, but he paid no heed. He set off across the heathland. He had not gone far before he came upon a twisting narrow track that wound between the white stems of the heather. He stopped, and sniffed the ground carefully.

There was no doubt about it. Another of his kind had passed this way, and only a short while ago. For some reason he could not understand, the knowledge filled Borun with a strange excitement. He moved off down the trail, quickening his pace as the scent grew stronger, until he came to a hollow in the side of the hill, where the ground was bare of vegetation and sharp flints shone among the pale ocher of the gravel. At the foot of a twisted old gorse bush a hole had been dug, and the sweet musky aroma that had so excited and disturbed Borun hung all around it. He moved closer and called, and the constriction he felt at his throat half strangled what he had meant to be a whickering greeting, so that it emerged as a soft purr.

He waited, but no response came, so he called again, louder, and this time he heard a muffled padding deep in the earth. Respectfully, he drew back a little, continuing to call, but standing very still as cautiously, inch by inch, the other badger emerged. She was smaller than he, very trim and slender, and she stood blinking in the strong morning sunlight, one paw raised and her nose questing the air. Borun moved slightly, and for a moment she made as if to dive back into the hole, but then she came forward, until the two animals touched noses, and then sniffed each other over face, ears, and neck. Both badgers were trembling, he with eagerness and anticipation, she with slight fear and nervousness.

Then she turned, and made her way slowly back into the set. Borun stood outside, irresolute, anxious, wanting to follow but unsure of his welcome. He turned away, half determined to depart, to find some other shelter for the day, but then he heard her call, and saw that she was back at the mouth of the set, watching him and waiting for him to make the next move. He walked toward her, and she backed slowly away from him, leading him down out of sight, into the cool darkness of the set.

There was only one tunnel, quite short, but it led under a great slab of sandstone, and then widened out into a sleeping chamber lined with a deep litter of fern. Borun was vaguely conscious of her snuffling near him, and rustling the fern, and then a great wave of exhaustion swept over him, and he fell into a deep sleep.

15. Handa

The female's name was Handa. She had been born in the same year as Borun. She and her brother had left their parents' set the previous autumn, and for a while they had shared a home on this heathland. Then one night a month ago her brother had wandered away alone and failed to return. Since then she had led a solitary and none too happy existence. Several times she had been on the point of abandoning the set, to seek the company of other badgers. Now Borun had come into her life. The knowledge of his presence, as he slept beside her in the darkness, filled her with contentment, and she drowsed happily through the day.

It was late in the evening when Borun woke, to find himself alone in the sleeping chamber. Handa was waiting for him outside the set, and she trotted over to greet him as he emerged. The sun was setting, illuminating the sky in the northwest, and shedding a soft rosy luster over the shaggy cloak of the hillside. Together the two badgers lay on the bare baked earth, still warm from the sun's rays, listening and waiting as the first pale stars appeared and dusk stole out of the valley below, welling like a dark tide up the slopes of the hill. A few rooks flew lazily overhead, winging their way back to roost after a long day's toil in the fields, and an owl wafted low over the heather, dropping out of sight and then rising with a small burden clutched in one of its talons.

As if by tacit assent the pair rose and moved off downhill, Handa leading the way. Gradually the heather gave way to rough grassland, sour and ill drained, invaded by bracken and coarse rushes. Glow worms shone like fallen stars amid the grass stems, and white moths fluttered over the fern, to fade and vanish among the dark alders that lined the riverbank. Slugs and snails were feeding on the damp vegetation. The two badgers sought them out, selecting the fattest slugs and rolling them carefully to and fro on the grass until they had removed all the slime. It was a slow and painstaking business, but the badgers were in no hurry, and an hour passed as they worked their leisurely way across the marshy pasture.

They came at last to the river, where they paused to drink. There they disturbed a moorhen roosting in the reeds with her half-grown chick, sole survivor of a brood of seven. The mother flew out of the water, calling to her youngster to follow, but the witless bird panicked and ran away from the river. Handa gave chase, and Borun followed, driving it further into the field. Yet try as they might, they could not catch the moorhen chick, for no matter how foolish and hysterical it might be, it could easily outrun both of them. The chase became fast and furious, and more of a sport than a serious hunt for the badgers, so when at last the wretched bird dodged past Borun and plunged into the river, the pair watched it go without any great show of regret. They trotted along the riverbank together, side by side, jostling and pushing each other and pulling each other's ears. Gradually their play grew more boisterous and frenzied. Then, quite suddenly, they paused, and in that moment Borun made Handa his mate.

Their honeymoon lasted until late August, when all the wheat and barley had been harvested, and the fields lay tawny and sere under the maturing sun. They began to grow fat, gleaning the grain that had fallen on the stubble, and feasting on the blackberries that shone in juicy clusters of ripe black fruit in the hedgerows and thickets. They found mushrooms and other fungi, and from time to time a wasps' nest. All around them the earth burgeoned with wealth, as the full-blown beauty of the summer mellowed into misty autumn.

Then came the acorn crop. The hard fruit spattered down like hail from the high branches of the oaks, while from the chestnut trees fell spiky green purses, from which burst succulent, shiny brown nuts. This year too, the beechmast ripened, an uncommon event, and the squirrels that peopled the woodlands went quite silly burying far more of the seed than they could ever eat during the winter, even if they were able to find their stores again.

With the first frosts the bracken fern yellowed and died. When it was sufficiently withered and dry Handa raked out all the bedding from the set and replaced it with new, collecting great armfuls and dragging it down, until the bed chamber was packed to the ceiling with springy fresh material. She dragged the old bedding away from the vicinity of the set and scattered it among the heather, where it would decay and replenish the earth.

Although she was putting on weight, and three months had passed since she and Borun had consummated their union, there was as yet no sign that she was about to bear young.

Yet the alchemy of love that had brought them together was still at work within her, and all was well. The union of two animals is more, far more, than a mere physical mating. It is a moment when the forces of the universe, the slow traverse of the seasons, the long journey of the earth through space around the sun, the pull of the moon and the tides, all conspire to fuse in a flashpoint of desire; and this moment is but one in a carefully programmed cycle of events.

Neither Borun nor Handa had known another mate. Nor were they ever likely to, for badgers bond for life. Their coming together stimulated appetites which until then had remained dormant. There is little doubt that it was excitement and pleasure at Borun's company that caused Handa to ovulate.

Now three fertilized ova lay at rest in Handa's womb. They would remain dormant until the winter solstice, the longest night of the year, when her body would then accept and nourish them. Why all this should be so is a question to which there is as yet no answer. It is a mystery perhaps understood by the silent oaks beneath whose roots the badgers have so long survived, but it may forever elude the inquiry of man.

The purple plaid of the heather darkened to deepest brown, and the western gorse, which had worn a coronet of gold flowers, resumed its garb of somber green. Gales came, stripping the birch of its brassy leaves, and rain lashed the earth, turning the waters of the river to muddy beige, in which dark drowned alder leaves danced a slow and stately dance. Then the sun shone again, on a changed world, in which the nuances of color were soft and indistinct, a muted landscape of faded browns and greens, yet against which the wine purple of the bare birch twigs glowed, with a rare beauty that would pass unnoticed in a harsher light. At night a hunter's moon hung in a sky curtained with stars, and in the mornings frost rime silvered the skeletons of the flowers of summer.

Men armed with mattocks and spades came late one afternoon on a gray autumn day when mist hung over the river and moisture clung to every twig and dried fern and grass blade. They filled a plastic bag which had once held fertilizer with gravel and stuffed it down the mouth of the set. Then they shoveled more earth over the entrance, and stamped it down flat before they left.

A fox hunt was due to be held the next day, and the master was anxious that it should be a success. Previously there had been complaints from the farmers that foxes were getting too numerous, and hunt followers grumbled that too many escaped the hunt by going to ground. So the hunt committee had agreed to pay two laborers for the task of stopping as many holes as they could find, and although strictly speaking the holes should have been stopped up on the morning of the hunt, there were too many to be dealt with in the time available. So the two men privately agreed to find as many as they could on the previous day, and so avoid too early a start in the morning.

Borun and Handa heard the muffled thumping and banging as the earth stoppers did their work, but the sounds soon ceased, and as silence returned to the set the two badgers curled up in sleep once more. The atmosphere in the set grew hot and stuffy, but it was not for another two hours that the occupants were to discover that they were entombed.

It did not take Borun long to dig free. The plastic bag tore readily in his sharp claws, and the loose gravel spilled out. It took longer, once Borun had broken through, to clear the earth and gravel from the tunnel entrance, but long before the moon had risen above the crest of the hill the pair were off foraging. Yet Handa was nervous and uneasy, and twice during the night she returned to the set to check that all was well. Just before dawn they both retired to pass the day, but Handa remained restless and wakeful, listening at the entrance of the bedchamber.

So she was the first to hear the clamor of the hunt, and the deep belling voices of the hounds as they surged across the heath, close on the heels of a young dog fox that had led them down the valley and across the river. The fox was wet and bedraggled, his head and brush hung low, and his weary limbs faltered as he toiled across the coarse heather. Twice he had run to earth, only to find his escape route blocked by sticks and stones, and now he was making a last bid to find cover.

Handa heard the harsh rasp of his breathing as he slid into the tunnel, and her warning snarl brought him up short a yard from the sandstone slab beneath which the badgers lay. He moved forward cautiously, but then he heard Borun's voice in addition to Handa's, and knew he dare venture no nearer. To squeeze through the crevice, with two badgers on guard on the other side, would be to court certain death.

Now all three animals lay silent and still as they heard the frantic clamor of the hounds at the entrance to the set. They heard the thunder of hooves, shouting, and curses, and then silence, followed by a soft, low snuffling.

After roundly cursing all laborers who were not worthy of their hire, the master of foxhounds had ordered a terrier to be sent down the hole. The little dog went in eagerly enough, and after a moment the assembled hunt heard its excited yapping as it came face to face with the fox. An old huntsman dismounted, and put his ear to the ground. Rising, he shook his head, and moved a yard or so further on, to kneel and listen again. Then he nodded, and tapped the ground beneath his heel, as an indication as to where to dig.

For the second time in twenty-four hours, Borun and Handa heard the thump and clink of spades, and soon after, the rattle of loose earth into the tunnel. They did not see the fox hauled out and thrown to the waiting hounds, and his death scream was drowned beneath the triumphant yelping of his tormentors. Loose earth blocked the entrance to the bedchamber, and no one paid the slightest heed to the little terrier still scratching in the tunnel.

The day was rapidly drawing to a close. Everyone was bone tired, cold, and hungry, and for many there was a long hack home, horses to be fed and watered and bedded down for the night, hounds to be tended to, and harness cleaned and dried before there was any chance of a bath and a meal. Most of the hunt followers agreed that after such a fine run, the digging out of the quarry was somehow a distasteful anticlimax, a necessary job to be done, but one which somewhat soured the day. One by one they left the field. The hounds were whipped in, and the terrier, which was still scratching in the tunnel, was hauled out by the scruff of his neck and thrown across a saddle.

As the last light faded from the land, the hill lay deserted, dark, and unchanged save for the ruins of the badger set, which yawned like an open grave. Close by, on the heather, there was a patch which from a distance resembled a scattered tribute of dark red roses, rapidly turning black in the fast gathering dusk.

16. The Long Journey

Borun and Handa waited for a long time after the hunt had left before they dared try to venture out of the blocked bedchamber, and it was only then that they discovered that freedom was not to be gained merely by scraping away a few armfuls of loose gravel. A large block of sandstone, which had once formed part of the roof of the tunnel, had fallen across the entrance, and was held in place by loose earth which the terrier had been unable to scratch away.

The block was too big to drag through the crevice, and too firmly embedded in the earth to be pushed aside. It took many hours of patient scraping and burrowing, dragging soil and small stones, a pawful at a time, into the sleeping chamber, before Handa was at last able to squeeze through, and past the rock. Then she was able to dig from outside, and it was not long before Borun could push aside the rock and crawl free.

Outside, in the fresh damp air, the badgers shook themselves vigorously, to free themselves of the loose particles of soil that covered their coats. Then, although they were weary, hungry, and thirsty, they began a slow and meticulous inspection of their home. The set was ruined beyond repair. The tunnel had caved in, and the sleeping chamber was drafty and exposed. Everywhere the ground was redolent of the smell of fox, hounds, horses, and humans, defiled and polluted to a degree that repelled both animals. When Handa found the remains of the fox on the heather, it was the last straw. With a gruff bark of anger and dismay she bolted away downhill, and Borun followed at a gallop, anxious not to lose track of her.

Once clear of the vicinity of the set, Handa quieted somewhat, and Borun began to forage for food. Soon Handa joined him. When Borun unearthed a cache of acorns, buried by a squirrel in the leafmold under the parent oak, she ate heartily of the fruit and began to forget the tragedy that had passed. Neither animal had any intention of returning to the ruined set, but they were not unduly concerned about the problem of finding shelter. Each knew every detail of the countryside around the set, and could call to mind half a dozen suitable refuges: holes dug by foxes and referred to as "earths" by the country folks, abandoned badger sets, and passages under the sandstone rocks that littered the hills. Even some of the older rabbit warrens had tunnels wide enough and spacious enough to accommodate them. So it was not until an hour before the dawn that Handa led the way up the side of the hill, to where, she knew, a fault in the eroded rock face allowed access to a dry and roomy cavern.

It was no good. The entrance had been blocked with a massive slab of stone, which had required the combined efforts of the two earth stoppers to lever into place. Handa scratched and pushed at the stone for a few minutes, then turned away, heading downhill to the site of an old quarry, in the corner of which a vixen had dug an earth and raised her young. The earth had long since been abandoned, and no taint of fox remained, but here again Handa was disappointed, for once more the earth stoppers had done their work well. A tree stump had been thrust into the mouth of the hole, and loose earth and stones heaped over it. Given time, the badgers might well have cleared the blockage, but daylight was fast approaching, and both animals were bone weary.

Now Borun led the way, to an earth mound that lay in the middle of a small beech wood. The mound was an ancient grave, the tomb of a Bronze Age chieftain who had been laid to rest there, with his weapons and his jewelry, with clay pots filled with food, and rich garments of wool and fur to keep him warm on his journey to the other land. There was a way into the tomb, Borun knew, at the base of the oldest beech tree, and when last he had visited it, there had been a spider's web spun across the entrance, a sure sign that it was deserted.

The hole was still there, and it had been overlooked by the earth stoppers, but there was no spider, and no web. Instead there was an old and irascible badger, driven half mad with toothache and pains in his joints, who was in no mood to welcome others of his kind, however great their need of shelter. He stood just inside the entrance to the tomb, growling and snarling, and Borun, who was quite big enough and powerful enough to master the old warrior, hovered timidly outside, wheedling and cajoling, in the hope of being allowed in. It was all to no avail, and Borun and Handa turned away. They could not ignore those instincts that taught them to respect the territorial rights of others. They left the tomb, and its testy old custodian backed off, muttering, into the dark recesses. Soon, his bones would join those of the other old warrior, and their spirits would become as one.

It was full daylight when the pair finally found refuge, in a small cave at the foot of a low sandstone cliff. A dense mat of ivy hung down the rock face, screening the entrance to the cave, and so the earth stoppers had missed it, too. Yet it was a poor sort of refuge, drafty and damp and cold, and the badgers lay huddled together on a bed of loose stones, in the driest corner they could find. For a while they forgot their discomfort in sleep, but nightfall found Borun wakeful and restless, padding to and fro at the entrance to the cave and looking out, beyond the ivy curtain, across the valley to where the limestone escarpment was stark against the winter sky.

Something about the shape of the hill pulled at his mind, evoking half-forgotten memories of a valley and a wood, a wood where it seemed it was always summer, and the voles were fat and sweet and plentiful, where rabbits ran among the fern and no man came near. As soon as darkness fell he left the cave and set off toward the river, moving purposefully down the wooded hillside without pausing to search for food. Handa followed, not knowing where she was going or why, but content merely to go with her mate.

Borun himself had no clear intention, no positive plan. He knew only that as long as he traveled toward the hills, he felt satisfied and content. The moment he stopped, or turned aside, his restlessness returned. So he journeyed on, until at last he was brought up short by the broad expanse of the river, now brown and turbulent with the winter rains.

Here he checked. Then, on impulse, he turned right and followed the river upstream. With every step he felt he was going more and more astray, and after a hundred yards or so he turned, retracing his steps, still following the river but heading downstream, and immediately he felt better. Handa plodded behind, as patient and trusting as ever.

Without map or compass to guide him, Borun's instinct led him true. After his capture by the Romanies, he had without knowing it been carried across the river in the van. Now it lay before him, sprawled like a great snake across the valley floor, swinging in wide curves as it meandered down to the sea. But it lay aslant his path rather than across it, and by heading downstream Borun was in fact drawing nearer to his goal, even though he was traveling at a slight tangent to it. How he was going to cross the river was a problem which had not even occurred to him.

The going was easy, along a wide track worn bare by the booted feet of countless fishermen, and the pair made good progress until Handa rebelled. A tree trunk lay beside the path, its bark crumbling and rotten. Rich yellow clusters of fungi clung to the decaying wood, and moss hung in trailing green tendrils, on which beads of moisture glistened in the starlight. The thought of all the food hidden under the bark was too much for Handa, and she called a halt in order to feed.

Borun, once his interest was aroused, was happy to join her, for his earlier restlessness had now much abated. Together they ripped the log apart, licking up the gray woodlice that scattered in all directions, and crunching the colonies of snails that were hibernating there. Beneath the bark, in the spongy timber, lay the fat white grubs of boring beetles, and best of all, in the soft ground under the log, they found a congregation of frogs, deep in their winter sleep.

His hunger appeased, Borun was once more ready to move, but Handa felt certain that yet a further treat lay in store beneath the log. She lingered for some minutes, searching in vain, while Borun bickered and chivied her, anxious to be off. She gave in after a while, and followed Borun along the path, grumbling to herself a little, but obedient to his will.

Ahead of them now the river was spanned by a bridge, but to gain access to the bridge they had to climb a high earthen rampart, that lay at right angles to their path. Together the pair clambered up the bank, some twenty feet or more in height, and found themselves on a wide level track. Two parallel steel rails ran along the length of the track, shining dully in the starlight, and Borun approached them nervously, with Handa close behind. He was halfway across the first rail when he realized that it was singing, and the song, a high-pitched whine, grew steadily louder, accompanied all the while by a rhythmic clicking sound.

Borun started back, almost bowling Handa over in his fright, and the pair of them retreated crouching in the thick dry grass as the whine grew to a hurricane of sound, a deafening roar and a whistle, together with a mighty pounding that made the earth shake. As they watched, too terrified to move, the train thundered past, the lights from the carriage windows flicking over their faces as they crouched low to the ground. Then it was gone. The noise faded into the distance, and then died.

It was more than half an hour before Borun and Handa dared venture once more onto the railway track, and this time they approached the rails with even more caution than before. The rails were silent, however, and Borun led the way across the bridge and over the river. Fortune was with them, for if Handa had not lingered that extra while at the tree stump, the train would have caught them halfway across the bridge, and probably killed them both.

The two badgers followed the railway for about half a mile, until it joined another track running roughly east to west. Borun hesitated only briefly before crossing the track, sliding over the smooth shining rails that lay in orderly rows before him. Once again, fortune favored him, for had the line been electrified, he would have died immediately. They slid down the embankment, crossed a small field, and pushed through the hedge, only to be caught up short by another obstacle, a broad stretch of water extending interminably in either direction.

Years ago, men had cut the canal across the country, to link two ports, and for a time it carried a heavy volume of traffic. Barges towed by horses ferried coal and timber, iron ore and hides, all manner of imperishable goods, especially fragile articles, such as pottery, which would not stand a jolting journey over the rough roads of that time. Then came the railway, swifter by far, and slowly, the canal fell into disuse. The locks crumbled and decayed, and nature came to reclaim her own. In summer water lilies carpeted the surface of the water, and flag irises bloomed along the banks. Birds nested amid the rushes, and fat tench lay basking in the sunlit shallows. Each autumn the weeds died down, to decay into thick black mud. Slowly, very slowly, the canal was being filled up, and there would come a day when it would once more be dry land.

Both railway and canal had been cut as nearly as possible in a straight line along the valley through which the river wandered, crossing and recrossing the natural waterway, and forming a pattern which resembled a gigantic dollar sign. Yet in spite of all their care in planning, the engineers were bound from time to time to follow natural contour lines, to avoid the expense of cuttings and embankments. So Borun found himself on a stretch of canal running due east to west, and was at a loss to know whether he should go left or right.

In the end he turned east again, following the overgrown towpath that led along the side of the canal. Withered sedges rustled in the breeze, a moorhen called anxiously as they approached, and swam away from the shore. A sleeping swan awoke, and raised his long white neck to hiss at them as they passed, and a water vole dived into the water with a musical plop. Then Borun stopped, listening.

All this while his mind had been recording the noises of the night, decoding them and classifying them as harmless, but now he had picked up one which refused to be categorized. It came again, from the middle distance, and just around a bend, a splashing sound. He waited, but the long seconds ticked by, and there was no repetition of the noise, so he moved on. Then it came again, louder this time, and nearer, as though some vast bulk had reared out of the water and fallen back. Handa was visibly nervous, and ready to flee, but for the moment Borun stood his ground, waiting and listening, trying to determine what manner of beast it might be that lived in the canal.

He did not have to wait long. There was an upheaval in the shallow water near the bank. A great head appeared, with monstrous ears crowned by a wreath of rotting, mud-stained weed, and behind that the indeterminate bulk of some huge body. Handa fled, with Borun close behind, and the pig, which had escaped from his sty to enjoy the luxury of a midnight bath, gazed after their fleeting forms in mild surprise.

Again, it was in a way fortunate that the badgers had met the pig. Had they carried on the way they were going, they would have crossed an aqueduct, and in due course they would have found themselves back on the other side of the river. As it was, they came shortly to a narrow bridge, which led them across the canal, and into a small copse. Here they found a rich harvest of wild hyacinth bulbs, and they dug the crisp juicy roots from the soft mold, feeding until dawn whitened the sky, and forced them to seek refuge in a hollow log.

With the coming of the night Borun was again restless and anxious to be on the move, but Handa insisted on feeding first. For a while Borun joined her, but as soon as his appetite was appeased the urge to travel grew strong in him again, and he bullied and nagged at his mate until at last she followed him out of the wood.

The direction he had to take was now strong and clear in Borun's mind, but the way was not easy. After crossing several fields they came to a busy highway, and when they had successfully negotiated this hazard they found themselves in a narrow lane. High banks topped with sheep fencing kept them from gaining access to the fields on either side, and once a passing car braked and swerved to avoid them as they darted in panic across the road.

The lane led them to Summercombe village. The badgers wandered through a maze of gardens, past darkened cottages where dogs barked from behind closed doors, one so loudly and persistently that a light appeared at an upstairs window and a man's head appeared. Deep in the shrubbery by the garden wall Borun and Handa froze, not daring to move until the window banged shut and the light went out.

Once clear of the village, their troubles were over. Borun led the way uphill, through fields and hedgerows, until he came to a rough tangle of fern and stone. Here he stopped, to sniff the air appreciatively, before leading Handa around the edge of the hill fort, and into Summercombe wood.

A few minutes later they arrived at the set. All was well. One Eye had long since departed, and time, together with the industry of innumerable scavengers, had all but obliterated the traces of her brief tenancy. Although some of the smaller entrances had caved in, the tunnels were largely intact. After a thorough exploration, Handa set about clearing up the main sleeping chamber, raking the old debris and dragging it out of the set. Beneath the trees there was dried fern in plenty, and deep drifts of leaves, crisp, brown, and fragrant, which Handa dragged into the set until the sleeping chamber was full. Long before dawn the set was habitable again. The badgers had returned to Summercombe wood.

17. Parenthood

It was the time of the winter solstice. As the path of the planet earth drew ever nearer its sun the north pole leaned away, sheltering its icy wastes from heat and light under a veil of darkness. At the hour of the perihelion, when the north star blazed with white fire over a land chilled with frost, and the tall trees stood silent and still, Handa's body accepted the dormant eggs within her and began to nourish them with her blood.

She was not aware of any change within her, and the month of January passed, cold and bleak, with icy winds from the east holding the land in thrall. In February the wind blew from the west, turning the snow to a gray blanket of slush that vanished in a night, save for a few drifts that lay lost and forgotten in the sunless hollows of the hills. A thrush shouted from the topmost branch of an ash tree, and the plump catkins on the willow shone silver in the sun.

One evening, as the sun blazed blood red beneath massed banks of cloud, suffusing the white petals of the wood anemones with rosy pink, Handa emerged alone from the set and disappeared into the prickly thicket of holly that grew close by. A rabbit, long dead, had once dug a burrow under the roots of the parent holly tree, and Handa began to scratch and dig, enlarging the hole so that it was just big enough for her to squeeze into.

Digging was easy in the soft sand, and she was already well underground when Borun sleepily emerged, to sit scratching himself at the mouth of the set. He could hear Handa at work in the holly thicket, but he paid little heed. Digging was second nature to the badgers, and they were both frequently at work, clearing debris out of a tunnel where the roof had partially caved in, or enlarging a sleeping chamber because it was too cramped. For the moment Borun was content to lie at the mouth of the set, waiting for Handa to join him on the night's forage.

After two hours had passed, however, he began to grow impatient, and padded over to the holly thicket. Deep underground he could hear a muffled thumping and a rattling of loose stones, but when he tried to enter the tunnel he found it was too narrow for his bulk. He withdrew his head, and the next moment he was pushed aside by Handa as she emerged backward, dragging a large stone in her arms.

He called to her, but she ignored him, bustling away down the tunnel, to reappear almost at once with an armful of sand, most of which, when she scattered it, went over Borun. He withdrew out of range, and settled down to wait once more, but it was late in the night, and the moon was westering, before she condescended to join him in a search for food.

She was hard at work again the following night when

Borun woke, and this time he did not wait for her, but went off foraging alone, returning from time to time to call for her, until at last she was ready to join him. By midnight on the third night she had finished her task, and when Borun appeared, she was taking in bedding.

The nursery she had dug was a model of its kind. The entrance under the holly tree was small and discreet, the excavated soil scattered and lost under the dense canopy of dark evergreen leaves. Just inside, it took a right-angle turn, sloping slightly upward to pass between two rocks. Again it turned through ninety degrees, this time to the left, still sloping uphill but leading deep into the earth. A step up, over a slab of stone, and then down into a nursery chamber from which no cub could stray, and to which no harm could come, especially with Handa on guard. The slab of sandstone rock was a vantage point from which she could drop on any intruder.

Not until the nest chamber was lined to her satisfaction did Handa consent to join Borun in foraging, and even then she would not stray far. Long before dawn she led the way back to the set, but instead of following Borun into their sleeping chamber, she vanished quietly into the nursery. Borun waited a while, but she did not reappear, so he retired to sleep alone. The following evening he called to her at the mouth of the nursery set, but there was no response, so he padded off alone into the darkness beneath the trees. He was not to know it, but he was the father of three lusty cubs, two female and one male.

From the moment of their birth, the cubs flourished under Handa's tender care. She was able to feed them well, for she was young and healthy, and although January had been a lean month, for the rest of the year the land had been kind to her. On the first night she took no food, apart from the afterbirths she had devoured, but thirst troubled her, and a little before dawn she went to the spring to drink. On the second night she met Borun, and the pair exchanged a brief greeting before she returned to her young. On the third night she joined him for a short foray, and ever after that, on mild evenings, she would leave her cubs for a brief spell while she foraged with her mate through the woods.

By the middle of March she had decided that the nursery was no longer big enough to accommodate her brood, and she took over part of the main set, refurbishing an old abandoned sleeping chamber for the purpose. Some excavation was needed, and in digging, she turned out some old bones, yellow and crumbling with age. One was a skull, the teeth long fallen from the sockets, and Borun sniffed at it curiously as it lay on the sand outside the set. It was the skull of his great-grandfather, who had died in that very bedchamber, and who had been walled in by a sorrowing widow almost thirty years previously.

Once the new nursery had been furnished to her satisfaction, Handa brought her cubs across, one by one. So Borun met his family for the first time, and though at first Handa would not let him touch the cubs, and snarled a warning at him when he tried to enter the nursery, she gradually relaxed her rules. By now the cubs were snub-nosed miniatures of their parents, tottering about the nursery on rubbery little legs, and Borun was able to play nursemaid, allowing the youngsters to tug at his ears and hair, while Handa took a much-needed respite above ground.

There was no shortage of food. The rabbits and voles were breeding more than ever before, and although the spring was cold and dry there was a good yield of fresh green grass. During the drought of the previous summer every tree and shrub had thrust their roots deep into the earth, searching for water, and inadvertently tapping rich new sources of minerals in their quest. Now they were reaping the benefit of the hot, dry weather, and every tree, as it blossomed, showed promise of a heavy fruit crop to follow. The yellow catkins of the hazel were thicker and longer than ever before in the memory of man. The blackthorn bloom spread like snow over the land, and the flowers of the oaks, which normally passed unnoticed, flourished until the trees looked as if they had been sprayed with liquid gold.

For some time now Farmer Fletcher had been suffering more and more from a progressive disease of the hip joints, which made walking tedious and painful. His doctors had promised him that in time an operation could be performed, which would remove the pain, but meanwhile he would have to wait until the condition developed beyond a certain stage.

The daily routine grew increasingly arduous, and while he managed to cultivate the flat lands adjacent to the farm, Fletcher found the hilly fields too steep to climb. So, gradually, the green fields began to return to forest, the forest that had flourished for thousands of years before the coming of the first farmer, and which may one day flower over the bones of the last. Slowly the bracken fern invaded the pastures, and the bramble thickets spread outward, providing shelter for seedling thorn trees and wild briars, which in turn created food and shelter for small birds and beasts.

On a warm afternoon in late April, a boy toiled across the slope of the hill. He was tall for his age, and skinny, with bony elbows and knees and thin red wrists that stuck out from the sleeves of his sweater. A solitary child, his interest lay in birds and insects and flowers rather than conventional sports and pastimes, and so he shunned his schoolfellows, preferring to rake the mud at the bottom of a field pond in search of aquatic insects, or to comb the hedgerows for birds' nests. These habits, together with his appearance, made him an object of ridicule among his peers, and so he grew shyer and more alone than ever, preferring to follow the lanes and byways, and hiding or running away whenever he met one of his tormentors.

His proudest possession was a small museum and zoo,

which he kept in a shed at the bottom of his garden. Here he tended his specimens of pond life, contained in an array of glass jars. Here he also kept a live bank vole and a dormouse, and an owl with an injured wing. His great fear in life was that one day his father would carry out his threat to "pour all that rubbish down the drain." His mother was neutral. She avoided the garden shed and the unmentionable horrors that lay within.

He wore a small haversack, in which he carried what he called the tools of his trade: a magnifying glass and a notebook, a pair of tweezers and a trowel, an assortment of plastic bags and a knife, some pieces of string, and other odds and ends. There was also a fine-mesh net on a wire frame, which, if necessary, he could fit onto the long handle he carried in his right hand, and used as a walking stick. Fear of ridicule inhibited him from carrying the net ready assembled, even in so isolated a spot as this.

He had walked a long way, and he was hot and tired and thirsty, but there was no shade, and no fruit or berries to quench his thirst. Ahead lay the wood, and the dappled shade of the budding trees looked cool and inviting. Perhaps, too, there might be a stream or a spring from which he could drink. Questing along the hedge in search of entry he came upon the badger track, and it was easy for him, with his stature, to squeeze through the gap and follow the trail.

It led him to the spring, where he drank gratefully, before stripping off his boots and bathing his feet in the ice cold water. Resting thus, and reclining against the rock, he noticed the pad marks in the mud of the soft ground around the spring. He examined them carefully, unsure as to what species of mammal had made them. A solemn boy who was very serious about his hobbies, he took out his notebook and made a sketch, exactly lifesize. He also made a note to obtain some plaster of Paris, so that he could return and make plaster casts of the prints. Then he dried his feet on a handkerchief and put his boots back on, before following the trail further into the wood.

As soon as he saw the badger set he recognized it for what it was, and the origin of the prints became clear. Although he had never seen a badger, nor stumbled across a set before, he had read about them in the natural history books in his school library. Thrilled at his discovery, he poked about in the sand thrown up at the mouth of the main entrance, and soon found the skull of Borun's ancestor, which he stowed in his haversack. He found several black and white hairs too, shed from Borun's shaggy coat, and these he placed carefully between the leaves of his notebook. Finally he drew a sketch of the set, showing the entrances in relation to trees and rocks, and with an arrow indicating north. At last, regretfully, he moved on, knowing that the badgers would not emerge until dusk, and that to stay away from home for so long might cause his father to carry out his dread threat.

He came to a small clearing among the trees, a lush green glade of grass with a solitary ash sapling sprouting in the center. A movement on the edge of the clearing caught his eye and he froze, watching and waiting to see what manner of creature he had discovered. There was a rustling of dried leaves, and then a small gray form appeared, with a bright dark eye. At first the boy thought it was just a rabbit, but then he saw the bushy waving tail and realized that it was a gray squirrel. As he watched, it ran a few paces out into the clearing and then sat bolt upright, its tail curled like a question mark as it held some tidbit in its forepaws, and nibbled at it with its bright orange teeth.

The gray squirrel had been introduced into Britain from North America many years before the boy had been born. He had read how the gray squirrel had spread through the country, and knew that it caused some damage to forestry, but guessed, rightly, that many reports were exaggerated. He had read, too, that the gray squirrel had somehow driven out the native red variety, but more recently he had learned that the red squirrel had been growing rare before the advent of the gray, and that destruction of the old primitive forests was more likely to be the cause of its extinction.

All the same, he knew that the gray squirrel was not popular with owners of woodland, and simultaneously the thought came to him that it might be fun to keep the gray squirrel as a pet, and teach it to sit on his shoulder. The squirrel was now near the base of the ash sapling, busily foraging among the grass at its roots, and it occurred to the boy that if he were to startle the squirrel, it would instinctively climb the tree, and from there he could shake it down onto the grass, and then grab it. No sooner had the idea occurred to him than he put it into practice, letting out a wild yell and rushing into the clearing.

The squirrel did just as he expected, leaping up into the tree and climbing to the top, and next moment the boy was shaking the tree violently. For a few seconds the squirrel held on, and then, losing its grip, it fell, snatching frantically at branches on the way down, gaining momentary holds, but finally landing asprawl in the grass at the boy's feet. As it began to leap away the boy laid hold of it, one hand clutching it tightly around the neck, and the other gripping its haunches.

18. Thomas Slips Back

For a few moments the squirrel lay limp, temporarily paralyzed with shock and fear, and the boy had time to feel the
soft, warm, rounded curves of the small body, and the silki-
ness of its fur. Unconsciously he relaxed his grip a little, and
the squirrel, sensing this, twisted violently in his hand, and
sank its chisel-like teeth deep into the fleshy ball of his
thumb.

The boy screamed in pain, and tried to throw the squirrel
to the ground, but the squirrel held on, its teeth locked
together in the boy's flesh. In panic now, the boy tried to
shake his attacker off, but the squirrel, twisting and writhing,
refused to let go, until at last its teeth tore through the skin,

leaving a raw and jagged hole from which blood poured in a steady stream.

Free at last, the squirrel began to leap away through the long grass, but the boy, half mad with pain and rage, pursued it, lashing out at it with his foot. His boot caught the squirrel behind the ear, so that it screamed and died, and at that moment the boy's rage left him. He fell on his knees beside the still palpitating corpse, and with his uninjured hand tried to massage life back into the small body, praying all the while that it was only stunned, but knowing that it was beyond saving.

Had anyone told him that morning that later in the day he would wantonly destroy an animal, his reaction would have been one of stunned disbelief. Even now, he could not understand what had happened. Grief, remorse, and pain from his injured hand all fused in an agony of despair that could find outlet only in an outburst of weeping, and thus Polly found him as she burst into the clearing.

The warm spring sunshine had lured her away from her garden to wander into the woods for an hour, and she had heard the boy scream as the squirrel bit him. Long experience with children had taught her to distinguish between the normal range of whoops and yells and a genuine cry of pain or terror. She knew that something was seriously wrong, and so she had at once hurried to the spot. She could not at first understand what had happened, but she could see that he was in no immediate danger, so she knelt down beside him and laid one arm over his shoulder. The boy ignored her, and continued to sob.

"Come on, young fellow," she said gently. "Dry your eyes and tell me your name. Have you got a handkerchief?"

Dumbly, the boy fumbled in his pocket and produced a very dirty rag. Polly smiled wryly, wondering how after all her years as a schoolteacher she could be so stupid as to ask a boy such a question. Then she saw the wound on his hand.

"Come on," she said, "this won't do at all. I'll take you to my home and fix that hand."

Without protest, the boy allowed her to raise him to his feet, and followed her obediently through the wood to the cottage. Polly took him into the kitchen and sat him down in a chair while she bustled about with a bowl of warm water and her first-aid kit, and ten minutes later his wound was dressed and swathed in a snow-white bandage. Then she bathed his tear-stained face with fresh cold water and poured him a glass of milk. "Now," she said brightly, "tell me your name."

The wave of emotion had passed, but the boy was still white and trembling with shock. "It's, it's Thomas, Miss. I, I didn't mean to do it."

"Do what?" queried Polly. "I'm still not sure what happened. Tell me about it."

Slowly, hesitantly, Thomas told her what had happened, the tears springing afresh to his eyes at the recollection, tears now of shame and guilt. Polly listened in silence until he had finished and sat staring at the kitchen floor.

"Tell me a bit more about yourself," Polly said. She wanted time to reflect. She recalled vividly, as if it were yesterday, the sudden attack by a young badger on a defenseless hedgehog, and it seemed to her that there was a parallel here somewhere. "Tell me about your school, and your hobbies. What were you doing in the wood today?"

Bit by bit Thomas began to tell her of his likes and dislikes, and soon he was describing his museum and zoo, and showing her his notebook. As he talked about his hobbies he grew more enthusiastic, and his face became flushed and animated. Polly was particularly interested in his account of the badger set. She had not herself ventured so far into the wood, so she had not discovered the set for herself. Now she found herself wondering whether this was the home of the young badger she had fed two autumns ago. She was on the point of telling Thomas about this when she suddenly realized that he had become crestfallen and silent again, and guessed he was thinking about the squirrel.

"I think you have reproached yourself enough about what happened this afternoon," she said kindly. "I think you just slipped back for a moment."

"Slipped back?" echoed Thomas. "How do you mean, Miss? Slipped back to where?"

"Back to the days of your ancestors," answered Polly. "Once, many thousands of years ago, our ancestors were hunters, roaming the hills and woods, just as you were this afternoon, only they were searching for food, and if they had found a squirrel, as you did, they would have reacted in exactly the same way. Only," she added, "they would have been more careful not to get bitten."

The boy shook his head. "But I don't like killing. I've never killed anything before, and I certainly won't ever again."

"No, I don't think you will," replied Polly slowly. "But don't you see, you are still a hunter, only now you hunt knowledge instead of food. You no longer have any need to kill, and the more you learn about the lives of other creatures, the less you want to kill them, but just for a moment, out there in the wood this afternoon, pain and shock made you lose control. You forgot who and what you were, and reverted back to your ancestry. Instinct told you what to do, and you did it without question, even though it was strictly against your principles. In future, now you know the enemy within you, you will have more control."

She paused for breath, and for a silent prayer that she was right. Still, deep down she felt confident that she had read young Thomas correctly. Whether he had understood half of what was said to him was another matter.

But Thomas was nodding his head solemnly. "I didn't want to kill the squirrel," he said. "But I wanted to own it, to keep it, and that's nearly as bad as taking its life. Taking its freedom, I mean. I have no right to do that. I was so stupid. Next time I feel like doing something like that I'll remember the squirrel, and stop and think.''

"Then perhaps the squirrel did not die in vain,'' said Polly. "Come on. I'll drive you home. Only I think, if anyone asks, we'll just say the squirrel fell out of a tree, and you got bitten when you went to pick it up. That's nearly the whole truth, and the rest will be our secret.''

She drove Thomas down to the village, and gave a brief explanation of the afternoon's events to the boy's mother, a vague, harassed woman who seemed to stare vacantly into space all the time she was talking to her. After extracting a rather half-hearted promise from her that she would take Thomas to a doctor to have his hand dressed properly, Polly hurried away.

On the way back to the cottage she found her thoughts turning toward the badger set that Thomas had described to her. She now knew roughly where it was, and though it was too late in the day to go search for it, she resolved to go exploring first thing the next morning.

A bright day dawned, with a blustery wind from the northwest sending white clouds scudding across a sky as blue as a thrush's egg, and setting the leaves of the oak trees to dance and shimmer in the sunlight. Small brindle butterflies hovered and floated over the young nettle plants, and bees were busy among the white star flowers of the wild garlic. Polly found herself wondering if the resulting honey would be garlic flavored.

She walked on, through the sun-dappled shade of the woodland, breathing the heavy perfume of the wild hyacinths, the leaves of the previous autumn crisp and dry underfoot. She came to the badger track and followed it, as it twisted and wound under the trees. Once she had to crouch down to pass through a low tunnel of blackthorn, and once she had to scramble over a fallen tree. The badger track itself passed under the trunk, and Polly noticed how smooth and worn the bark was at that spot.

At length the track opened out into a wide arena beneath the trees, and Polly saw the yawning mouths of the entrances to the tunnels, black in the morning light. She did not go near them, but instead circled around until she was above them, seeking about her for a vantage point to which she could return that evening, when she hoped to see the badgers emerge into the open. She found it in an old ash stump, shaped for all the world like a large armchair, with back and arm rests, and even a footstool. All it needed to make it really comfortable was a cushion, and that was easily arranged.

She devoted the rest of the day to her garden, finishing off the last of the spring planting, hoeing between the tall green spires of the onions, and staking the peas newly emerging from the soil. Although slapdash and untidy in her housekeeping, she was almost fanatically orderly and neat in her vegetable plot. The beds were raked and rolled to billiard-table smoothness, the seeds set in exactly parallel rows, and the young plants spaced with mathematical precision. Not a weed was permitted to survive.

So the time passed, with one task suggesting and leading to another. The afternoon was well spent when the sudden appearance of Vandal, the white cat, reminded Polly that once again she had forgotten to collect the milk from the farm. For a moment she was tempted to go without it, but she knew that Vandal would expect his daily ration, and if he did not get it, he would spend the evening rubbing around the refrigerator and miaowing at the top of his voice. With a sigh, Polly put away her gardening tools and set off to the farm.

Mrs. Fletcher greeted her with that subdued air of triumph that befits the bearer of grave but important news. "Have you seen the papers, Miss Shaw?" she trumpeted, as Polly crossed the farmyard. She was confident that Polly had not. She took no papers whatsoever, as Mrs. Fletcher well knew. That was why she had waited impatiently all day for this moment.

Polly allowed herself to be led into the farm kitchen, where the front page of the *Advertiser* lay displayed for her to see. There was no doubt as to which news item had aroused Mrs. Fletcher. Glaring banner headlines leapt out of the page: NEW BY-PASS PROPOSED. SUMMERCOMBE WOOD THREATENED BY PROGRESS.

19. The Sacrifice

Swiftly, Polly ran her eyes down the column of print. "If a proposal by the County Council meets with approval from the Department of the Environment, the village of Switchwick will win a long-awaited reprieve. A new by-pass is being planned which will divert traffic wishing to gain access to the motorway from the existing road, which passes through the village.

"For some time now residents have complained that the ever-increasing volume of traffic has brought dust, noise, and atmospheric pollution to the village, and lately fears have been expressed that there could be danger to life and property. Residents of Summercombe, too, will welcome the news. They claim that the junction of their road with the

Switchwick road is hazardous, and that there has already
been one near fatal accident there.

"The proposed route will carry the by-pass along the side
of the hill, below the iron age fort, and across land which is
mostly unproductive and infertile. The main casualty will be
Summercombe wood, which will be divided in half by the
new road."

There was a large-scale map of the area, with a dotted line
drawn to indicate the path of the proposed new road. It was
smudged and indistinct, but Polly could see that Summercombe wood was in danger of being bisected along its whole
length, and worse, the by-pass would skirt the front of her
garden. She stood looking at the map for a few moments,
knowing that Mrs. Fletcher was eagerly waiting to see her reaction. She took a deep breath, determined at least that she
would not give the woman the satisfaction of seeing that she
was distressed.

So she was smiling as she turned to face Mrs. Fletcher.
"I'm afraid the *Advertiser* is a little premature with its news.
After all, this is, as yet, only a proposal, little more than a
pipe dream. It's hardly fair, in my view, to raise people's
hopes when so much still needs to be considered."

Mrs. Fletcher was nettled. "Everyone I've spoken to so far
thinks it's a fine idea. I've no doubt myself that it will go
through as planned. After all, the council exists to serve the
rate payers, and if they want the new road, the council must
surely build it."

"I hope the rate payers can afford it," mused Polly. "My
yearly contribution won't go far, I know."

"The country's rich enough," sniffed Mrs. Fletcher.
"And anyhow, they'll probably get a grant from the Department of the Environment, since the new road is to serve the
motorway." She omitted to mention that if the new road was
built across Summercombe wood and the adjoining fields
along the shoulder of the hill, Mr. Fletcher would be hand-

somely reimbursed for land which had become nothing more than a nuisance to him.

Polly took her milk and fled, but in spite of her apparent lack of concern, her heart was heavy as she made her way back to the cottage. As she turned in at the gate she tried to visualize a major road snaking across the fields. Already in her imagination she could hear the sullen roar of diesel engines, an unending procession of heavy trucks thundering past by day and by night. As she stood meditating a blackbird flew to the hedge with a worm in his bill. For a few moments he perched on a dead branch, and as Polly watched she heard him warble a snatch of song.

She wondered how many people knew that a blackbird could sing with a beakful of worms. How many cared? How many ever got a chance to find out? How many could afford the luxury of standing in the fragrance and peace of an evening in spring, and hear the song of a bird? Suddenly she was aware of the privilege of her position, in enjoying the best of both worlds. She accepted without question the gifts of progress. She took for granted a pure water supply, skilled medical service, and an efficient police force. She had electric light, television, her record player, and more clothes than she could ever wear out, a greater store of material possessions than perhaps any previous resident of the cottage ever had. Without these objects, and other benefits, would she still retain the numinous sense of wonder and awe for the rest of the natural world, or would she become just another drudge, ill nourished and in poor health, cursing an alien environment?

She did not know, but she was honest enough with herself to admit that perhaps she did not care to find out. She also had to admit that if she herself expected and took for granted a high standard of living, then she had no right to deny it to anyone else. The new by-pass was intended as part of that system by which living standards were maintained, for the motorways brought petrol for her car to her garage, petrol derived from oil that lay fathoms deep beneath the North Sea. The motorway carried new potatoes from the coasts of Cornwall and Wales to the cities, and fertilizers from the manufacturers to the fields. They brought everything from sugar to cigarettes, from new books to nylon underwear to the local shops, and if the system was not ideal, at least it worked. One day there might be a better transport system, for after all the railways had replaced the canals, and in a very short space of time the motorways had ousted the railways. Meanwhile, mankind had to learn to live with the motorway.

Polly found herself reflecting rather bitterly that this was a society that would not dream of depriving her of her material possessions, without being given extremely good cause, but which would, without any misgivings, rob her of the immeasurable and indefinable wealth of her surroundings, and so considerably reduce the quality of her life. Immediately, she realized that this was perhaps unfair of her. The building of the by-pass would greatly improve the quality of life for the residents of Switchwick, and when it was built perhaps they would be able to stand in their gardens and hear a blackbird sing. If they wanted to, that was.

Polly suspected that the majority would be more concerned about the quality of reception on their television sets. Certainly the planners were motivated by the economics of speedy transport, rather than the welfare of the villagers, and anyway, the residents were not gaining anything new, but merely getting back the peace and quiet they once enjoyed. This was not progress; it was maintaining the status quo.

She herself was the sacrifice, and not much of one at that. She was well past middle age, and she had no dependents. She might well be dead before the by-pass opened, or unfit to manage alone. Already she could feel twinges of rheumatism in her shoulders and hips after a day in the garden.

Suddenly she pulled herself together, scolding herself for what in anyone else she would have regarded as maudlin self-pity. She marched into the house, put the milk in the refrigerator, and poured herself a large iced tea. "Here's to progress," she said aloud, and then corrected herself. "No, to Mother Nature. She always wins, in the end."

Of one thing she was certain. She could not appeal against the planning of the new road. It meant too much to everyone else. To fight a lone battle would merely succeed in making her very unpopular, and it would be a long and wearisome struggle that would in the end prove futile. She would just have to wait and watch events, and if those events made life too unbearable, she could always sell out and move somewhere else. After all, no dream lasted forever.

Suddenly she remembered the badgers and the wood, and realized that she was not the only sacrifice to progress. The badgers, too, would be dispossessed of their home, as would all living things that lay in the path of the proposed by-pass. Did it matter? Life had survived the ice ages of the past. Surely it could survive this ice age, when glaciers of concrete crept across the island, and vast areas of the naked earth lay buried not under snow fields, but under tons of bricks and mortar.

Was it possible that a breed of man would one day emerge who could learn to live as one with the rest of the natural world? There had been such people in the past, and she wished fervently that once again it could be so. Then she thought of herself and her garden. She flattered herself that it was semi-natural, and used no pesticides or herbicides, nor any artificial fertilizers. She liked to think it was a haven for wildlife, especially birds, but in the vegetable plot no weeds were permitted. Each week she ruthlessly destroyed thousands of small plants she would not dream of harming in woodland or hedgerow, and she waged continual war against slugs and snails, caterpillars and greenfly, ants' nests and earwigs. It was no good denying it, she was as guilty as the next person in waging war on the wild, and the by-pass, when it came, would be no more than a logical extension of her activities in the garden. As long as mankind needed to eat, the war would continue.

She was still brooding as she set off through the woods to take up her vigil on the ash stump. The blackthorn had shed its bloom, and the white petals lay like snowdrifts among the purple haze of the hyacinths. Rooks were calling to each other as they drifted lazily overhead, and a thrush sang in a rich contralto. The aroma of the woods rose strong and sensual on the warm evening air, a scent so pungent that it was almost animal, and everywhere the beauty of the new green leaf was bewildering in its rippling diversity of shade and texture, like the silks and satins of an empress's wardrobe, spilled out for all to admire. Some half-forgotten lines of poetry came to her mind, lines written by Patrick Pearse, the Irish rebel leader, on the eve of his execution for his part in the Easter Rising, 1916:

> "The beauty of this world has made me sad,
> This beauty that will pass."

She had to permit herself a wry smile at the recollection of the next lines.

> "Sometimes my heart has shaken with great joy,
> To see a leaping squirrel on a tree."

Thomas had "shaken with great joy," and his joy had quickly turned to anguish.

She reached the ash stump and climbed into it, settling herself comfortably on the cushion she had brought with her. Below her the clearing lay silent and empty, as the green-dappled light of day slowly turned to yellow in the setting sun. There was no breeze, and as Polly sat watching and listening, her senses slowly became attuned to the tiny sounds that dropped into the pool of silence, the buzz of a beetle, the soft clap of a bird's wings, a slow, smooth rustle that marked the passage of a snake. Stealthily, secretly, the magic of the woodlands wooed and possessed her, so that she became as one with the ancient oaks and the fragrant fertile earth, and the affairs of mankind grew small and far away.

Suddenly, a loud sniffing noise alerted her and brought her back to reality. Peering down into the clearing, she saw to her delight that a badger had emerged from one of the openings and was standing in the arena, its back to her and its head nodding as it stared into the trees. As she watched, it flopped over onto one haunch and proceeded to scratch its flank vigorously. Then it rolled over and repeated the process on the other flank, its claws making a loud rasping noise against its hide.

Polly was surprised to find that her mouth was dry and her heart was beating furiously. She was terrified that she would cough or sneeze, or make some movement that would alert the animal to her presence. She held her breath, as Borun lurched to his feet, gave himself a thorough shaking, and padded leisurely away to the latrine area. A few minutes later he returned to the mouth of the set, and to Polly's joy a second badger emerged, to repeat the process of shaking and scratching.

For a short while the pair pottered about the clearing, scraping at the ground here and there, and poking around at the entrances to the sets. Polly did not realize it, but the two badgers had picked up the scent of Thomas after his visit on the previous day, and were now checking to see if they had received a further visitation. Fortunately, Polly had not gone near the sets, and the badgers, finding only stale, cold scent, were unperturbed.

Without warning, Borun moved off into the wood, and Handa, after watching him depart, returned to the darkness of the set and her cubs. The clearing, which a moment before had seemed alive with small and busy people, once more lay silent and deserted, and Polly was aware of a sense of deflation and loss. For the very first time since she had moved into her cottage, she felt lonely.

She was also stiff and cramped and cold, and she had forgotten to bring a torch with her. The sun had dipped below the shoulder of the hill, and already the fields below the wood were bathed in purple mist. If she was to find her way home through the wood in safety, she would have to be on her way. Quietly, she slipped out of the ash stump and stole away.

20. Woodland Encounter

The following night she returned to the wood, and her vantage point in the ash stump, and once again she was rewarded with a glimpse of Borun and Handa. It was the same on the next night, and the next, and gradually the nocturnal visits grew to be an obsession with her. Throughout the day she followed her normal routine, without giving more than a passing thought to what she had come to refer to as the little gray bears of the wood. But each evening, as the sun began to slant toward the shoulder of the hill, and the shadows of the woodland lengthened beneath the trees, the confines of the cottage became almost unbearable to her, and she felt drawn to the twisting path beneath the oaks.

Sometimes she was rewarded with a glimpse of the adult

137

badgers. At other times they failed to appear. It did not matter. It was the ageless brooding mystery of the twilight that drew her, quickening her senses, sharpening her hearing, enhancing her sense of smell, as darkness deepened and her eyesight became of secondary importance. Each evening she returned to the cottage, stiff, cold, and itching from mosquito bites, barking her shins as she stumbled through the wood.

Not surprisingly perhaps, at the end of a week she succumbed to a feverish chill, which confined her at first to bed, and then to the cottage. Gradually she grew stronger, and as health returned, so did the urge to visit the woods. At the end of a fortnight she could bear it no longer. The day had been warm and sunny, with the promise of a mild night, and she felt fit and strong again. Dressed in warm clothes, and carrying her cushion, she set off.

She was surprised to see how far spring had advanced since her last outing. Entering the woods was like plunging into a deep green pool, a dim-lit lake where all was liquid movement. Late-foraging bumblebees droned heavily among the thick clusters of blossom, that clung like clotted cream to the spiky twigs of the hawthorns, and all around the air was loud with bird song, as from every thicket and brake each individual songster proclaimed his territorial rights for others of his kind to heed.

She settled into the ash stump, a little shaky and breathless, but eager to see what the night would bring. A half-hour passed, and gradually the bird song diminished in volume, until at last there was only the robin, still staking his claim from the top of a sycamore tree. The thin, high song ceased abruptly as the hoot of an owl echoed down through the trees, and in an interval of silence the dusk deepened in the valley.

Then Borun emerged, and a few seconds later the clearing was alive with bustle and noise, as the three cubs poured out of the set. Spellbound, Polly watched them begin a wild and joyous romp, racing in and out of the bushes, yelping and bickering and chasing each other's tails. For some twenty minutes the cubs played, lying in ambush and pouncing on each other, until the games ended in a prolonged and strenuous wrestling match, with all three rolling in the dust. Handa and Borun kept watch, making sure that no cub strayed too far, but otherwise interfering little with the cubs' boisterous play.

A vigorous grooming session followed. Handa inspected each protesting cub in turn, holding it down with a firm forepaw, and releasing it only when she was satisfied that the required standards of cleanliness had been met. It was late now, and the moon had risen, filling the arena with silver light, and plunging the bushes into deep shadow. Suddenly, Polly realized that she was alone. The badgers had faded into the night. She waited a while, half hoping they would return, but also giving them time to get well clear, so that she would not alarm them as she made her way back to the cottage. She could hardly wait for twilight to come again.

The long day passed, a day of increasing concern for Polly. She had slept badly, her dreams disturbed by woodland scenes, through which small, gnomelike creatures capered madly in the moonlight. She woke in the early hours, wondering what was to be the fate of the badgers, and then could not sleep again. Would the sets be destroyed by the building of the by-pass? Would the youngsters have left home by then? She did not know. She would have to get maps, and try to relate the proposed route to the position of the sets. Even then she could not be sure, for the line of the by-pass was not yet fixed. She would just have to wait until she had more positive information to go on. She tried to dismiss the problem from her mind, but it kept returning, in spite of all she could do to keep herself occupied.

She was relieved when at last the day was far enough advanced to allow her to escape to the woods. There at least she would find solace, and relief from her anxieties. The evening was sultry and humid, and in the distance the mutter of thunder heralded the coming of a storm. Nevertheless, she set off, her cushion under her arm, moving slowly through the trees.

Long practice had taught her to move without sound, so that now she could pick her way through the woods without rustling a leaf or stirring a branch. Thus she had come to learn much more about the ways of the woodland, and was rewarded by small cameos; a stoat poised in a clearing, one paw raised as its nose quested the air, a hen pheasant nervously leading her chicks across a path, a grass snake lying coiled beneath the fern. All these images she stored lovingly in her memory. She was alert to sounds too, and could distinguish between the short, sharp rustle that told of a bank vole diving for its nest, and the scratching of a lizard as it scurried for cover over the dried leaves, a sound exactly like a pen nib scratching over parchment.

So when she heard a rustle in the undergrowth, a few yards away to her right, she stopped and listened. It came again, and at first she thought that it was just a blackbird scratching in the leaves, a sound that had often deceived her in the past, but then she heard what sounded to her like an exasperated groan. She moved forward cautiously, not knowing quite what manner of beast might be hiding in the woods, but curious to find out.

A bearded face stared out from a clump of elder, a face with gimlet dark eyes and black curly hair. For one idiotic moment she thought she had come face to face with the woodland god Pan, but just as she was beginning to doubt her sanity a twig snapped under her foot, and the face spoke. "Is anyone there?"

Pulling herself together, and trying to keep her voice under control, Polly answered, "What is it?"

"I wonder if you would care to render a little assistance here."

Striving not to laugh, so great was her relief, Polly climbed up the slope. The voice was so precise and controlled, the request so polite, that in this setting it sounded incongruous.

It was not Pan who lay half reclining in the thicket, but a man, well past middle age, attired in a neat jacket of Norfolk green, with a matching shirt and tie. He made no attempt to rise as she approached, but contented himself with a rather deprecatory wave of his hand. "I'm afraid I've got myself into a rather ridiculous predicament here. Your arrival is most timely, ma'am."

"What happened?" queried Polly.

The man pointed in the direction of his foot. "I slipped, walking along the side of the hill, and my foot has somehow got trapped under a root."

Polly looked, and sure enough the man's leg was gripped tight, just above the ankle, between a tough elder root and a rock. "Perhaps, if I could get your boot off . . ." she began.

"I fancy my foot is now too swollen, but if you could loosen the laces, it might be more comfortable."

He sighed in relief as Polly did as he asked, but it was clear to her that she could not remove the boot without cutting it. She had no way of knowing whether the ankle was broken or merely sprained, and she hesitated to touch it in case she caused further injury. Suddenly it occurred to her that the obvious solution was to cut through the root.

"If you could just be patient for a little while longer," she said. "My cottage is not far away. I'll go back and get a saw, and then you'll soon be free."

"I would be most grateful," said the man. "I promise you I won't go anywhere."

Polly laughed. Then she remembered her cushion. "Perhaps if you put this behind your head," she offered. "It might be more comfortable."

"Such luxury," sighed the man, settling back. "I'm so

glad you came along. If I might make one more small request? My haversack is lying just up the hill where I dropped it. In it are my cigarettes and matches. With them I can wait content.''

Polly scrambled further up the hill and retrieved the haversack from the fern. It was surprisingly heavy, as though it was full of rocks, and the handle of a hammer stuck out of the flap, but it was not until she was halfway back to the cottage that its significance struck her. Even then there was no time for speculation, for the impending storm was now much nearer. The skies were darkening, and an ominous breeze ruffled the leaves of the trees.

Still, she voiced her question in the form of a comment, as she sawed through the elder root with a small bow saw. ''You're a geologist, Mr. . . .''

''Firth, ma'am, Rupert Firth. Yes, I am. That is why I find myself here, and all because a group of megalomaniac bureaucrats think they can build a by-pass here.''

Polly's interest quickened, but just then the root parted, and the geologist was free. Gingerly he stood up, testing his leg with his weight. ''Not broken, I think,'' he grunted. ''Only sprained, and swollen with the constriction.''

''I brought a long-handled broom back with me,'' said Polly. ''I'm afraid I'm not strong enough to bear your weight, but if you put the head of the broom under your armpit, you can use it as a crutch.''

''A splendid idea,'' murmured Firth. ''I must be in favor with the god Pan for him to have sent you, of all people, to save me.''

''I thought you were he,'' laughed Polly ''when I first saw you.''

''Oh, he was very near,'' said Firth seriously. ''I felt his presence just before you arrived. Not for nothing did he give his name to panic. Fortunately, he's a jokey sort of fellow. He likes to tease.''

Polly shivered. "You've probably noticed that there is a storm brewing. I think we ought to vacate the woods as quickly as you are able. We'll make for my cottage, and then I can look at that ankle."

A flash of lightning gave point to her remark, and they set off through the woods, he leaning on his makeshift crutch, and she following, burdened with cushion, saw, and haversack.

21. The Geology Lesson

Twenty minutes later Rupert Firth sat in Polly's armchair, sipping some hot tea as Polly applied cold compresses to his ankle, while outside the full fury of the storm unleashed itself upon the woods. Rupert glanced out the window and shuddered, thinking about his predicament had he not been rescued. "Miss Shaw," he began, "you really are a paragon. I can't think how I can ever repay you for your resourcefulness and kindness."

Polly could, but for the moment she held her peace.

"My chances of rescue seemed so slim," continued Firth. "And then you came along. It's none of my business, I know, but could you satisfy my vulgar curiosity by telling me why a lady of your mature years was walking through the woods at that hour, carrying, of all things, a cushion?''

"Simple," said Polly. "I was setting out to watch badgers.''

"Ah yes," nodded Firth, as though it was the most natural thing in the world for an elderly lady to do. "I saw the sets earlier today. The whole hillside is honeycombed with them.''

"They won't be there much longer if the by-pass is built," said Polly quietly.

There was a long silence, as Firth sipped his tea. Finally, he spoke. "I expect that while I was trapped under that root I was delirious and babbling, so that if in one of my more lucid moments I let slip certain information, I could trust you to treat it with the same confidence that a nurse or a doctor would?''

Polly grinned. The more she saw of this man the more she liked him. "Yes, you can trust me. I gather your report won't be a good one.''

Firth's eyebrows shot up. "My reports are always good. Models of accuracy and detail. Whether they are favorable or not to the parties concerned is of no consequence to me. I am a consultant geologist, and I get the same fee whatever my findings. My opinion, which I believe is quite well respected in several countries, is bound in the end to be upheld. What do you know about geology?''

"Nothing," admitted Polly.

"You ought to know something," said Firth sternly. "You can't begin to understand the hills and valleys unless you know something about their anatomy. Have you a few slices of bread?''

Polly got to her feet. "I'm so sorry. I quite forgot. You must be starving.''

Firth laughed. "Please. I want the bread for quite a different purpose. Fetch it, and you'll see.''

Polly brought four slices of bread on a plate, and Firth stacked them neatly, one on top of the other. "The rocks that form the backbone of this hill may be anything up to two hundred million years old," he began. "They are sedimentary rocks. That is to say, they are formed of sand washed down by rivers long extinct, or blown by winds from ancient deserts. These rocks once lay on the floor of a shallow sea, shifting sands, moved here and there by the currents until they were coated with a calcareous solution, and then compressed by further layers of sediment until they became limestone.

"From time to time the sea dried, and boulder clay covered the limestone. Then came a layer of sand, and then the seas returned, to lay down a layer of limestone again. So these layers were built up, like these slices of bread, with perhaps a smear of butter or jam in between. The first thing to remember, then, is that sedimentary rocks are always laid down on top of each other, almost horizontally, and then compressed, so that after a few thousand years the layer is about a foot thick. The second thing to bear in mind is that the oldest rocks are at the bottom."

A peal of thunder drowned his voice, and he glanced up at Polly. "Am I boring you?" he asked.

Polly shook her head, and he continued. "The fury of the elements tonight is nothing compared with the storms that have raged in ages past, that swept the sediments down to the sea. Now the earth lies in chains, and we tend to think she is overpowered, but from time to time she stirs, she moves, and strives to break her bonds."

He took the slices of bread by the four corners, bending the sides upward, so that all four sloped inward and down toward the center. "Sometimes this happens, and we call it a syncline, but sometimes this formation occurs."

He pressed the corners of the bread to the plate and pushed inward, so that the center of the top slice rose in a hump, forced upward by the other slices underneath. "We call this an anticline, and as you can see, the layers of rock that form the hill slope down and out, so that if one was to cut into the side, or otherwise disturb the formation, the slabs would slide away downhill.''

"And this hill is an anticline?" queried Polly.

"Right," said Firth. "And if anyone was to interfere with it, then, on such a night as this, as water seeped between the layers of rock, lubricating their surfaces, parts of the hill could well slide away. In fact, I would go so far as to say that they definitely would slide, only I couldn't predict quite when or where.''

"Could the hillside not be buttressed, to keep it from sliding?" asked Polly.

Firth nodded. "Sure. But in this instance it would have to be supported above and below the road, and whoever undertook the roadwork would have to be prepared to write a blank check, for no accurate estimate of the cost could be made. Even then the work could not be guaranteed.''

Polly felt a great surge of relief. "So the by-pass will never be built?''

"It will be built somewhere, no doubt. Probably along the floor on the opposite side of the valley. You'll see it from here, but it will be at least a mile away at its nearest point. Oh, my report will be rejected, and my clients will employ commercial geologists, who will take the taxpayers' money for giving the sort of answers the planners want to hear to their questions. There may be trial borings, but in the end they will have to give in. If a major trunk road was being planned, or a motorway, things might be different, but for a few miles of village by-pass, no politician is going to risk his career by squandering public funds.''

Suddenly Polly felt ten years younger. "Well, Mr. Firth, you've amply repaid me for rescuing you. For a moment, when I first realized why you were in the wood, I was tempted to leave you where you were.''

"Call me Rupert," begged Firth. "I think that is about the

one thing you wouldn't be capable of. And now, somehow, I must relieve you of the burden of my presence.''

"On a night like this? You'll do no such thing. I'll fix a meal, and then you can occupy the spare bed. I'm sure that at our age we can dispense with the proprieties. In the morning I'll drive you to the doctor to get that leg examined.''

A sudden thought struck her, one that filled her with unaccountable dismay. "Oh, I didn't think. Someone might be wondering where you were . . . might be concerned.''

Firth shook his head. "There's no one. I'm a widower, have been for a long time. I had planned to find a hotel for the night."

"That's settled then," said Polly. "Help yourself to more tea while I scramble some eggs."

She was abashed to discover she was blushing, and scurried away into the kitchen, where she rattled plates while she scolded herself for being a stupid old maid. All the same, she could not suppress a lilting happiness at the thought that whatever else this night's work had begun, it had laid the foundations of what she hoped would be a long friendship.

Much later, Firth raised his cup to the storm. "To you, Pan," he murmured. "Thanks, you noisy bounder."

Polly smiled, remembering an earlier defiant toast she had made. "No," she corrected. "To Mother Nature. She always wins, in the end."

Epilogue

Work began in earnest on the new by-pass late one December. At the end of the first day, as the excavators ground to a standstill, and the mechanics slouched wearily over the wasteland they had created, back to their waiting cars, a badger stood in a thorn thicket, his striped head nodding slightly as he surveyed the scene. Borun and his kind would not alter their ways, and it may be that in their very resistance to change they have sealed their own fate. Yet equally it could be argued that by continually changing his lifestyle, man might one day hit upon one which, all unforeseen, could prove to be the one that would ensure his own extinction. Perhaps, indeed, he has already chosen that path.

Further down the valley Polly, too, gazed across the fields

at the raw yellow scar, now mercifully becoming veiled in the gauze of the twilight. If, as she fervently believed, all nature was part of a whole, and the universe revolved with meaning, and if man was part of nature, as she was sure he was, then even the inscrutable working of his mind was part of the plan, however aberrant and devious his behavior might appear to be.

Certainly it was unbelievable that an intellect that could conceive an oak tree in an acorn would permit a mere man to wreck the plan. In spite of this, she knew she could not complacently accept the world as it was, as long as she lived, and carried within her the realization of what it could be. Perhaps this knowledge, too, was part of the plan, and it might be that the very possession of life prevented her from learning its secret. Death might provide the key, and with this thought she was content, accepting without rancor the knowledge that she had but a relatively short time to wait.

At the edge of the thorn thicket Borun glanced skyward, and a star shone in his eye, the same star that had shone on the unseeing eye of his dead father, that had shone on the building of Stonehenge. How many more changes might the star yet witness, before the sun burnt itself out, leaving the world locked in a pall of ice? For the badgers of Summercombe, and Western civilization, time was perhaps running out. The badgers at least had for the moment won a short reprieve.

BEYOND DIPLOMACY

A Background Book on American Military Intervention

Other books by Richard J. Walton

THE REMNANTS OF POWER:
The Tragic Last Years of Adlai Stevenson

AMERICA AND THE COLD WAR

BEYOND DIPLOMACY

*A Background Book on American
Military Intervention*

By RICHARD J. WALTON

Introduction by James J. Storrow, Jr.

Parents' Magazine Press • *New York*

Each Background Book is concerned with the broad spectrum of people, places and events affecting the national and international scene. Written simply and clearly, the books in this series will engage the minds and interests of people living in a world of great change.

Copyright © 1970 by Richard J. Walton
All rights reserved
Printed in the United States of America
International Standard Book Numbers: Trade 0-8193-0392-5, Library 0-8193-0393-3
Library of Congress Catalog Card Number: 70-93861
Maps by Don Pitcher

To My Parents

ACKNOWLEDGMENTS

THE AUTHOR ACKNOWLEDGES, with thanks, permission to quote excerpts from the following books (specific citations of page numbers appear in the Notes, which begin on page 259):

The Latin American Policy of the United States, copyright, 1943, by Samuel Flagg Bemis. Reprinted by permission of Harcourt, Brace & World, Inc.

America's Road to Empire: The War with Spain and Overseas Expansion by H. Wayne Morgan, copyright 1965. Reprinted by permission of John Wiley & Sons, Inc.

The Year of Decision: 1846 by Bernard DeVoto, copyright 1942 and 1961. Reprinted by permission of Houghton Mifflin Company.

Intervention and Dollar Diplomacy in the Caribbean, 1900–1921 by Dana G. Munro (copyright © 1964 by Princeton University Press). Reprinted by permission of Princeton University Press.

Dominican Diary by Tad Szulc. Published by Delacorte Press, © 1965 by The New York Times Company. Reprinted by permission.

The author also wishes to thank his editor, Lillian McClintock, who is both tough and very good.

CONTENTS

INTRODUCTION

BEYOND DIPLOMACY DISPELS MANY OF THE delusions under which students—and teachers, however well-intentioned— have labored for more years than one cares to count. It "debunks" many of the historical myths which have so long captivated us. It is concerned with the past century and a quarter and deals, as its title attests, with how and why the United States has repeatedly cast aside diplomacy and resorted to armed intervention in the affairs of other nations. Two of these episodes—with Mexico and Spain—we called "wars"; thereafter we resorted to euphemisms. These, and our other armed intrusions into Spanish-speaking nations—Cuba, the Philippines, Colombia and Panama (which we succeeded in separating), Guatemala, Nicaragua, the Dominican Republic —are here recounted, briefly and tellingly, just as they happened. This is a book, not of opinions or judgments, but of solid, unadorned information; the facts presented here are unequivocal and convincing.

George Washington was the Father of his country. This of course made him first in the hearts of his countrymen. He once chopped down a cherry tree and promptly imparted the news to his father (he never in his life told a lie). Also—on a later occasion—he threw a silver dollar across the Potomac.

Abraham Lincoln was the Savior of his country. He was born in a log cabin, did his studies in front of the fire, where he wrote on the back of a shovel, and once made his living splitting rails. He was about eight feet tall, and wore a stovepipe hat and a shawl.

Nuggets of information such as these have been conveyed to generation after generation of schoolboys. Their proper name is myth. If not exactly factual, they seem pretty harmless, even when they were conscious creations. Who, after all, could get angry at Parson Weems, whose earnest purpose was simply to instill in young minds a healthy love of their country and a respect for its founders?

All peoples need myths, and all have produced them. Myths are necessary and useful molds in which national pride and identity are cast. A myth is not truly a fabrication; it usually has a core of truth and hard experience. Nelson Glueck, in *Rivers in the Desert,* has remarked on the unexpected accuracy of Old Testament geography. Along with Joshua's account of how the sun stopped in the sky over Jericho, we have a precise and verifiable description of the lay of the land. Both elements are essential substance of the Bible. And the Old Testament in turn has been essential to the survival of a people through millenia of diaspora and persecution. The People of the Book have the Book largely to thank for their existence.

When Americans decided to be a people and to reject English rule, they quickly cast aside also their English past, its legends, and its heroes. King Arthur and King Alfred,

Robin Hood and his merry men were English all, no longer claimed by ex-Englishmen become Americans. A new people, suddenly alone in a hostile world, cut off from their origins in corrupt old Europe, possessed a vast, rich continent—and a psychological vacuum. To cement their identity as a people they wanted heroes and traditions. Myths were needed, and were not long in arising.

Instant identity, heroes to order, traditions out of whole cloth: in human history it had not happened. There is no parallel. The Hebrews entered into Canaan in fulfillment of a promise; Alexander's Greeks conquered the known world; Romans brought law and culture to the ends of the Mediterranean. These things were happening in America; a promised land claimed, a territory conquered, a savage people to be civilized. But not by Hebrews, Greeks, or Romans. Nor by Englishmen, Frenchmen, or Dutchmen. By a brand new people. An instant people: Americans.

The making of American myth began, and has continued ever since. The process has been called The American Dream and Manifest Destiny by true believers, Dollar Diplomacy and American Imperialism by "lesser breeds without the Law." But its real nature was fantasy.

A myth which has had a natural growth reflects the inner truth of a people. But one made to order, forced into being, is another matter. It can of course be harmless nonsense; it can as well be tragic delusion—monstrous, as unnatural growths often are.

The American Indian, for instance. A Child of Nature. A cruel barbarian. The noble savage. The only good one is a dead one. . . . These people were, of course, neither noble nor savage. We robbed them of their inheritance simply because they refused to adopt our white European set of values. We had a very dubious love affair with the Indian: we loved him to death with firewater, the Colt .45, and smallpox germs.

The dark-skinned tenth of our population *did* come to terms with our culture and survived. Have they fared better? White views of black people still are shaped by myth; the offensive stereotypes, too familiar to need enumeration, would fill pages. The appalling thing is that after three hundred years of living in juxtaposition, the average white mind is dark as ever concerning its black neighbor.

Having disastrously failed to comprehend people living in our midst, small wonder we do not understand Latin Americans (or Arabs, Russians, or Chinese) any better. Nor have we made any fair assessment of our country's proper relationships with theirs. The failures of our foreign policy are directly traceable to our national delusions, assiduously nurtured.

The fact is that we have long been taught to delude ourselves. The elder Henry Ford is supposed to have said that history was bunk. He never spoke a truer word. Much of the history taught in school to the generation of men now in power was heavily larded with bunk. One could go through a course in American history without getting an inkling that the subject might have a few blemishes. Our Indians had, sort of somehow, largely disappeared; it just happened so. (The word "genocide" did not appear, even in Unabridged Webster's.)

We of course knew that since the abolition of slavery, the Negro had attained his proper place in society. If he wasn't *quite* on a par with his white compatriots, it must be due to, let us say, natural differences between the races. The conclusions we were expected to draw were inescapable, though of course never given words.

Looking out over the world, we learned: yes, Latin Americans were poor but, as with the poor in our midst, it was unfortunate they just didn't like to work quite as hard as we did. We were naturally the most enlightened and diligent of the world's people, and had the duty to understand and sympathize with less fortunately endowed humans; but one shouldn't really expect too much of them. We had never, of course, lost a war, but then we never would have fought in an unjust one, or in one which had not been forced upon us.

I dwell upon this hermetic creed for one purpose only: to try to make credible to a new generation how it happens that they are inheriting what appears to be a working model of insanity. The achievement of *Beyond Diplomacy* is that this book, through example, makes explicitly understandable the process by which this has come about. It is not to excuse. There will never again be the opportunity to make the same mistakes; young people see the consequences very clearly, since it is they who are the chief sufferers. But it helps to know how it happened.

Beyond Diplomacy provides illumination to those who may be wondering, painfully and earnestly, how it was that we became involved in the direst "foreign entanglement" in our history. It is a valuable and a necessary work for anyone who is concerned that today we may be the victims of the most tragic myth, and the most disastrous delusion, of all.

James J. Storrow, Jr.,
Publisher, *The Nation*

AUTHOR'S PREFACE

IN DISCUSSING THE HISTORY of American foreign policy, particularly until the beginning of World War II, it is conventional to speak of isolationism, the reputed tendency of the people of the United States to be primarily concerned with their own affairs to the exclusion of substantial participation in the affairs of the rest of the world. But like most conventional wisdom, it is, at best, only partially true. It is entirely true that the people, and the successive governments, of the United States were suspicious of the constant power struggles that beset Europe. These successive governments, until the time of World War I, generally followed the advice of George Washington in his farewell address:

> Europe has a set of primary interests which to us have none, or a very remote relation. Hence she must be engaged in frequent controversies, the causes of which are essentially foreign to our concerns. Hence, therefore, it must be unwise in us to implicate ourselves by artificial ties in the ordinary vicissitudes of her politics, or the ordinary combinations and collisions of her friendships or enmities.

Our detached and distant situation invites and enables us to
pursue a different course. If we remain one people, under an
efficient government, the period is not far off when we may
defy material injury from external annoyance; when we may
take such an attitude as will cause the neutrality we may at
any time resolve upon to be scrupulously respected; when
belligerent nations, under the impossibility of making acquisi-
tions upon us, will not lightly hazard the giving us provoca-
tion; when we may choose peace or war, as our interest,
guided by justice, shall counsel.

Why forgo the advantages of so peculiar a situation? Why
quit our own to stand upon foreign ground? Why, by inter-
weaving our destiny with that of any part of Europe, entangle
our peace and prosperity in the toils of European ambition,
rivalship, interest, humor, or caprice?

From this message of September 17, 1796, it is not so
far to the Monroe Doctrine of 1823. (See Appendix I.)
Whereas Washington said that the United States should not
get entangled in European affairs, Monroe conversely warned
Europe not to become involved in western hemisphere affairs,
and here the area of concern was broadened to include not
only the United States of America but all independent states
of America.

For a century, from the War of 1812 to World War I,
the United States remained substantially clear of European
entanglements. But at the same time, the sense of "manifest
destiny" that drove Americans ever westward caused many
to believe that it was the mission of the United States to
spread the blessings of democracy to the peoples of the
"uncivilized" world. This sense of mission inevitably became
intermixed with the commercial considerations that sent
American merchant fleets ranging the world over and with

the sense of national pride that was common to all the western nations in what came to be known as "the age of imperialism."

Thus "isolationist" America became involved with the peoples of Latin America and the Pacific. Usually this involvement took the customary shape of trade and diplomatic contact, but sometimes, more often than many Americans realize, it went beyond diplomacy. Sometimes this involvement beyond diplomacy took the shape of political and/or private armed intervention, as in Texas at the time of the Alamo; or political and economic intervention as in much of Latin America for the past century and a half; or covert intervention such as Central Intelligence Agency activities in Iran and Guatemala and elsewhere; or even the sponsoring of an exile invasion at the Bay of Pigs in Cuba in 1961. But that is too broad a canvas for this one book. So too beyond the scope of this book are World War I and World War II, the Korean and Vietnam Wars. The two World Wars are clearly different in character from the interventions discussed herein. On the other hand, the Korean and Vietnam Wars are clearly related in motivation to the interventions in Lebanon and, especially, the Dominican Republic, but they are of such magnitude as to require separate treatment.[1] This book will consider those other interventions beyond diplomacy in which the United States openly committed its armed forces, ranging from the Mexican War in 1846 to as recently as April 1965, when the United States again sent Marines to the Dominican Republic.

Perhaps the reasons for those interventions, and the results, will shed some light on the American present and perhaps even on the future.

AUTHOR'S NOTE

ALTHOUGH THE WORDS "AMERICA" and "American" apply, of course, to the whole western hemisphere and not just to the United States, I have for the sake of editorial convenience used both words as they are commonly, perhaps chauvinistically, used in the United States as referring solely to this country. In referring to other parts of the hemisphere, I use such terms as "Latin America" and "Central America." I hope that in the context of *Beyond Diplomacy* this usage is clear—and forgivable.

—R.J.W.

Part I
THE MEXICAN WAR

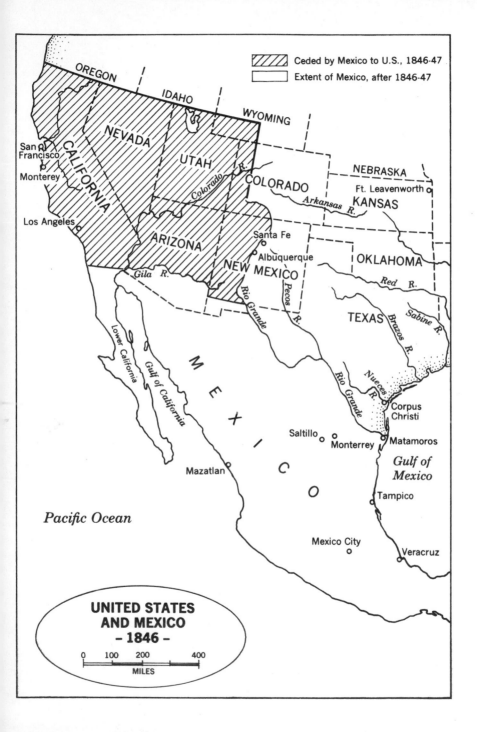

Ceded by Mexico to U.S., 1846-47

Extent of Mexico, after 1846-47

OREGON

IDAHO

WYOMING

NEVADA

UTAH

CALIFORNIA

San Francisco

Monterey

Los Angeles

Colorado R.

COLORADO

NEBRASKA

Ft. Leavenworth

Arkansas R.

KANSAS

ARIZONA

Santa Fe

Albuquerque

NEW MEXICO

OKLAHOMA

Gila R.

Pecos R.

Rio Grande

Red R.

TEXAS

Brazos R.

Sabine R.

Lower California

Gulf of California

M E X I C O

Rio Grande

Nueces R.

Corpus Christi

Saltillo

Monterrey

Matamoros

Mazatlan

Gulf of Mexico

Tampico

Pacific Ocean

Mexico City

Veracruz

UNITED STATES
AND MEXICO
– 1846 –

0   100   200   400

MILES

THE MEXICAN WAR

Chapter One

IN EARLY MAY 1846 an anxious President Polk was trying
to decide whether or not Mexican "provocations" were sufficient to persuade Congress to declare war on Mexico. But,
although Polk did not know it, war had already come. On
April 26 General Mariano Arista had sent a strong Mexican
force across the Rio Grande into what is now Texas. Camped
nearby, the American commander, Brigadier General Zachary
(Old Rough and Ready) Taylor heard reports of the movement and sent out scouts. Captain Seth B. Thornton cantered
out of the dusty camp at the head of sixty-three cavalrymen.
A while later they blundered into the Mexicans. Seventeen
Americans were killed and the rest, save for one man,
captured. He escaped to tell the story.

As soon as Taylor learned of the disaster, he sent a dispatch off to Washington: "Hostilities may now be considered as commenced. . . ." And thus began a war that
even now, a century and a quarter later, is controversial. By
modern standards it wasn't much of a war—less than two
thousand Americans were killed—but a quick glance at the
map of North America shows how important it was. Mexico

was cut in half and the United States won by conquest the present-day states of California, New Mexico, Arizona, Nevada, Utah, and part of Colorado. This vast area, together with Texas, which had also been part of Mexico, was about a third of the present United States. How different the history of the United States—and Mexico—would have been if that enormous tract, with its great riches and splendid harbors, had remained Mexican.

President James Polk—and many Americans too—wanted that land. They believed that it was America's "manifest destiny" to spread "from sea to shining sea" and there were even those who thought that all of Mexico and Canada too should enjoy the benefits of American democracy.

There is no dispute about President Polk's desire to have California and the rest of that almost boundless territory then called New Mexico. What historians dispute is whether he intended to take it by force and whether the United States or Mexico began the war.

Although Samuel Morse had already invented the telegraph in the spring of 1846, it was not yet in widespread use, so President Polk had not heard that the war had already begun the way he hoped it would: with the first military blow struck by Mexico. He had just about decided to go to Congress and ask for war when, on the evening of May 9, he heard the news of the clash along the Rio Grande.

Most of the next day he devoted to his war message, taking time out only to go to church with Mrs. Polk and his niece and nephew, for it was a Sunday. When he finished the message, late in the day, senators and representatives began to stream into the White House. It was easier to see the President then than now; in those simpler times he was just another political leader, albeit the most important. They kept coming until 10:30 P.M., a late hour in those days. The next day at noon he sent his message to both the Senate and the House, declaring that ". . . after reiterated menace, Mexico has passed the boundary of the United States, has invaded our territory, and shed American blood upon the American soil." (See Appendix II.) Sufficient cause for war, it would seem, but little about that now-distant conflict was as simple as it seemed.

As senators and representatives were quick to point out, there was considerable doubt that the skirmish took place on American soil. Some argued that the territory north of the Rio Grande to the Nueces River was disputed territory, that Mexico had never conceded that the Rio Grande was the Texas boundary, and that Texans had never controlled the territory. Other lawmakers asserted that the territory was not even in dispute, that the United States had absolutely no claim to it, and that by sending Taylor and his army to the Rio Grande he, Polk, had been the one guilty of aggression.

But whoever owned the soil, American blood had been spilled, and as history has demonstrated many times before and since, people of any nation seldom stop to think or ask many questions at a time like that. The House voted war that very day, 173 to 14, and the Senate the next day, 40 to 2. Yet the great southern senator John C. Calhoun was to write that if there had been deliberation of even a single day and if even a single important Democrat had come to his side, the declaration of war would not have passed. We will never know if Calhoun was right, but certainly criticism mounted in the days and months to come. Indeed, Polk's

War, as some came to call it, was attacked a year and a half later by a young representative from Illinois, Abraham Lincoln. And on January 3, 1848 the House passed, by one vote, and on a strict party line, a resolution which asserted that the war had been "unnecessarily and unconstitutionally begun by the President of the United States."

Whatever the current and subsequent criticism, Polk moved rapidly to prosecute the war. Congress authorized him to raise an army of fifty thousand volunteers and to spend $10 million—which, in 1969, would pay for only a couple of hours of the Vietnam War. Polk, his Secretary of War and of Navy, and a few generals did their best, but the nation was not ready for war; perhaps it was not yet even a nation. As the Civil War would prove only a generation later, America was not yet one land; it was too young, it was not yet formed. Thus the war was a curious one—by present standards, a hopelessly inept, even comic war. Orders from Washington took weeks—sometimes, as in the Far Western campaigns, months—to reach the field commanders. Often circumstances had drastically changed since the orders were written; often the orders were irrelevant the day they were written because Washington had no idea what the conditions were in the field. Often military commanders disobeyed orders and even Polk's Ambassador refused to come home from Mexico City when he was twice ordered to—and, as we shall see, it was probably just as well that he didn't. The President openly criticized his top two commanders and they replied in kind; and generals carried their disputes with one another to the newspapers. All in all it was an extraordinary war, which America could not have won had it not been that Mexico, an even younger nation, was in worse shape.

So the war began on the dusty plains of the Rio Grande on April 26, 1846. Or did it? Does any war begin on the day the first shots are fired? This war, like all others, began years before.

As early as 1805 Aaron Burr—the former Vice President who had killed Alexander Hamilton in a duel the year before—was involved in a group that wanted to conquer Mexico. By 1819 John Quincy Adams, then Secretary of State, negotiated a treaty with Spain by which Spain relinquished its claim to Florida and the United States accepted the Sabine River, now the boundary between Texas and Louisiana, as the boundary between the United States and the Mexican province of Texas. When Adams became President, he tried to buy Texas for $1 million in 1827, but the Mexicans were not interested.

During Mexico's revolution against Spain it was helped by many Americans, and after Mexico gained independence in 1821, it made generous land grants to attract settlers to sparsely populated Texas. Developments in Texas led to the war. The Mexican government became alarmed as American settlers in Texas rapidly outnumbered Europeans and native Mexicans. The new Texans gave their allegiance not to Mexico but to the United States. The Mexican government tried to stop the influx, to abolish slavery in the territory, and to rule the Texans as Mexicans, but it was powerless to do so. Inevitably, many of the Texans wanted their new colony to become part of the United States. President Andrew Jackson in 1829 again tried to buy it, this time for $5 million. Partly he wanted Texas for itself, partly he was trying to remove the cause of the growing tension between the young nations.

In 1835 the Texas Revolution broke out and the leader of the rebels, Stephen F. Austin (after whom the state capital is named), appealed to President Jackson for help, declaring that "This is a war of barbarism against civilization, of despotism against liberty, of Mexicans against Americans." But this was Jackson's response:

> The writer does not reflect that we have a treaty with Mexico, and our national faith is pledged to support it. The Texians [*sic*] before they took the step to declare themselves independent, which has aroused and united all Mexico against them, ought to have pondered well, it was a rash and premature act, our neutrality must be faithfully maintained.

But if the United States government was officially neutral, the people, particularly the frontiersmen of the South and West, were entirely committed to the revolution. American pioneers flocked to the Texas cause and one of the great legendary episodes in American history involved two of the most famous pioneers, Davy Crockett and Jim Bowie. On March 6, 1836, four days after Texas declared its independence, a force of 3,000 Mexicans under Santa Anna finally took the Alamo mission in San Antonio. For more than a week the Mexicans had been held off by only 187 men, among them Crockett and Bowie. When Santa Anna finally seized the mission, the remaining defenders were massacred. And three weeks later another 300 were massacred when they surrendered to General José Urrea at Goliad. The cry, "Remember the Alamo," became the battle cry of the retreating Texans. But suddenly they turned on the pursuing Mexicans and, under Sam Houston, a few hundred men, shouting "Remember the Alamo," routed Santa Anna and took him captive on April 21. On May 14 he signed a treaty pledging independence for

Texas. The Mexican Congress immediately repudiated the treaty but it was powerless to do anything effective.

The Texas Revolution further inflamed relations between the United States and Mexico. The Americans not only believed that Texas rightfully belonged to the United States but they were outraged by the massacres at the Alamo and Goliad. For their part, the Mexicans were embittered by what they saw as the theft of Texas by the *norteamericanos*. And no doubt many Mexicans believed that the Americans would not be content with Texas.

Because of these inflamed passions, Jackson refused to initiate legislation to annex Texas even though the Texans themselves and many Americans were clamoring for annexation. Jackson's successor, Martin Van Buren, followed the same course, a decision that was to change the direction of American history, for it cost him the Democratic nomination in 1844 when he again sought the Presidency after being defeated for re-election by William Henry Harrison in 1840. Both Jackson and Van Buren were convinced that the Mexicans meant what they said when they declared that the annexation of Texas would mean war.

That historic step was not far off. Van Buren was the front runner for the Democratic nomination for the 1844 election but his southern opponents were able to produce a letter from Andrew Jackson, still the leading figure in the Democratic Party, in which Jackson called for the annexation of Texas. This put Van Buren on the spot. If he supported annexation, he would lose essential support in New York and New England, where it was believed that annexation would result in the creation of four or five slave states. This would give control of the Senate to the South. If Van

Buren opposed annexation, he lost the support of Jackson and the southerners.

In an attempt to defuse the situation, Van Buren and his most likely Whig opponent, Henry Clay, both published letters in which they said annexation without Mexican consent would probably lead to war. But the stratagem didn't work. Although Van Buren led clearly on the first ballot in the Democratic convention, southern forces were able to insist on a two-thirds majority for nomination. Van Buren couldn't quite make it and, on the ninth ballot, with Jackson's support, the nomination went to James K. Polk of Tennessee. The first "dark-horse" candidate was an ardent expansionist. Clay, as expected, was the Whig nominee and Polk won in a close election: 1,337,243 to 1,299,068. Clay would have won, but a third-party candidate, James G. Birney, running almost entirely on an anti-slavery platform, took enough votes from Clay in New York to deprive him of that state and thus the election.

The incumbent President, John Tyler, who had succeeded to office on the death of William Henry Harrison, read the election results as a mandate for annexation, and he wanted to accomplish it before Polk's inauguration (inauguration took place in March until 1936). He had tried some months before to have the Senate ratify an annexation treaty but it was rejected by 35 to 16. This time he put the matter before Congress as a whole, requesting a joint resolution. The new tactic worked, although just barely. On February 27, 1845 the Senate approved Tyler's resolution by 27 to 25. The next day it was passed by the House, 132 to 76. Thus on March 1, just three days before Polk was inaugurated, Tyler signed the joint resolution.

At that same time the Mexican minister, General Juan N. Almonte, demanded his passport and stormed away from Washington, attacking "the greatest injustice recorded in the annals of modern history . . . despoiling a friendly nation . . . of a considerable part of its territory." Soon thereafter diplomatic relations between the two countries were completely severed when the American minister, Wilson Shannon, was asked to leave Mexico.

War was on its way. Before we examine the rapidly developing events that led to it, let us take a look at the young nation whose men the United States would be facing on the way to the "halls of Montezuma." This description comes from Bernard DeVoto's marvelous book *The Year of Decision: 1846.*

> . . . it is a fundamental mistake to think of Mexico, in this period, or for many years before, as a republic or even as a government. It must be understood as a late stage in the breakdown of the Spanish Empire. Throughout that time it was never able to establish a stability, whether social or political. Abortive, discordant movements of revolution or counter-revolution followed one another in meaningless succession, and each one ran down in chaos from which no governing class ever arose, or even a political party, but only some gangs. . . . Furthermore, the portions of Mexico with which we are con-concerned, Texas, New Mexico, and California, were precisely the portions where Spain's imperial energy had faltered and run down. To this frontier Great Spain had come and here it could go no farther, here it began to ebb back.[1]

Chapter Two

WHEN JAMES K. POLK of Tennessee, the eleventh President of the United States, took the oath of office on March 4, 1845, he was faced with two great international problems: the growing antagonism between the United States and Mexico, and a dispute with Britain over the great Oregon Territory that included the present states of Oregon and Washington and extended deep into what is now the western part of Canada. Many Americans were willing to fight to preserve all of the U.S. claim, and the slogan "Fifty-four forty or fight" has passed into our history. But Polk knew it was one thing to contemplate war with the new, revolution-torn state of Mexico and quite another to fight mighty Britain, then the most powerful nation in the world. So he was willing to compromise. He dropped America's claim to that part of the Oregon Territory extending into Canada as far north as the parallel 54° 40′, and Britain dropped its claim to that portion of the Territory below what is now the American-Canadian border.

While working toward that compromise, Polk also took steps to achieve his great goal: the possession of California. But the path to California led through Mexico. And the American steps swiftly followed the compromise. On June 15, 1845, Secretary of State James Buchanan (later to become President) promised Texas that it would be protected from Mexico if it agreed to the annexation recently approved by the American Congress. That same day Zachary Taylor, veteran of innumerable Indian fights, was ordered to move his small army from Fort Jessup, Louisiana, "to the mouth of the Sabine, or to such other point on the Gulf of Mexico, or its navigable waters, as in your judgment may be most convenient for an embarkation at the proper time for the Western Frontier of Texas." On June 23 the Texas Congress approved annexation and on July 4, a date hardly an accident, a convention of Texans ratified its action.

The Mexican response to these events came on July 21 when President José Joaquín Herrera asked his Congress for a declaration of war to take effect whenever the United States either annexed Texas or sent its troops there. Ten days later General Taylor established his camp at Corpus Christi on the western bank of the Nueces River, just inside the territory claimed by Mexico. On August 27 a Texas convention adopted a state constitution and on October 13 both annexation and the constitution were ratified by the Texans in a special election. On December 29, 1845 Texas became the twenty-eighth state of the Union.

War was now practically inevitable, but there seemed to be one last chance to avoid it. In mid-September 1845 an American confidential agent in Mexico, Dr. William S. Parrott, wrote that Mexico wanted to reestablish diplomatic relations with the United States. Polk decided to send an envoy, John Slidell of New Orleans, who spoke Spanish fluently. He was authorized to offer fifteen or twenty or even forty million dollars for California and New Mexico.

Like almost everything else connected with the Mexican War, Slidell's mission had some of the aspects of a farce. In brief—for a complete report would take pages—Slidell left for Mexico City after the U.S. had moved the flotilla cruising near Vera Cruz, which Mexico regarded as threatening. Slidell arrived on December 6, but the Mexican Foreign Minister declined to see him. Internal conditions had so deteriorated that the Foreign Minister feared that the presence of an American envoy might topple the government. By December 20 the Mexican government definitely decided it could not afford to see Slidell.

In response, he sent a sharp note in which he said, among many other things, that if war came "the fault will not be with the United States; the sole responsibility of such a calamity, with all its consequences, must rest with the Mexican Republic."

At some other time the Mexican Foreign Minister might have made an equally sharp reply, but the government was toppling, and on December 29, the day on which Texas joined the Union, it fell, with General Mariano Paredes y Arrillaga seizing power. Slidell had no better luck with the new government, which on March 12, 1846 not only announced its refusal to receive him but denounced at length what it termed American expansionism. Slidell then demanded his passport and left for Washington. He arrived on May 8 while Polk was trying to make up his mind whether or not to ask Congress for war. Slidell recommended war.

But war, as mentioned earlier, had already begun. It was the all but certain result of decisions made by Polk almost a year before. On May 28, 1845, General Taylor had been warned that he would be receiving orders to move his force of less than 1,500 men from Fort Jessup to the western frontier of Texas. The specific orders came on June 15 and by mid-August Taylor had established his little force at Corpus Christi, then only a village of thirty houses on the west bank of the Nueces River. He was thus inside disputed territory.

Gradually Taylor's army swelled to 4,000 men and even Taylor's admirers have criticized his administration of the camp. There was little discipline and the sanitary conditions were terrible. As his biographer Holman Hamilton writes:

> That Taylor tolerated an almost complete lack of sanitation certainly did him little credit. Few soldiers died from disease, but the record shows that diarrhea and dysentery kept an average of ten percent of the officers and thirteen percent of the men bedridden throughout the late autumn and winter months. Actually, in November and December [1845] the number of those affected was even larger.[1]

On February 3, 1846, when Washington had concluded that Slidell was likely to be unsuccessful in his attempt to buy California and New Mexico, Taylor was ordered to move south and west to the Rio Grande, but it was more than a month before he got the army marching. As the little army moved deeper into disputed territory, some of its officers were reluctant. Lieutenant Ulysses S. Grant, later commander of the Union armies in the Civil War and still later President, wrote in his *Memoirs:* "I was bitterly opposed to . . . the war . . . as one of the most unjust ever waged by a stronger against a weaker nation. . . . We were sent to provoke a fight, but it was essential that Mexico should commence it . . . Mexico showing no willingness to come to the Nueces to drive the invaders from her soil, it became necessary for the 'invaders' to approach within a convenient distance to be struck." Grant, called Sam in those days, was not the only one. Lieutenant Colonel Ethan Allen Hitchcock wrote: "As to the right of this movement, I have said from the first that the United States are the aggressors. We have outraged the Mexican Government and people by an arrogance and presumption that deserve to be punished. . . . My heart is not in this unholy business; I am against it from the

bottom of my soul as a most unholy and unrighteous proceeding; but, as a military man, I am bound to execute
orders."[2]

On March 20, for a few anxious minutes, it seemed as if
Taylor's unchallenged march was over when the force was
confronted by a Mexican array, complete with fifes and
kettledrums, whose commander announced that any attempt
by the Americans to cross the Arroyo Colorado—a deep,
high-banked salt lagoon—would be regarded as an act of war.
But Taylor told the Mexicans that if they attempted to stop
him, he would turn artillery on them. The Americans were
vulnerable as they began to wade across. The Mexicans could
have taken a heavy toll and perhaps influenced the course of
the war that was soon to come. But instead they wheeled
and galloped off.

On March 28 Taylor's army arrived on the north bank of
the Rio Grande across the river from the little city of
Matamoros, where Mexican flags flew. Officers of the two
sides met, and the Mexicans declared that Taylor's march
constituted an act of war. But the Americans said they did
not consider it such and would remain where they were until
the two governments settled the matter. They added that
Taylor would consider the crossing of the Rio Grande by
any armed party of Mexicans an act of war, and would pursue
it accordingly. The Americans had marched deep into territory
claimed by Mexico and yet said that for the Mexicans to
cross a river into that territory would be an act of war.

It was a curious confrontation. As the Americans built a
fortification and armed it with guns aimed at the public
square of Matamoros, the military bands serenaded each
other. In this military endeavor at least the Mexicans were

superior. Taylor and his officers were confident. Although
the Mexicans were at least the equal of the Americans in
number, they were, as Taylor wrote, "very inferior in quality
& equipment, & should we come to blows there can not
be a doubt as to the result. We must beat them." There
is an interesting sidelight to this little army in which Taylor
had such confidence. Nearly half of it was composed of
foreigners: mainly Irish (24 percent) and Germans (10
percent).

On April 24 a new Mexican commander arrived at
Matamoros, General Mariano Arista. He immediately wrote
Taylor that recent events had been "clearly hostile to Mexico,"
and that Mexico was "oppressed and forced into a struggle
which we cannot refuse, without dereliction of the most
sacred duty of men." And he proclaimed that: "Hostilities
have commenced, and I do not hesitate to assure your ex-
cellency that arms are hereafter to be used, and that you
must not be surprised that the troops under my command
should wait for no further signal."

Taylor replied that his occupation was not warlike, that
the matter should be settled by diplomacy, and that friendly
relations might be maintained on the frontier, but ". . . if
hostilities are to ensue—the responsibility must rest with
them who actually commence them." Old Rough and Ready
didn't have long to wait. That very day, April 26, Arista
sent 1,600 troops across the Rio Grande. As soon as Taylor
heard of this movement, he sent Captain Seth Thornton out
to reconnoiter. Some hours later, Chapita, a Mexican guide
—the one who had escaped—returned to Taylor's camp. He
described the engagement that began the open hostilities.
Taylor, even before he notified distant Washington, sent off

hurried calls to the governors of Texas and Louisiana asking for 5,000 volunteers.

By May 1 Taylor decided he had better hurry back to his base camp on the Gulf of Mexico before Arista cut it off. He left five hundred men and eight cannon at the fortification, Fort Texas, and led a forced march to the Gulf. He succeeded only because the boats in which Arista's army was to cross the Rio Grande did not arrive in time. Thus the Mexicans lost a good opportunity to inflict a serious defeat on the Americans.

But the sound of cannon fire alarmed Taylor and his entire force, for they knew it meant that little Fort Texas was under attack. For two days they had no word, but the continued firing assured them that the fort was holding out. By May 7 Taylor had received enough reinforcements from New Orleans and from the navy flotilla to give him confidence that his base camp could defend itself. Taylor calmly told the army that he was looking for a fight and he reminded the infantrymen that "their main dependence must be in the bayonet," for Old Rough and Ready was a great believer in cold steel. Lieutenant Sam Grant was impressed by Taylor's calm: "No soldier could face either danger or responsibility more calmly than he. These are qualities more rarely found than genius or physical courage." Many writers have criticized, probably with justice, Taylor's capacities as organizer and tactician, but have not been able to fault his quiet courage, and it was that which in the end brought him victory.

On May 6 Arista had called on Fort Texas to surrender but the Americans "respectfully" declined. The final assault was scheduled for May 7 but the Mexican commander learned of Taylor's advance and decided to concentrate instead on defeating Taylor's main force. As Taylor, with his army of 2,200 men and more than 200 wagons, moved ponderously toward the pond of Palo Alto, he got word that Arista in full battle array was deployed two miles farther on, across the line of American advance. Calmly, Taylor halted his army, allowed his men to fill their canteens and refresh themselves, and then formed the troops into attack columns. All the while Arista pranced on his horse and, riding up and down along his line, told the cheering troops that victory and glory were ahead. And they might well have been if Arista had attacked instead of allowing Taylor to form his troops.

Taylor was outnumbered at least two to one but he had more and superior artillery. He decided to use artillery instead of his favorite bayonet, and it was artillery that won the Battle of Palo Alto. For, as was written in a contemporary Mexican account, "The artillery of the Americans, much superior to ours, made horrid ravages in the ranks of the Mexican army." But the Mexicans were brave. As Grant wrote his wife-to-be, "Every moment we could see the charges from our pieces cut a way through their ranks making a perfect road, but they would close up the interval without showing signs of retreat." And Taylor wrote in his report that the "constancy with which the Mexican infantry sustained this cannonade was a theme of universal remark and admiration." And that was how the Mexican War was to go. The Mexican soldiers were brave but often were irresolutely led and almost always poorly equipped.

When darkness fell on that historic day of May 8, the Mexican army had suffered cruel punishment at a cost to the Americans of eleven killed or fatally wounded and some fifty less seriously wounded. As dawn approached on May 9, some of Taylor's officers were content with the victory and wanted to entrench and wait for reinforcements. Taylor listened patiently and then announced that he would press on. When dawn came, the Mexicans were in retreat, demoralized by rumor and dissension. At 10 A.M. Arista halted his retreat and established a defense line but evidently did not really expect Taylor to attack again so soon. So Arista stayed in his tent while Taylor did indeed attack. Again it was the American artillery backed by infantry charges, this time with cold steel, and before Arista realized the severity of the assault, it was too late. He led a gallant cavalry charge, but the Americans mowed down the Mexicans. Again they had to retreat but this time it was a rout, with the Americans in full pursuit, "yelling like mad."

The Mexican army was smashed on this second day and the American battle deaths were only thirty-nine. Thus, on May 9, 1846, the Battle of Resaca de la Palma ensured the success of the first American campaign in the Mexican War. This day, the very one on which Polk was to learn that war had begun, also ensured the White House for Zachary Taylor, for Americans throughout their history have often rewarded victorious generals with the highest prize they possess: the Presidency.

Taylor's victories both pleased and dismayed the Democrat Polk, for he was convinced that the Whig Taylor had his eye on the White House fully as much as on the Mexican army. That may have been true later when honors began to be heaped on Taylor, but it is unlikely that the plain old soldier had such aspirations at first. And there was another result of these twin American victories, although a decade and a half would pass before its full impact could be seen. A young lieutenant, Ulysses S. Grant, had learned what artillery could do:

> . . . Lieutenant Grant had learned about fire power . . . and a great part of the defeat of the Confederate States of America was inflicted in the muggy Mexican sun on May 8, 1846. For the far more brilliant Lee, who had as much chance as Grant to learn the lesson, never learned it. He remained confident that the courage of the Southern infantrymen could prevail against the Northern barrage and sent them against it too often. . . . There is no reproach in that fact: the texts show that a full year of the first World War had passed, and half a million men had been killed in their tracks, before any commander learned about the power of massed fire what Ulysses Grant, whose campaigns all of them had studied, learned in the six hours of Palo Alto.[3]

After his victories, Taylor was not quite sure what to do next. He occupied Matamoros on May 18 and then sat. There was no enemy nearby and any possible objective was far distant across inhospitable deserts. Further, he didn't know what Washington wanted him to do. There was an exchange of correspondence in which Taylor asked for supplies and suggested that he conquer the northern provinces of Mexico rather than move on the capital, Mexico City, because of supply difficulties.

But these were not quiet days for Taylor. War fever had swept the United States, particularly the frontier regions, and volunteers were descending in hordes upon Taylor's headquarters. They were trigger-happy and spent hours each day firing their guns off in random fashion. Lieutenant George Meade, later to be a Union Army commander in the Civil

War, wrote: "Bullets come whizzing by us as thick as in action and I really consider spending a day in my tent, uninjured, equivalent to passing through a well-contested action." And Lieutenant George B. McClellan, also to be a Union commander, wrote: "The people are very polite to the regulars . . . but they hate the volunteers as they do Old Scratch himself. . . . The volunteers carry on in a most shameful and disgraceful manner; they think nothing of robbing and killing Mexicans." But when the time came, these volunteers could fight.

While Taylor was waiting around for instructions and for the steamboats he needed to proceed inland along the Rio Grande, the United States was trying to organize itself for war. It must be remembered that the telegraph and the railroad were just coming into use and that the war was being fought thousands of miles from the still-young industrial centers. The task of getting men, supplies, and transport where they were needed, and when, was supremely difficult, complicated by American ignorance about Mexican climate and terrain. All the advantages would seem to have rested with Mexico, which, of course, had much shorter supply lines. But Mexico as a nation was only twenty-five years old, it had virtually no industry, at best its government was disorganized, and it was continuously racked with revolution.

And it was just as well, for the situation in Washington, too, was almost incredible. President Polk was extremely suspicious of his two top generals, Taylor in the field and Winfield T. Scott in Washington. Indeed, there was open hostility between Polk and Scott, a Whig, who had his eye on the White House. Polk tried to undercut Scott, though he was eventually forced to give him authority because he was the only one qualified to head the army. Scott wrote long and indiscreet letters that soon became public knowledge and increased the bitterness between the President and his top commander. And there were all kinds of political infighting that involved the army and the navy, for in those days there was little or no attempt to keep the military out of politics.

This extraordinary situation may be a bit more understandable when you consider that Washington was just a town then, with a population of only forty thousand, that all the leading figures knew each other personally, that it was still a frontier society, and that high government office did not yet have the aura that later was to confer on its holder a certain respect. These men, whose names now live in history, treated each other with the rough informality of frontier society, and neither rank nor title awed them, for they knew each other too well. This was a far different society from the more formal and structured one we now know.

Yet somehow Polk and his Secretaries of War and Navy, and General Scott and Quartermaster-General Thomas S. Jesup, prepared for Taylor's campaign and the campaign against Mexico City. There were blunders and bottlenecks, to be sure, often driving Taylor and Scott to distraction. But it wasn't so bad considering that the amount of preparation was limited by the fact that not a cent was appropriated for the war until after the Battle of Resaca de la Palma.

Two months after Resaca de la Palma, Taylor began to move troops toward his first goal, Camargo, more than 100 miles inland. Many of them had to march through scorching,

parched deserts, often collapsing from thirst and heat. Some
were able to travel in the tiny steamboats, but it was slow,
tortuous going, for the boats lacked power, had to fight a
strong downstream current, and had only green mesquite wood
to burn for fuel; and the river twisted and turned so that
the distance was 400 miles by water. In early August Taylor
and his staff left for Camargo and the campaign was on—
nearly three months after the early victories. But Camargo
was not an auspicious starting point: the heat sometimes
reached 112 degrees, the town of three thousand had
recently been hit by a flood, there were plagues of disease-
carrying insects, and the water was polluted. Many men
died.

Nonetheless, Taylor organized his army and on August 20
it set out for its major objective, the city of Monterrey. But
while Taylor marched, a strange drama was unfolding that
was to have a profound effect on the war. The chief character
was General Antonio López de Santa Anna, already known
to Americans for the massacre at the Alamo and his surrender at San Jacinto, which had made Texan independence
possible. Santa Anna was almost too extravagant to be
believed, but perhaps Bernard DeVoto came close to describing him:

> Santa Anna is the set piece of Mexican history, complete
> with rockets, pinwheels, Greek fire, and aerial bombs. He had
> been president of Mexico, dictator, commander in chief, much
> too often and too variously for specification here. He had con-
> trived to persuade a good many different factions that he was
> their soul, and he never betrayed any of them till he got their
> funds. He was enormously rich. . . . He had the national
> genius for oratory and manifesto, and a genius of his own for

courage, cowardice, inspiration and magnificent graft. . . . Since [Jacinto] he had procured further revolutions at home, had lost a leg defending his country against a French invasion, had established a new dictatorship, and had been overthrown by the uprising that put Herrera in power.[4]

The Mexican people had tired of the self-styled "Napoleon of the West" and, as the Mexican War approached, he was living in exile in Havana, Cuba, with his child-bride. Believing it was his destiny to rule Mexico, he saw the ominous developments as an opportunity. This incredible tale begins on February 13, 1845, when a Colonel A. J. Atocha, a Spanish-born American, met privately with President Polk. Polk believed that both Santa Anna and his emissary Atocha were unreliable but he thought he could use them, so he listened with interest to Atocha's proposal. It was extraordinary. Santa Anna, above all, wanted tranquillity for Mexico and that was possible only with a friendly United States. He was willing to obtain that friendship by ceding to the United States much of New Mexico and California. Of course, there would be a certain expense: about $30 million. And of course the Mexicans would never agree to being sold out by their government, so the cession would have to appear to be forced. Perhaps Polk might want to have General Taylor invade Mexico. Polk didn't feel it necessary to tell the Colonel that had already been planned. And so the interview ended with both men feeling confident that much had been achieved. Again DeVoto:

> Neither [Polk] nor his Cabinet seems to have appreciated that Santa Anna's proposal was one of the most outrageous in the history of nations. Worse, they were unaware that they were being used as aides to gang politics in Mexico—in plain

American, that they were being played for suckers to assist in the overthrow of Paredes.[5]

The Polk–Santa Anna scheme, which had matured in further direct and indirect contacts between Santa Anna and the United States, began to go into effect in August 1846. Another Mexican revolution overthrew General Paredes, and General José Mariano Salas assumed office, but everyone understood that he was just standing in for Santa Anna. On August 16 Santa Anna, aboard the British ship *Arab,* steamed, by arrangement, through the American blockade and landed at Vera Cruz with his beautiful seventeen-year-old wife and staff members. His reception was lukewarm but the "superb egoist" brushed that off and made for Mexico City, where he arrived in mid-September.

By this time word of the dealings between Polk and Santa Anna had begun to leak out and it was even reported in British newspapers. There was great suspicion of Santa Anna in Mexico but he managed to allay it somewhat by immediately rushing off to raise an army to oppose Taylor in the North. What happened to his deal with Polk? Perhaps Santa Anna was scared away from it by the response of the Mexican people or perhaps he had been using Polk all along when Polk thought he had been using Santa Anna.

But Santa Anna was not yet ready to take the field and it was General Pedro de Ampudia who opposed Taylor at Monterrey. As Taylor's force of some six thousand men, about evenly divided between regulars and volunteers, approached Monterrey, it became apparent that this battle was not going to be as easy as those of Palo Alto and Resaca de la Palma. Here the Mexicans were well fortified and had superior artillery, for Taylor had left his heavy guns behind because of transport difficulty. This victory, if there were to be one, would depend on the courage of the men who would have to take Monterrey by frontal assault.

After studying reports of the reconnoitering parties, Taylor decided that Monterrey was weakest in the rear and he assigned the attack there to General William J. Worth. Worth some months before had stormed away from Taylor's camp because of a dispute as to whether he or General David E. Twiggs was second in rank to Taylor. But he had returned when fighting broke out and Taylor, although still put out at Worth's earlier departure, recognized his qualities as a fighter. As it turned out, Worth proved himself at Monterrey a better tactician than Taylor. Worth mounted his attacks with resolution and intelligence, whereas Taylor, although as courageous as ever, directed his attacks where they cost the most men and didn't attack at all at the moment when Worth most needed support. Nonetheless, in four days of hard fighting—often charging up steep hills into severe Mexican fire—the Americans carried Monterrey. Indeed, some of the hills were so steep that the Americans could climb them only by clinging to bushes and jagged rocks. When they reached the crest, despite sustained Mexican fire, they resorted to Taylor's favorite weapon, Old Betsy, the naked bayonet, and swept the defenders before them.

In the final assault, Worth's men used a technique developed by the Texans in 1836. Rather than brave the withering artillery and musket fire that swept the streets, the Americans, using pickaxes, crowbars, and improvised battering rams, smashed their way through walls from house to house. On September 23 the Americans overcame the

Mexicans' brave resistance, as Taylor strolled casually through the streets with bullets buzzing around him.

Before dawn on the 24th the Mexicans offered to surrender if Taylor would let Ampudia withdraw his army and its equipment. Taylor refused, but in a face-to-face confrontation with Ampudia agreed to let a commission of three officers from each army work out the terms of surrender. The negotiations dragged on until late that night but the final terms were generous. The Mexicans were to surrender Monterrey, but Ampudia's troops could retain their arms and one field battery of six pieces with twenty-one rounds of ammunition. The Mexicans were to evacuate the city within a week and withdraw to a line about forty miles away Taylor agreed to this remarkable restraint, for which he later was severely criticized. Although pressing forward might have ended the war before Santa Anna could raise another army, Taylor agreed not to advance for eight weeks, or at least not until orders could be received from the two governments. Evidently Taylor believed that a pause might lead to a political settlement of the war. But Polk wasn't interested in a political settlement any more, and when on October 11 he finally learned of Taylor's victory, he wrote in his diary no praise for the victory, just criticism for the armistice:

> In agreeing to this armistice General Taylor violated his express orders and I regret that I cannot approve his course. He had the enemy in his power and should have taken them prisoners, deprived them of their arms, discharged them on their parole or honour, and preserved the advantages which he had obtained by pushing on without delay farther into the country, if the force at his command justified it.

The next day the Cabinet unanimously agreed that Taylor had made a grave misjudgment, that he might have ended the war then and there if he had disarmed Ampudia's troops. And the Cabinet also agreed unanimously to send orders to Taylor to end the armistice immediately and prosecute the war "with energy and vigor." But then ten days later Polk reversed himself, not on the armistice but on pushing farther inland, and again the Cabinet was unanimous in agreeing "that under existing circumstances General Taylor should not advance beyond Monterrey. . . ."

Taylor's victory added further to his fame even though the credit really belonged to General Worth. The victory was costly, with about seven and a half percent of Taylor's force being killed or wounded. One hundred twenty men were killed, virtually all of them at the eastern end of Monterrey, where Taylor was in direct command. But Taylor was the top commander and he gained the laurels as he would have received the blame if the battle had been lost.

After Monterrey there was another of those long pauses that characterized the American prosecution of the Mexican War. In Washington Polk was seeking frantically for a politically acceptable general to lead the campaign against Mexico City that would end the war. Despite Taylor's string of victories, Polk didn't want him; and he didn't want General Winfield T. Scott, the Army Commandant, even though he was clearly the best-qualified general in the nation. But more about that after we take a look at the war in the West.

Chapter Three

ALTHOUGH THE MAIN BATTLES of the Mexican War were
fought in Mexico proper, Polk's real goal was those vast
and rich lands known as New Mexico (much bigger than
the present state of New Mexico) and California. To get
them he had to defeat Mexico, for Mexico would not sell
them. While Taylor was engaged south of the border,
Polk also took direct steps to seize New Mexico and California. In May 1846 Commodore John D. Sloat, commander
of the Pacific Squadron of the Navy, was ordered, if war
with Mexico came, to seize San Francisco, blockade other
Californian ports, and do all he could to establish good
relations with the Californians. And then Colonel Stephen
Watts Kearny, commander of Fort Leavenworth, Kansas,
was blandly ordered to seize New Mexico, whose capital,
Santa Fe, was a mere nine hundred miles away across desert
and through fierce Apache, Pawnee, Arapaho, and, fiercest of
all, Comanche territory. And he was to do all this with an
army of seventeen hundred, about half volunteer.

   We have already seen what Taylor's volunteers were like.
Kearny's weren't much better. Bernard DeVoto describes
them this way:

> They were volunteers, they were farmers mostly, they were
> incredibly young, they were Missourians and frontiersmen—
> close kin to the Big Bear of Arkansaw. All good armies grouch;
> probably none has ever bellyached so continuously as this one.
> They groused about their officers, their equipment, the food,
> the service regulations, the climate, the trail, the future. They
> would accept direction or command no more easily here than
> at home, and were always assaulting their non-coms on the

ground that Joe's stripes could not neutralize his native stupidity and did not sanction him to put on airs. They howled derision of the officers whenever it was safe and frequently when it wasn't, made fantastic plots against the most inflexible of them, and when a vacancy occurred resolved to elect no one except from the rank of private. They abominated neatness, they hated the routine of guard duty and the care of horses, they straggled worse than any other troops in history that would fight. Till the army was concentrated at Bent's Fort, its component parts were just where whim took them—a battalion strung out for five miles while the individual soldier wasted ammunition on imaginary antelope, or three quarters of it marching in a clump with the guard just to see what the country was like.[1]

But, as DeVoto pointed out, "It could do nothing well except march and fight, and would not do those by the numbers." They drove the West Pointers crazy until they learned to accept the inevitable. But fortunately Kearny did not keep them in camp for boring weeks as Taylor had done with his volunteers in Mexico.

March these volunteers did. On June 5, 1846 Kearny sent off the first detachments. Others followed. Kearny and his staff left on the last day of the month. It was quite a trek. To provide supplies in the hostile country ahead, Kearny took with him 1,556 wagons, 800 head of cattle, 459 horses, 3,658 mules, and 14,904 oxen, a logistic triumph of no mean proportion. Although the Santa Fe Trail itself was well worn by years of emigration west, there was no road—not even a path from Fort Leavenworth to the trail. Deep ravines, steep-banked creeks had to be crossed, and prairie soil so soft that wagons sank to their axles. But they got through and the regulars and the volunteers learned to help one another

cheerfully. March these volunteers could, for on July 28 two
infantry companies of volunteers strode into Bent's Fort on
the Arkansas River, having covered six hundred miles in
twenty-nine days, beating mounted men who had left before
them.

On August 18 Kearny marched into Santa Fe without
having fired a shot or spilled a drop of blood. A couple of
times Mexican forces made a show of resistance, but they
always faded away when Kearny showed he was not about
to turn back. And Kearny proved himself a wise and humane
conqueror. He immediately pledged "a free government with
the least possible delay, similar to those in the United States."
And he declared that "the people of New Mexico will then
be called on to exercise the rights of freemen in electing
their own representatives to the territorial legislature." It is
not often that a conquered people welcomes its conquerors
but such was the case in New Mexico. For the Mexican
government had never really been able to govern in that
territory; it was too distant and too weak. Thus the
governors, uncontrolled by the Mexican capital, were often
despotic and corrupt, nor could they protect the settlers
from the terrible raids of the Comanches and other Indians.

Kearny appointed two lawyers from the Missouri Volunteers,
Colonel Alexander Doniphan, whose great adventure was
yet to come, and Private Willard Hall, to write a constitution for the territory. Then Kearny began to prepare for
the long trek to California, for, as he wrote the Adjutant
General in Washington, "the territory is now so perfectly
quiet" that he intended to leave on September 25. He did,
and having heard that the Navy had secured California, took
only three hundred men with him.

The Navy had taken California. In May 1846 Commodore Sloat heard of the fighting between Taylor and Mexico, but he was not quite sure that war had been declared. In the first few days of June he got further information but still hesitated. Finally, on June 7, Sloat learned that the Navy had begun operations in the Gulf of Mexico and that decided him. He weighed anchor, sailed from his position off the Mexican port of Mazatlán north to Monterey, some distance south of San Francisco. Sloat paid a courtesy call on the Mexican officials and then met with the United States Consul, Thomas O. Larkin. Larkin, who had received earlier instructions from Polk to do what he could to influence California toward the United States, was still not sure that war had begun. But Sloat put aside his doubts and on July 5 he sent ashore a force that raised the American flag above the customhouse. And Sloat proclaimed that "henceforth California will be a portion of the United States" and he pledged that all "peaceful inhabitants would retain their rights, their property and their freedom of religion." Sloat then sent orders to do the same to Commander John B. Montgomery, captain of the *Portsmouth,* which was anchored in San Francisco harbor.

It all seemed very easy, for in that great rich and fertile area of California there was a population of only 25,000. About 15,000 were Indians and of the settlers only about 800 were Americans. Most of the rest were Mexicans, at least theoretically. There were three leading men: Governor Pío Pico, pro-British; General José Castro, publicly pro-Mexican but with an eye to ruling an independent California; and M. G. Vallejo, a big landowner, pro-American. But from this time on, things got terribly confused in

California and even a century and a quarter later it is hard
to sort them out. During the next few months there were
the mysterious and unpredictable actions of John Charles
Frémont, who became known as the "Pathfinder," ran as the
first Republican candidate for the Presidency, and was a
disastrous Civil War general. The son-in-law of Senator
Thomas Hart Benton, one of the most powerful men in
Washington, Frémont had great aspirations. He saw himself
as a man of destiny, and thought, among other things, that
he should be the first governor of California. He was forever
appearing where he had no right to be, doing things he had
no right to do, making the pacification of California infinitely
more difficult, and, as a matter of course, disobeying orders.
All the while he was writing dramatic letters to his father-
in-law in which he pictured himself as achieving triumph
after triumph. Actually, he ended up being court-martialed
and convicted of mutiny, disobedience of orders, and conduct
prejudicial to good order and military discipline. Polk approved
the judgment but remitted the sentence, and Frémont, not
a whit chastened by the experience, continued to play a
flamboyant role in American politics for another decade and
a half.

In August Commodore Robert F. Stockton had succeeded
Sloat as naval commander in the Pacific. He led a force—
which included Frémont and Consul Larkin—that took Los
Angeles unopposed. Mexican troops fled in all directions,
even though Stockton's command consisted of only a few
score men. Stockton wrote of his accomplishment with the
modesty that characterized most of the leading figures in
the Mexican War:

Thus, in less than a month after I assumed command of the United States force in California, we have chased the Mexican army more than three hundred miles along the coast; pursued them thirty miles in the interior of their own country; routed and dispersed them, and secured the Territory to the United States; ended the war, restored peace and harmony among the people; and put a civil government into successful operation.

It certainly looked good. On August 22, 1846, while Taylor was on the road to his victory at Monterrey, the very day that Kearny had claimed all of New Mexico, Stockton organized a civil government for California with himself as temporary governor. Frémont, he declared, would be appointed permanent governor later. This was the picture Kearny got when, on October 6, pushing west toward California, he encountered the legendary scout Kit Carson. Carson, with sixteen men, was headed across the continent with dispatches for Washington from Stockton and Frémont. He told Kearny that all was quiet. Kearny decided therefore that he didn't need all three hundred men and detached two hundred to return to New Mexico. He also persuaded Carson to turn his dispatches over to the force returning to New Mexico and to guide Kearny into California.

There was only one thing wrong. Stockton had been wildly optimistic, and on September 23, even before Kearny encountered Carson, Mexicans had risen against their conquerors. Indeed, DeVoto writes that Stockton's grandiose proclamation had alienated the Mexican Californians, who, till then, had shown no hostility to the Americans. DeVoto argues that Stockton and Frémont made war when there was no reason to. Whatever the cause, by early December, when

Kearny's exhausted and famished party reached an American ranch in California, the territory was in full revolt. Despite the dreadful condition of his small command, Kearny moved immediately to the attack. Unfortunately, however, he encountered a superb force commanded by Andrés Pico, brother of the former governor; ". . . well-mounted and among the best horsemen in the world," Pico's men charged with lances. As Kearny reported, "On account of their greatly superior numbers but few of us remained untouched." The clash was a costly one. Out of Kearny's hundred or so men, nineteen were killed, including three officers. And Kearny himself received two wounds.

Kearny's command was in bad shape. They dragged themselves toward the coast as wolves, attracted by the smell of blood, howled alongside. Their provisions were exhausted, their horses dead, the mules staggering, the men fatigued and emaciated, pulling the wounded behind them on rough litters, and all the while Pico's force harassed them. Finally Kit Carson and two others went for relief to San Diego, twenty-nine miles away. Relief came on December 10, and two days later Kearny, after seventy-nine days on the trail, marched his tattered, exhausted band into San Diego.

Characteristically, Kearny immediately urged Stockton to attack Los Angeles. The attack took a couple of weeks to prepare and Kearny led it, although Stockton insisted that he was in overall command. After some brief skirmishes Kearny occupied Los Angeles on January 10, 1847, and now, after three months, the City of Angels was back in American hands.

But no sooner had peace been established in California than one of those almost comic situations developed that

seem characteristic of the Mexican War. Even though Kearny
had been ordered by Polk to establish a government in
California, Stockton claimed that the orders given his prede-
cessor, Sloat, gave him that authority. And he claimed—
presumably with a straight face—that he had already succeeded before Kearny arrived. Stockton appointed Frémont
governor. Kearny wisely decided not to force a crisis and
bided his time. It came on February 13 when orders arrived
from Washington clearly establishing Kearny as the highest
authority. Frémont at first refused to relinquish his post but
finally backed down and, under Kearny's orders, accompanied
him back to Fort Leavenworth, where Frémont was arrested.
The court-martial, which lasted three months, was held in
Washington with Senator Benton as his son-in-law's unsuccessful defense counsel.

Before leaving the Western campaign, brief mention must
be made of what is certainly one of the great sagas in American history. Although it did not have a profound influence
on the war, the Missouri Volunteers under their elected
colonel, Alexander W. Doniphan, made a forced march
that can have few equals in the annals of warfare. First, the
Missourians under Doniphan marched from Fort Leavenworth to Santa Fe, some nine hundred miles. Then, following
Kearny's orders, Doniphan led his men to the support of
General John Ellis Wool in the Mexican province of
Chihuahua. Doniphan left late in October 1846 and in just
over four months marched the almost incredible distance of
three thousand miles through snow-covered mountains and
across burning deserts. Along the way he pacified the Mexican
population, conquered and made peace treaties with the
Navajos, and twice defeated much larger Mexican forces, all

at a cost of two men killed. It is no wonder that William Cullen Bryant, poet, scholar, and journalist, compared Doniphan and Xenophon, the Greek writer-soldier, as "two military commanders who have made the most extraordinary marches known in the annals of warfare of their times."

Chapter Four

BACK IN WASHINGTON President Polk must have been both pleased and perplexed. By early 1847 Taylor had decisively defeated the Mexican forces in the northern provinces and Kearny had achieved Polk's primary goal, the conquest of California and New Mexico. Yet unaccountably the Mexicans would not give up, and obviously they would not do so until Santa Anna had been defeated and Mexico City occupied. But the first enthusiasm for the war had worn off. Indeed, the Whigs had scored victories in both Congressional and state elections in 1846. And there was no shortage of dissent. Abraham Lincoln, a majority of the House of Representatives, many Senators, and such wise private citizens as Emerson and Thoreau opposed the war.

But James Polk did not have time to worry overmuch about criticism and dissent. He had a war to win, a war that Mexico had already lost, although strangely it would not admit it. Polk needed a general. He considered Taylor unfit, but whether this was a political or a military judgment is hard to say. If not Taylor, why not Scott? He was clearly the best-qualified man. But Polk didn't like Scott's Whig politics either and he didn't like the letters Scott had written. For a while he even toyed with the extraordinary idea of trying to get Congress to allow him to appoint the wholly unqualified Senator Benton as supreme commander of the final thrust against Mexico City. Eventually Polk had to settle on Scott; there was no other rational choice.

In Mexico, Taylor bitterly received the news that not only would Scott direct the final campaign, ". . . but, my dear general, I shall be obliged to take from you most of the gallant officers and men (regulars and volunteers) whom you have so long and so nobly commanded." Needless to say, Taylor did not take this graciously. Now, added to all the infighting in Washington, was the fact that the two top field commanders in Mexico were not on speaking terms. The troops were sorry to leave Taylor, and Lieutenant (Civil War General) George C. Meade wrote: "I must confess I regretted exceedingly parting with the old man. He has been most outrageously treated by the administration, which hopes to play off General Scott against him . . . to break him down and destroy his popularity."

Taylor, whose forces now numbered less than five thousand, only five hundred of them regulars, was specifically ordered to remain on the defensive. But in this war it was hardly surprising that Taylor refused to leave Saltillo and return to Monterrey, pushing forward toward Santa Anna instead. Taylor compounded his disobedience by declining to meet Scott, who was waiting for him a short distance away at Camargo. By the middle of January 1847 Santa Anna had raised an army of 21,000 men. When he learned that Taylor's force had been drastically reduced, he decided to finish off Taylor and then turn back and deal with Scott. He was confident that when Scott landed—the fact that an expedition was being mounted was hardly a secret—*el vómito,* yellow fever, would serve to occupy Scott for a while.

It was a good plan, for Santa Anna was good at plans and he was a genius at organizing armies. The only trouble was that, once he had an army, he wasn't quite sure what to do with it. Besides, this time nature was against him. Santa Anna began the march toward Taylor with 18,000 men, but the force was quickly hit by unseasonable rain, wind, and bitter cold. And when the storm blew itself out, burning heat succeeded it. There was not enough food or water and when Santa Anna mustered his troops at La Encarnación on February 21, he had lost four thousand dead, deserted, sick, or straggling. Even so his force was nearly three times as big as Taylor's.

Taylor had sent out scouts. When he learned of the superior force advancing on him, he decided to fall back to more defensible ground. As Santa Anna advanced on Agua Nueva, the Americans put the torch to the supplies they could not carry away. Seeing the flames, Santa Anna thought the Americans were falling back in disorder, that they were in a panic. He should have known better. Whatever Taylor's faults, a tendency to panic was not one of them. The Americans were falling back to a position at Buena Vista that General Wool had chosen two months before as "the very spot of all others I have yet seen in Mexico, which I would select for battle, were I obliged with a small

army to fight a large one." Taylor had approved the choice
and here the Americans awaited Santa Anna. This is the way
Taylor described it:

> Our troops were in position occupying a line of remark-
> able strength. The road at this point becomes a narrow defile,
> the valley on its right being rendered quite impracticable for
> artillery by a system of deep and impassable gullies, while on
> the left a succession of rugged ridges and precipitous ravines,
> extends far back towards the mountains which bound the
> valley. The features of the ground were such as nearly to
> paralyze the artillery and cavalry of the enemy, while his
> infantry could not derive all the advantages of its numerical
> superiority. In this position we prepared to receive him.

Santa Anna could have circled around Taylor and captured
the American base at Saltillo. He could have waited a day
or two for his men to recover from the arduous march.
Instead he chose imperiously to demand Taylor's surrender.
Although Taylor's exact words have been lost, they were
reported as being "forcible." So Santa Anna pressed the
attack despite the difficult terrain and he pressed it reso-
lutely. With Taylor's old adversary Ampudia heading one
of the columns, the Mexicans hit the Americans with cavalry,
infantry, and artillery. The Americans fought well, the advantage of the terrain helping them to take a fearful toll
of Mexicans. They fought all the afternoon of February 22,
shouting Washington's name. The fighting ended with darkness, but the next morning Santa Anna again pressed the
attack. The Americans were still taking a heavy toll but the
strength and resolution of the Mexican attack were beginning to take effect. Ampudia was beginning to roll up the

American left. The Mexicans captured some American cannon, and panic began to spread in the American ranks as troops fled from the battle line toward the rear.

General Wool galloped up to Taylor and said, "General, we are whipped." Calmly Taylor replied, "That is for me to decide."

Then came one of those moments that decide whether a battle is won or lost. Fifteen hundred brilliantly costumed Mexican lancers, flags flying, moved against Colonel Jefferson Davis, later to be President of the Confederacy. He positioned his Mississippi Volunteers and some Indiana troops in a "V" with the open side facing the Mexicans. As the Mexicans got within about eighty yards of the "V", they unaccountably slowed to a walk. At that moment the Americans opened up. "It was appalling. The whole head of the column was prostrated," wrote Captain J. H. Carleton. And he went on to say that if the Mexicans had galloped into the Americans without slowing down, their losses would have been high but they would have smashed through and carried Taylor's rear.

The battle continued for the rest of the day with the Mexicans attacking courageously and the Americans continuing to impose high losses. But the Americans were suffering severe losses too and, when night fell, Taylor's men did not look forward to the next day. They did not know how much longer they could hold on. They were just about whipped.

But when the sun rose and the morning mists cleared away, the Americans, to their astonishment, found that they alone occupied the field. Santa Anna had fled, to the disgust, wrote one Mexican historian, of his men. They perhaps had perceived what he had not, that another day of hard fighting would have brought them victory. The Americans were delirious with joy, for they realized how close they had been to defeat. It was an old story in this war. The Mexican soldiers were brave, but their generals often combined recklessness one day with over-caution the next. It was a costly battle for the Mexicans with 591 dead and 1,037 wounded, but the Americans, too, had paid a high price: 267 dead, 456 wounded, and 23 missing. This punishment of Santa Anna contributed to the final victory. If Santa Anna had won, he would have gained the momentum and the confidence that would have made him a much more dangerous foe.

Though he didn't know it, that was Taylor's last fight. The final victory was to be Scott's. On March 9, 1847, after assembling a force at Tampico, Scott at Vera Cruz made the first amphibious landing in modern warfare. Soldiers poured into small boats that were rowed quickly to shore under the protection of Navy guns. As keels grated on the sand, the soldiers leaped ashore, officers waving swords, men with fixed bayonets. The landing was unopposed. No one knows why, for it was widely agreed that if General Juan Morales had positioned his men in the dunes, they could have inflicted serious, perhaps fatal, losses on the invading force.

Scott then laid siege to Vera Cruz. Many of his officers wanted to storm the walled city, but Scott did not have the eagerness many officers have to shed blood. He wanted a victory, but he did not want casualties. On March 22 Scott began shelling the city from land and sea. On the 27th the city surrendered and on the 29th Scott's forces were inside the walls. The cost: only nineteen lives. It was a brilliant triumph but largely overlooked in the United States, where Taylor's costly victory was hailed. As in all lands in all times, the magnitude of the triumph seemed to depend more on its cost in lives than on what was achieved.

Scott was now eager to get inland, away from the hot coastal plain where *el vómito* was about to make its annual visitation, but now he felt the frustration Taylor had felt before him. He did not have enough wagons or animals to draw them, but he started contingents inland anyway. By this time Santa Anna had sufficiently recovered from his self-proclaimed "victory" at Buena Vista to march to Mexico City, where he again became President, the result of still another revolution.

Scott and Santa Anna met for the first time at Cerro Gordo on April 17–18. The Mexicans had drawn themselves up in favorable rough terrain, but the Americans were too resolute for them. At a cost of 63 killed and 367 wounded, Scott routed Santa Anna (whose dinner was eaten by a couple of captains) and captured more than 2,000, including five generals. It is during this battle that we first encounter a name that is to figure greatly in American history. In his report Scott was "impelled to make special mention of Captain R. E. Lee." Robert E. Lee, who was to lead the Confederate armies during the Civil War, was remarked "as again indefatigable . . . in reconnaissance as daring as laborous [*sic*] and of the utmost value. Nor was he less conspicuous in planting batteries, and in conducting columns to their stations under the heavy fire of the enemy." Other high-ranking officers wrote in similar language.

In addition to Lee and Grant, the two great commanders of the Civil War, dozens of other senior Civil War generals served their apprenticeship under fire south of the border. The Mexican War, among other things, was the dress rehearsal for the much crueler Civil War. What did Robert E. Lee think of war? He wrote his son Custis after Cerro Gordo, "You have no idea what a horrible sight a field of battle is."

Although the war was going well, the personal relations among the Americans were following their now customary course. Almost all the top-ranking generals were quarreling with one another and Scott and Taylor could agree on only one thing: that Polk was treating them both shabbily. Enter now another figure who plays an almost incredible role, Nicholas P. Trist, who had been a protégé of Thomas Jefferson. Although his title was merely that of senior clerk of the State Department, he was second in influence there only to Secretary Buchanan. Polk decided to attach him to Scott's army to make a peace treaty when the Mexicans were ready. Scott evidently didn't read his orders very carefully, for he immediately concluded that Trist was trying to undercut his authority. To this Trist, in the now commonplace manner, replied with an angry thirty-page letter. Polk became quite cross with both of them, but before his instructions arrived telling them to patch things up, they had become quite friendly. A gift of guava jelly from Scott when Trist was ill seemed to open the door. And subsequently both wrote to Washington asking that their nasty letters about each other be removed from the files.

But Trist's peace-making assignment was still some months off. Scott first had to take Mexico City. When reinforcements brought his army up to 10,000 troops, Scott, on August 7, began the advance to Mexico City. It was not a timid move, for from then on he would have neither base nor supply line. Scott, whose pen was seldom guilty of understatement, wrote to the War Department: "Like Cortez, finding myself isolated and abandoned . . . I resolved no longer to depend on Vera Cruz, but to render my little army a self-sustaining machine." By August 12 Scott had neared Mexico City and he devoted several days to reconnaissance, for the walled city would be a difficult prize, as events proved.

Although the Americans easily won an engagement at Churubusco on August 19, things were different the next day. Scott won another victory, but it was a costly one. A total of 1,056, or nearly fifteen percent, of the American troops engaged were dead, wounded, or missing. Mexican losses were even higher: some 2,600 prisoners and an estimated 4,000 dead and wounded. Santa Anna was shaken. He had been defeated at the very gates of Mexico City. He quickly asked for a year's truce while peace was negotiated. Scott and Trist agreed to reject that proposal but did offer a short armistice.

The truce lasted only a few days as Trist and the Mexicans could not agree on anything more permanent. On September 6 Scott informed the Mexicans that the armistice would end the next day at noon. Meanwhile Santa Anna had rallied his forces. The battle for Mexico City began on September 8 and the Americans assaulted the fiercely defended, fortified city for six bloody days. They scaled rocky hills with ladders and pickaxes and battered their way through walls with picks and crowbars. Santa Anna fled the city with most of his remaining troops and on September 14 the American flag was raised in the Grand Plaza and a contingent of Marines marched into "the halls of Montezuma."

The fighting was over, but Trist had no luck in negotiating a peace. The Mexican government was in such turmoil—Santa Anna had again renounced the presidency—that

Trist had difficulty in finding anyone responsible to talk to. On October 4 Polk decided to recall Trist "because his remaining longer with the army could not, probably, accomplish the object of his mission, and . . . might, and probably would, impress the Mexican Government with the belief that the United States were so anxious for peace that they would ultimately conclude one upon Mexican terms." A few days later another recall order was sent. Trist received both on November 16. When he informally told the Mexican government, they were distressed. Though the Foreign Minister informed him that he had just appointed commissioners to deal with him, Trist said he could not stay. However, on December 4 Trist changed his mind, having decided that successful negotiations depended on immediate action. So, in what must be one of the most extraordinary actions in diplomatic history, he calmly informed Polk he was staying in a lengthy, contemptuous letter. It takes thirty-five printed pages to reproduce.

Polk wrote in his diary:

> January 15, 1848— . . . A very long dispatch from Mr. Trist . . . is the most extraordinary document I have ever heard [of] from a diplomatic representative. . . . His dispatch is arrogant, impudent, and very insulting to the government, and even personally offensive to the President. . . . If there is any legal provision for his punishment he ought to be severely handled. He has acted worse than any man in public employ whom I have known. His dispatch proves that he is destitute of honour or principle, and that he has proved himself to be a very base man. I was deceived in him.

All true, but Trist did open negotiations with the Mexicans and did get a treaty that obtained just what Polk had wanted all along: California and New Mexico. Trist's treaty, that of Guadalupe Hidalgo, named after the suburban village where it was signed on February 2, 1848, fixed the American–Mexican boundary as it now stands except for the later modification of the Gadsden Purchase. For this, the United States agreed to pay Mexico $15 million and assumed, up to $3¼ million, the claims of American citizens against Mexico. The United States was now a continental nation possessed of lands of almost limitless wealth. Polk had no alternative but to accept the treaty. An extraordinary ending to an extraordinary war.

Several of the victorious generals immediately began a public dispute as to who was responsible for the victories of the final campaign, and Generals Scott, Worth, and Gideon Pillow, Polk's former law partner, ended up before courts of inquiry, with Scott even being removed from command of the troops occupying Mexico. Polk blamed Scott, who had won the war for him, for just about everything, but a more grateful Congress heaped honors on the general. And Zachary Taylor, whom Polk had tried to humble, succeeded Polk in the White House even though he had never voted in a Presidential election in his life and didn't bother to campaign in the 1848 election.

EPILOGUE

THE WAR WAS OVER. Polk had California and New Mexico, but the criticism of "Polk's War" continued as it has to this day. Why did war come to the two young and neighboring nations? One theory blames the South for the war, arguing that "slavocracy" wanted more slave states. A second theory says New England merchants wanted harbors on the Pacific; therefore, commercial interests caused the war. A third theory suggests that Manifest Destiny, that imperial urge of the nation as a whole, was the cause of the war. A fourth puts the blame almost entirely on James K. Polk himself. It was indeed "Polk's War," according to this theory. Some argue that Mexico, spoiling for a fight, started the war.

There can be no certain answer. Most likely each of the suggested causes was a contributing factor, but perhaps the most significant is what has come to be called Manifest Destiny, the belief by Americans of that age that it was America's destiny to spread its enlightened philosophy of democracy across the entire continent. Indeed, there are those who would argue that many Americans still believe that the American way of life should be spread over all the earth—an extension of Manifest Destiny.

In retrospect, it seems that the war could, and should, have been avoided. Even without war the United States would have eventually acquired California and New Mexico, for Mexico was simply too weak, too disorganized to hold on to them. It is difficult to dispute the Rev. Theodore Parker's words of more than a century ago:

> I maintain that aggressive war is a sin; that it is a national infidelity, a denial of Christianity and of God. . . . Treason against the people, against mankind, against God, is a great sin, not lightly to be spoken of. The political authors of war on this continent, and at this day, are either utterly incapable of a statesman's work, or else guilty of that sin. Fools they are, or traitors they must be. . . . Considering how we acquired Louisiana, Florida, Oregon, I cannot forbear thinking that this people will possess the whole of this continent before many years, perhaps before the century ends. . . . Is it not better to acquire it by the schoolmaster than the cannon, by peddling cloth, tin, anything rather than bullets? . . . It would be a gain to mankind if we could spread over that country the Idea of America—that all men are born free and equal in rights, and establish there political, social, and individual freedom. But to do that we must first make real those ideas at home. . . .

Part II
THAT "SPLENDID LITTLE WAR"

THAT "SPLENDID LITTLE WAR"

Chapter Five

ALTHOUGH THE EXPANSIONIST urge that many believe was
the primary cause of the Mexican-American War did not die
with the Treaty of Guadalupe Hidalgo, it was largely submerged for nearly a half century by the approach of the
Civil War, the war itself, and the turbulent years of Reconstruction that followed. But as the 19th century approached
its end, as the scars of the terrible War Between the States
began slowly to heal, this seemingly irresistible urge to stretch
outward began to reassert itself.

There were, however, strong and articulate political forces
who believed that America was big enough and rich enough
to achieve its great destiny within its own shores, that it
would be a perversion of the great American tradition of
government with the consent of the governed if the United
States were to impose its rule on subject peoples. This group
of anti-imperialists included such powerful figures as Grover
Cleveland, twice President; the leading writers of the time,
among them Mark Twain; the great industrialist Andrew
Carnegie; the influential political leader-editor, Carl Schurz;
and many leading Republican and Democratic figures from
both houses of Congress.

53

Yet strong as they were, they could not withstand the expansionist movement that seemed to seize the American imagination. This movement, too, had great leaders: the young Theodore Roosevelt; Henry Cabot Lodge, for decades one of the most powerful men in the Senate and grandfather of a namesake famous in our time; Navy Captain Alfred T. Mahan, whose book *The Influence of Sea Power Upon History* had a lasting impact the world over; John Hay, author of the Open Door Policy; Henry Adams, historian and descendant of two presidents, and many others of almost equal stature.

These were not modest men with modest goals; they were powerful men with great goals. Roosevelt and Lodge, among others, were confident that Canada would inevitably be absorbed by the United States, and they planned for American power, carried by a strong navy, to make itself felt around the world. Although this sense of destiny had long been felt by American leaders, it has never flourished with such vigor before or since, although critics of American foreign policy have seen streaks of imperialism in U.S. policy since the end of World War II.

Even while Grover Cleveland in his first inaugural address was expressing the isolationist strain in the American people, two well-known publicists were giving voice to the opposing interventionist strain. "John Fiske, historian and philosopher, wrote that the superiority of the Anglo-Saxon people, and that the natural growth of their power, could leave no doubt that, having already spread over two hemispheres, this favored race would continue to maintain its sovereignty of the sea and its commercial supremacy."[1]

And the evangelical leader Josiah Strong wrote that the

seat of Anglo-Saxon power had been transferred to the United States and from there would move "down upon Mexico, down upon Central and South America, out upon the islands of the sea, over upon Africa and beyond."

In their reflection of the impact of the theory of evolution upon racial conflicts, the views expressed by Fiske and Strong were extremely important. The idea of the Anglo-Saxon's innate superiority, his impressive lead in the struggle for racial survival, and his inevitable future triumphs, had become generally accepted in America by the 1890s. Had not Darwin himself stated that the wonderful progress made by the United States and the energetic character of the American people were the result of natural selection? Had not Herbert Spencer declared that Americans could reasonably look forward to the time when they would have produced a civilization grander than anything the world had known to that time?[2]

Most Americans, even anti-expansionists, shared Strong's view that they were a people chosen by God to do great things. Thus it was inevitable that the expansionists were able to justify their urge for empire in moral terms. American expansion would not be a grasping for territory and raw materials and markets; rather it would be a spreading of civilization and American democracy. This view was summed up in rolling verse not by an American but by the Englishman Rudyard Kipling, who, after visiting the United States, called upon the American people to "take up the White Man's burden."

> Take up the White Man's burden—
>   Send forth the best ye breed—
> Go bind your sons to exile
>   To serve your captives' need;
> To wait, in heavy harness,

On fluttered folk and wild—
Your new-caught, sullen peoples,
Half-devil and half-child.

Roosevelt and Lodge entirely approved of Kipling's call to action although Roosevelt, no mean writer himself, was much more dubious of Kipling's verse than Lodge.

The urge to empire was there but how would it manifest itself? The first flickerings began in mid-century after Commodore Matthew C. Perry made the historic voyage to Japan which opened up that nation to the West. He urged, in a remarkable foreshadowing of great events to follow a century later, the establishment of American protectorates over the islands of Okinawa and Formosa. And William H. Seward said that Asia was fated to become "the chief theater of events in the world's great hereafter." Perry and Seward wanted Hawaii and Alaska when almost no one dreamed that they would one day become states of the Union.

The pace toward empire quickened a bit in the late 1870s when the United States acquired Pago Pago, with its broad and beautiful harbor in the Samoan Islands, as a naval station. It quickened a bit more under Grover Cleveland, who enlarged and modernized the Navy, not for expansion but for continental defense and to provide some protection for America's increased trade. The Navy became popular as a symbol of national pride, and as it grew stronger, the need grew for fueling stations all over the world. Captain Mahan's writings became immensely influential and there was new interest in annexing Hawaii and in building a canal across the narrow waist of Central America to join the Atlantic and Pacific Oceans.

Again, late in the century, Hawaii became the focus. As early as 1820 Americans had influence in the Hawaiian Islands. Missionaries went there, then traders and whalers. By mid-century the United States was the most influential of the several nations that had dealings there. American settlers and their descendants came to dominate Hawaiian agriculture, squeezing out native Hawaiians. In 1887 the white Hawaiians carried off a bloodless revolution against the corrupt, authoritarian King Kalakaua and forced him to accept what the native Hawaiians called the "Bayonet Constitution." This gave whites control of the government, and its property qualifications disfranchised most native Hawaiians.

In 1891 King Kalakaua died and was succeeded by his tough-minded sister, Queen Liliuokalani. She strongly opposed white rule and refused to abide by the white-imposed constitution. In 1893 the whites overthrew "Queen Lil" with the help of the American minister to Hawaii, John L. Stevens, who ordered U.S. marines landed from the cruiser *Boston*. As the marines occupied government buildings, Stevens, without State Department authorization, recognized the new government. This government, under the leadership of Sanford B. Dole of the famed pineapple family, drew up an annexation treaty which was submitted to the Senate by President Benjamin Harrison. Democrats in the Senate blocked immediate passage, and when Grover Cleveland started his second term in the White House in March, he withdrew the treaty and sent a special commissioner to Hawaii to conduct a thorough investigation. After four months former Representative James H. Blount reported that Stevens' conduct had been improper, that most Hawaiians opposed annexation, and that the main force behind the revolution had been the sugar planters and their associates in the United States who hoped that annexation would mean a bounty for Hawaiian sugar.

Cleveland tried unsuccessfully to put Humpty Dumpty together again. He was willing to restore "Queen Lil" to power, but she refused to grant amnesty to the leaders of the revolution and Dole refused to step down. Cleveland was unwilling to use force, but he condemned publicly the means by which the white-dominated government had come into power and said he would not submit the annexation treaty to the Senate. On July 4, 1894 the Republic of Hawaii was proclaimed and the next month Cleveland formally recognized it. In 1897, when William McKinley was President, another annexation treaty was worked out, but the Senate refused to ratify it and there the matter lay until the public mood changed with the beginning of the Spanish-American War. Then, in July 1898, McKinley dodged the issue of Senate ratification by having Hawaii annexed as a territory of the United States as a result of a joint Senate-House resolution that required only a simple majority in each house. In 1959 Hawaii was admitted as the 50th state of the Union.

As the 19th century neared its end, the expansionist urge in the United States was clearly on the rise, and its specific form was to be determined by the struggle that was soon to come between the fading old imperial state, Spain, and the rising new international power, the United States. Just as it was more than a half century later, the focus of this historic conflict was the tropical island Cuba.

For decades some Americans had wanted to annex Cuba. But this interest was put aside during the tense years that preceded the Civil War and the isolationist years that followed. Only occasionally did Americans look to the Caribbean, where Cuban rebels were fighting for their freedom from Spain. One rebellion, begun in 1868, was caused by Spain's oppressive rule, economic exploitation, and cruel repression of attempted reforms. The bitter and bloody struggle lasted for an entire decade. During that time, American intervention consisted only of a continuous demand that Spain make widespread reforms.

Such reforms were announced by Madrid in 1878, but they existed on paper only and for nearly two decades the situation in Cuba smoldered. As it did, the United States gradually became more involved. American capital moved into Cuba in vast amounts, bringing modern methods to the sugar industry. Sugar became Cuba's vital export and the United States its most important customer. During these years the American temper was changing from isolationism to "jingoism," an aggressive chauvinism that took its name from a bit of doggerel that appeared in the Detroit *News*. Written in the late 1880s at the time of a fisheries dispute between the United States on one hand and Canada and Britain on the other, the verse went:

> We do not want to fight,
> But, by jingo, if we do
> We'll scoop in all the fishing grounds
> And the whole Dominion, too.

In the mid-years of the 19th century's final decade, millions of Americans seemed to want to fight, and it didn't seem to make much difference whom they fought. "The jingoes did not think in terms of dangerous national conflict, but rather of picturesque naval battles and exciting cavalry charges—flags, bands, and glory."[3] Thomas F. Bayard, first American ever to hold the rank of Ambassador, put it this way: he complained of those who proposed "to deal with the vast issues of war or peace between great states in the spirit of prize fighters or scuffling bootblacks." But the temper of the time seemed personified in Teddy Roosevelt, the hearty New York aristocrat who believed a good fight would put some spunk into the American people.

This was the setting when the Cuban rebellion flared again in 1895. Again Spain rushed to put down the revolt. It sent some 150,000 Spanish soldiers led by its ablest commander, Captain-General Valeriano Weyler, who soon earned in the American press the name of "Butcher." He embarked on a policy called "reconcentration," a new military tactic then, although in decades to come it would be used by a number of other nations, including the United States.

> . . . If the rebels would not fight in the open field, he would herd their women, children, and old people into cities and towns, construct elaborate defenses, and systematically reduce the countryside until it would not support the insurrection. It was a brutal method that inflamed American public opinion, the press, the pulpit, and government. A later generation, inured to the prospect of total annihilation, may find this hard to believe; but that era's concept of war did not encompass the destruction of non-military property, ravagement of whole provinces, and murder of non-combatants.[4]

While there were a number of historic forces moving Spain and the United States toward conflict, the most spectacular of them—but not necessarily the most significant —was the jingo press. Partly out of genuine horror at Spanish cruelty in Cuba, partly out of a chauvinistic eagerness for war, and partly to increase newspaper circulation, many American newspapers fanned the already spreading war fever. Two mighty newspapermen in New York were using every tactic, fair and foul, to outdo each other: Joseph Pulitzer of the *World* and William Randolph Hearst of the *Journal.* They chose to compete over Cuba. It was an incredible contest. There was no shortage of genuine atrocity stories from Cuba, but they weren't lurid enough for Pulitzer and Hearst. Their reporters made up stories ever wilder and wilder, their artists drew entirely fictional pictures; it was an orgy of irresponsible journalism, the height (or depth) of "yellow journalism." Americans were already deeply sympathetic with the Cuban rebels and would, in any case, have been willing, even eager, to go to their rescue. But with the yellow press in full cry, the pressure from public and jingo politicians alike was almost irresistible.

Nonetheless, Cleveland, in the last year of his second term, was determined not to have war with Spain. Even if Congress and the people wanted war, Cleveland wanted a peaceful solution and he pressed Spain diplomatically to make genuine reforms in Cuba. But he got nowhere. Even though many Spanish leaders had come to realize that their proud old nation was no longer strong enough to put down the rebellion and certainly not nearly strong enough to take on the young giant of the United States, traditional Spanish pride would not let them back down. Finally, even Cleveland grew angry. Although he did not want to commit the incoming McKinley Administration, he said in his last annual message on December 7, 1896: "The spectacle of the utter ruin of an adjoining country, by nature one of the most fertile and charming on the globe, would engage the serious attention of the Government and people of the United States in any circumstances." And Cleveland warned: ". . . the United States is not a nation to which peace is a necessity. . . ."

When William McKinley became President, he followed Cleveland's policy. Although he was under even greater pressure to intervene in Cuba, for the leading jingoes were fellow Republicans, he, too, tried diplomacy. At first it seemed to be working. Throughout 1897 he pressed Spain patiently. In Havana he kept on Cleveland's man, the colorful, mustachioed former Confederate brigadier, Fitzhugh Lee. Lee worked for America's interests but never hid his conviction that the United States should help free Cuba. McKinley thought of putting someone else in Havana but feared that would cause Spain to think he was changing U.S. policy. However, he decided he had to have a new man in Madrid and he got Stewart Woodford, a distinguished Republican lawyer from New York who had served under several Presidents.

By October 1897 it seemed as if the worst were over. A more liberal Spanish government recalled General Weyler, substantially modified the reconcentration policy, and said it was about to give the Cubans a larger measure of self-government. But when the Spanish Queen Regent proclaimed the new Cuban policy, it was nothing more than the old policy dressed up. The American press was again in full cry and soon events would tumble one upon the other so rapidly and with such consequence that war became almost inevitable. In early January, when an outwardly calm McKinley was still acting optimistic, as if the Spanish reforms would really take place, pro-Spanish elements in Cuba broke out in anti-autonomy riots. It became immediately apparent that even if Madrid were disposed toward reform, the Spanish colonists in Cuba would not stand for it.

Worse was soon to come in the shape of perhaps the worst diplomatic scandal in American history. A terribly indiscreet letter from the Spanish Minister to Washington, Dupuy de Lôme, fell into the hands of the pro-Cuban junta. The revolutionists lost no time in getting it into the hands of the press. Copies of the text went to a number of papers and a facsimile went to the jingoist New York *Journal*. On February 9, 1898 readers saw on the front page this headline: WORST INSULT TO THE UNITED STATES IN ITS HISTORY. Whether it was that is questionable but certainly Americans didn't relish reading de Lôme's description of McKinley as "weak and a bidder for the admiration of the crowd, besides being a would-be politician who tries to leave the door open behind himself while keeping on good terms with the jingoes of his party." Hardly strong language, for in any American political campaign candidates routinely say much harsher things about each other. But with much of the country already up in arms against Spain, few paid heed to the occasional newspaper that declared, as did the Washington *Post,* that the de Lôme letter should not affect American policy.

Much worse was to come just a week later when the jingo newspapers, already at frenzy pitch over the de Lôme letter, had a much more shocking story to print. On January 25 the battleship *Maine,* pride of the American Navy, had sailed into Havana for a "friendly visit," a hardly subtle attempt by the McKinley Administration to convince the Spanish they should make some genuine concessions in Cuba. The Spanish officials received the *Maine* cordially and all seemed well until suddenly at 9:40 on the evening of February 15 the *Maine* blew up, killing 260 of the crew. An outraged America hesitated not a moment in blaming the Spanish and the slogan "Remember the Maine" became the battle cry of the war that was only weeks away. Again a few sober newspapers called for calm until an investigation turned up the cause of the explosion. But war fever was raging in the American body politic and McKinley's continued silence did nothing to quiet it. Both the United States and Spain investigated. While the American board of inquiry was out, McKinley still hoped for peace, but he decided that if war were to come, the U.S. should be better prepared than it was. He asked Congress to appropriate $50 million for defense, in those days an enormous sum. On March 9 the bill was passed with the enthusiastic support of press and public. The Spanish were shocked. "It has not excited the Spaniards, it has simply stunned them," Woodford cabled from Madrid. "To appropriate fifty million out of money in the treasury, without borrowing a cent, demonstrates wealth and power. Even Spain can see this. To put the money without restrictions at your disposal demonstrated entire confidence in you by all parties. The Ministry and press are simply stunned."

Although McKinley was still working diplomatically for peace, the interventionist camp grew even stronger after a historic Senate speech by Republican Senator Redfield Proctor of Vermont. The Senate wasn't looking forward to the speech for it had heard many fiery denunciations of Spain. But Proctor didn't give a fiery speech. He spoke calmly and dispassionately for several hours on March 17 and his speech —in a time of near hysteria—was all the more effective for its lack of passion. It was a simple recitation of the horrors he had witnessed in Cuba and he concluded by saying that Spain neither wanted, nor had the power, to make effective reforms. The interventionists needed no further persuasion, but Proctor's speech was immensely effective with those who had previously opposed intervention. The last barriers to intervention were fast crumbling.

Now the public turned to the report of the board that had investigated the *Maine* disaster. The Spanish inquiry had already found that the *Maine* had been sunk by an internal explosion, but the American public was in no mood to accept that verdict. Now the American board reported that an external explosion had sunk the *Maine,* but it did not say what caused the explosion. Again the people's mood determined its judgment. Most Americans decided—indeed had long since decided—that Spain was responsible for the explosion, few of them stopping to recognize that Spain had the most to lose from the affair. The last thing Spain wanted was war with the United States, and blowing up the *Maine* would hardly enhance the chances of peace.

Chapter Six

BY NOW EVEN THE patient McKinley was getting impatient. And he was spurred on by Woodford in Madrid, who recommended that Washington insist on swift action. McKinley concurred and wired Woodford to tell the Spanish government that the U.S. wanted Cuban reforms and wanted them fast. He set a deadline of April 15, little more than two weeks away. In the meantime McKinley tried to buy time with an impatient Congress, press, and public, but the war fever was so virulent that the once popular President became the target of bitter attacks. Now McKinley, terribly worried by the national reaction, sent an ultimatum to Spain:

> (1) Spain must freely grant an armistice to last until October, both sides to accept McKinley's good offices. (2) Spain would end reconcentration forever and undertake massive relief in Cuba. (3) If peace terms were not reached by October 1, McKinley would settle the Cuban problem as arbitrator. (4) If necessary, the President would approach the Cuban rebels directly for their participation in the plan if Spain first agreed. Implicit but not spelled out was the administration's central demand: Cuba must ultimately be independent. A mere cease-fire or suspension of hostilities would not be enough. The whole plan depended on speed.[1]

In early April it began to appear as if Spain would give in entirely. On April 10 the Queen ordered her commander in Cuba "to grant immediately a suspension of hostilities for such length of time as he may think prudent to prepare and facilitate the peace earnestly desired by all." And Woodford cabled that he was confident that Spain would agree to a settlement that would give Cuba autonomy on terms satisfactory to the rebels, or give Cuba complete freedom, or cede it to the United States.

It is about these few days that historic controversy still swirls. Had McKinley won all he wanted from Spain and should he have held out against the interventionists and thus prevented war? Or are his defenders right in arguing that there was no more reason to believe Spanish promises then than earlier? Perhaps it was just too late; perhaps events had carried the United States too far to turn back. No one can answer these questions with certitude but it is certain that McKinley was showing the strain. Navy Secretary John D. Long wrote in his diary on April 4: "He has been robbed of sleep, overworked, and I fancy that I can see that his mind does not work as clearly and as self-reliantly as it otherwise would." And twelve days later, McKinley's secretary, George Cortelyou, confided to his diary: "The President does not look well at all. . . . His haggard face and anxious inquiry for any news . . . tell of the sense of tremendous responsibility."

The Spanish were being slow and imprecise and McKinley was under terrific pressure from the war wing of his own party (Lodge, Roosevelt, and others), from Congress generally, and from the hysterical press and the public. And there were other pressures for war. It would submerge growing discontent on the farms and the controversy over difficult currency problems. But most of all the nation seemed to want war. Perhaps no President could have stood up to this fierce pressure; certainly McKinley could not.

Finally, he succumbed and on April 11 sent a war message to Congress:

> The long trial has proved that the object for which Spain has waged the war cannot be attained. The fire of insurrection may flame or it may smolder with varying seasons, but it has not been and it is plain that it cannot be extinguished by present methods. The only hope of relief and repose from a condition which can no longer be endured is the enforced

pacification of Cuba. In the name of humanity, in the name of civilization, in behalf of endangered American interests which give us the right and the duty to speak and to act, the war in Cuba must stop. [See Appendix III.]

Although a war resolution was not voted by a cheering Congress until April 25, the United States began to take military steps before then. On April 22 the Navy began to impose a blockade around Cuba's chief ports. The Navy was in pretty good shape, for it had received presidential support for more than a decade and had been led by a series of effective Navy secretaries. When fighting came, it was led by the competent John D. Long and Assistant Secretary Theodore Roosevelt, who for months had directed preparations for the war he wanted and was sure would come. When it did come, he resigned his office and helped form the Rough Riders as their deputy commander.

But if the Navy was prepared, the Army was not. It had been allowed to disintegrate for decades and was down to about 26,000 officers and men, most of them in areas where there was still Indian trouble. On April 23 McKinley called for 125,000 volunteers and they poured into recruiting stations. They wanted adventure, they wanted glory, and they wanted to free the Cubans. The glamour of war—the volunteers were too young to remember the horror and ugliness of the Civil War—and the nobility of its cause were irresistible. We shall see shortly what happened to these innocent romantics. First, however, we must consider an extraordinary naval victory, one that was to change the course of American history.

The story begins two months before the war, shortly after the explosion of the *Maine.* On February 25 Navy

Secretary Long took the day off and Teddy Roosevelt "seized the opportunity" to send a cable to Commodore George Dewey to mobilize America's Asiatic Squadron at Hong Kong. Roosevelt, without his superior's authorization, instructed Dewey to be ready, if war came, to conduct "offensive operations in the Philippines." When Long returned to the office the next day, he was astonished to learn what Roosevelt had done. He wrote in his diary that "the very devil seemed to possess him [Roosevelt] yesterday afternoon" and he added that Roosevelt came "very near causing more of an explosion than happened to the *Maine.*" Nonetheless, Long did not change the orders and Dewey did mobilize the fleet.

Dewey carried out his instructions with dispatch. He painted his warships gray (they had been white during their good-will visits), bought a collier full of coal, and impatiently waited for the cruiser *Baltimore* to arrive. It was carrying needed ammunition, and Dewey also wanted its bottom scraped before war broke out and he would have to sail the fleet out of neutral Hong Kong. The *Baltimore* came just in time. It arrived on Friday, April 22, and two days later was ready for battle: scraped, painted, coaled, and provisioned.

The very day the *Baltimore* was finished, Dewey got his battle orders. They had been some days in the making. Secretary Long on the 21st had urged McKinley to order the ships to Manila, but the President thought the time was not yet quite ripe. "But early Sunday forenoon, the 24th, I conferred with him at the White House. . . . It was a lovely, sunny, spring day, a bright contrast to the grim business in hand. He sat on a sofa, thoughtful, his face showing a deep sense of the responsibility of the hour." McKinley gave permission and Long cabled: "War has commenced between the United States and Spain. Proceed at once to the Philippine Islands. Commence operations at once, particularly against Spanish fleet. You must capture vessels or destroy. Use utmost endeavors."

On April 27, 1898, at two o'clock in the afternoon, Dewey set sail for the Philippines, a place so remote to the America of that era that even the President conceded that he could not place it on the globe within two thousand miles. As the Asiatic Squadron steamed southeast, Dewey ordered the sailors of his six fighting vessels assembled so their captains could read a proclamation by the Captain-General of the Philippines, Basilio Augustín Dávila. In the rolling language so favored by the proud Spaniards, the Captain-General declared: "A squadron manned by foreigners, possessing neither instruction nor discipline, is preparing to come to this archipelago with the ruffianly intention of robbing us of all that means life, honor, and liberty . . . to treat you as tribes refractory to civilization, to take possession of your riches. . . . Vain designs! Ridiculous boastings!"[2] This bombast was greeted with derisive laughter by the American seaman.

Early Saturday morning, April 30, the great island of Luzon came into view and the squadron knew that its work was not far off. The ships readied for battle, expecting the Spanish fleet to be in Subic Bay, the best natural defensive area if shore batteries had been installed. But there were no Spanish men-o'-war and the American fleet turned toward Manila Bay, thirty miles distant, after pausing for a short time while Dewey conferred with his captains aboard the flagship *Olympia*. Aboard the flagship John L. Stickney of the New York *Herald* was acting as Dewey's aide and he wrote:

> The moon has risen, and although it was occasionally obscured by light clouds, the night was not one in which a squadron ought to have been able to run through a well-defended channel without drawing upon herself a hot fire. Consequently, at a quarter to ten o'clock, the men were sent to their guns, not by the usual bugle call, but by stealthily whispered word of mouth.

Another newspaperman, John T. McCutcheon of the Chicago *Record,* was aboard the *McCulloch,* a revenue cutter that had joined the squadron. He continues the account:

> About 11:30 the entrance to the bay can be seen. Two dark headlands—one on either side of the entrance—show up gloomy. . . . In the space between a smaller mass shows where the dreaded Corregidor lies. . . . It was understood the heaviest guns of the Spanish were at Corregidor. The entrance was also said to be planted with mines, and it was known that there were torpedoes waiting for the ships. . . .
>
> The *Olympia* turns in and steers directly for the center of the southern and wider channel. The *Baltimore* follows and in regular order the rest of the fleet slide on through the night toward the entrance. Still there is no firing from the forts, and it is hoped that the daring maneuver may not be discovered.

The Spaniards must have seen the fleet. It was a moonlit night and, furthermore, the soot in the funnel of the *McCulloch* caught fire a couple of times and fireballs blazed high in the sky. But for some reason the powerful guns on Corregidor did not open up and Dewey's fleet sailed unharmed into the great Manila harbor and silent and dark crept toward the city twenty-three miles distant. At dawn they reached the city and should have found the Spanish fleet there lying protected under shore batteries. But the Spanish naval commander, Rear Admiral Patricio Montojo y Pasarón, wanting to spare Manila from bombardment, took his less powerful fleet to the less-protected waters off the Cavite naval base.

At four o'clock the officers and men of the American fleet had been served coffee and hardtack. As the fleet steamed past Manila in close battle array (the *Olympia*, the *Baltimore*, the *Raleigh*, the *Petrel*, the *Concord*, and the *Boston*) the shore batteries fired a couple of wild shots. Soon the Spanish fleet was spotted, its battle flags flying in the morning breeze. Dewey headed right for it and soon they could hear the cheers of the Spanish sailors. More menacing, as Stickney reported:

> Suddenly a shell burst directly over us. From the boatswain's mate at the after 5-inch gun came a hoarse cry. "REMEMBER THE MAINE!" arose from the throats of five hundred men at the guns. . . . The *Olympia* was now ready to fight.

Calmly the white-mustachioed Commodore Dewey gave his famous order: "You may fire when ready, Gridley," and at nineteen minutes before six the *Olympia* opened up and with it the other American men-o'-war. Lieutenant Bradley A. Fiske was atop the *Petrel*'s mast and he could see the entire battle:

> . . . the American fleet paraded back and forth before the Spanish fleet, firing as rapidly as they could with proper aim. To me in my elevated perch the whole thing looked like a performance that had been very carefully rehearsed. The ships went slowly and regularly, seldom or never getting out of their relative positions, and only ceased firing at intervals when the

smoke became too thick. For a long while I could not form an opinion as to which way fortune was going to decide. I could see that the Spanish ships were hit a number of times, especially the *Cristina* and the *Castilla;* but then it seemed to me that our ships were hit many times also, and from the way they cut away boats from the *Raleigh* and from other signs I concluded the *Raleigh* was suffering severely. I could see projectiles falling in the water on all sides of our ships. . . .

Two of the ships in the Spanish column were evidently much larger than the others . . . and the Captain seemed naturally to direct the fire at them. I could see also that the Spaniards directed their fire principally at the *Olympia* and the *Baltimore,* which were our largest ships. . . . I think everybody was disappointed at the great number of shots lost. Our practice was evidently much better than that of the Spaniards, but it did not seem to me that it was at all good.

About the decks of the *Petrel* things were entirely different from what I had expected. I had seen many pictures of battle and had expected great excitement. I did not see any excitement whatever. The men seemed to me to be laboring under an intense strain and to be keyed up to the highest pitch; but to be quiet, and under complete self-control, and to be doing the work of handling the guns and ammunition with that mechanical precision which is the result we all hope to get from drill.

Although the American marksmanship was far from perfect, Dewey's force was otherwise efficient despite the fierce heat. In the engine rooms it was terrible; some reported nearly 200 degrees. A stoker on the *Olympia,* Charles Twitchell, later said:

The battle hatches were all battened down, and we were shut in this little hole . . . it was so hot our hair was singed. There were several leaks in the steam pipes, and the hissing hot steam made things worse. The clatter of the engines and the roaring of the furnaces made such a din it seemed one's head would burst. . . .

We could tell when our guns opened fire by the way the ship shook; we could scarcely stand on our feet, the vibration was so great. . . . The ship shook so fearfully that the soot and cinders poured down on us in clouds. Now and then a big drop of scalding water would fall on our bare heads, and the pain was intense. One by one three of our men were overcome by the terrible heat and were hoisted to the upper deck.

On deck there was still another view, as reported by Lieutenant John M. Ellicott, intelligence officer on the *Baltimore:*

The American squadron stood past the Spanish ships and batteries in perfect column at six knots speed, making a run of two and a half miles, then returned with starboard guns bearing. The first lap followed the five-fathom curve as marked on the charts, and each succeeding one was made a little nearer, as the soundings showed deeper water than the chart indicated. The range was thus gradually reduced (from about three miles, to as close as one mile). . . .

Under the miraculous providence which ordered the events of that day those six American ships steamed serenely back and forth unharmed for nearly three hours. . . . The pall of smoke which hung between the contending vessels prevented the effect of many shots from being seen, but close scrutiny with the glasses gave the comforting assurance after the first twenty minutes that the enemy was being hit hard and repeatedly, and as the range grew less, so that guns' crews could watch the fall of their shots with the naked eye, many an exultant cheer went up from every ship. Naked to the waist and grimy with the soot of powder, their heads bound up in water-soaked towels, these men who had fasted for sixteen hours now slung shell after shell and charge after charge, each weighing a hundred to two hundred and fifty pounds, into their huge guns under a tropical sun which melted the pitch in the decks.

Two of the Spanish ships were moored; the other five dashed frantically, purposelessly back and forth. They were brave but ineffectual, fighting solely for honor's sake, for they knew they were beaten. By 7:30 the *Cristina,* burning fiercely, was out of action and the *Castilla*'s guns nearly silenced. All but one other ship ran behind the mole at Cavite Arsenal, where they were trapped.

At that moment Dewey received the ominous but fortunately erroneous report that ammunition was short. He ran up the flags: "Withdraw from battle" and soon thereafter Dewey told his commanders to let their men have breakfast. How extraordinary! The enemy on the verge of defeat and Dewey calmly orders his exhausted, famished men to have breakfast. The captains conferred on the *Olympia* and then, at about 11 A.M., Dewey finished off the Spaniards, with the *Baltimore* first silencing the shore batteries. Then the light-draught *Petrel* steamed behind the mole, fired a few shots and then stopped when the Spaniards ran up a white flag at 12:20.

Dewey had won a great victory in the remote Philippines in a war presumably being fought over nearby Cuba. But few seemed to think that curious in the first wild flush of victory that made Dewey a national hero. For it was a great victory. The Spanish fleet had been crushed, nearly four hundred Spaniards killed or wounded, while no American ship was seriously damaged and only a few of Dewey's men slightly wounded. It would be some time before McKinley realized the full implications of Dewey's victory—that America was now, or about to become, an imperial power. How he dealt with this great question we'll consider after turning to the action in Cuba.

Chapter Seven

AFTER THE NAVY'S GREAT victory at Manila, the Army was rarin' to go on its glorious adventure to Cuba. But it didn't turn out that way. The Army was totally unprepared for war. The volunteers flocked into training camps but the food was bad and the sanitation often appalling, with diseases from measles to typhoid fever racing through some camps. McKinley and Army Secretary Russell Alger had had $50 million to spend since March 9 but they so narrowly construed the term "national defense" that the War Department did not purchase or order most of what they needed until after the war began. Thus the soldiers were armed with obsolete Springfield carbines, firing with old-fashioned black powder that gave away the rifleman's position with every shot, and the soldiers headed for tropical Cuba were outfitted in heavy blue winter uniforms.

Despite everything, the Army maintained its enthusiasm and as units began to concentrate at Tampa, Florida, the embarkation port, everyone's question was, "How soon do we sail for Cuba?" No one knew, for it all depended on how soon the American Navy could locate the fleet of Admiral Pascual Cervera y Topete, which reportedly had left the Cape Verde Islands on April 29. There was great fear that the Spanish fleet would make forays along the Atlantic coast, perhaps even attack New York. Alternately, it was feared Cervera would intercept the American invasion force at sea and do it terrible damage.

Admiral William T. Sampson, guessing correctly that Cervera intended to steam to San Juan to refuel, took his own fleet to that Puerto Rican port. But Cervera got word of Sampson's move and avoided San Juan, steaming to Santiago, Cuba. The Americans learned the whereabouts of the Spanish fleet, which, for some reason, did not make a dash for the open sea. Instead Cervera just sat there, and on June 1 Sampson clamped a blockade across the harbor mouth, even shining searchlights across the entrance every night. And there the two fleets sat. After a few days, when it became apparent that Cervera was not going to venture out, Sampson established a coaling base in Guantánamo Bay, where the American Navy has been ever since.

Since Admiral Cervera's fleet was no menace—at least for the time being—the first units of the Army thought they were ready to invade Cuba. But the order to General William R. Shafter on May 26 exposed the shocking unpreparedness of the Army. The War Department thought he could lead 25,000 men, thousands of horses and mules, and supplies for men and beasts all in a couple of days. And on May 30 an impatient War Department ordered him to capture Santiago and the Spanish Navy and asked when he would sail. Shafter, despite the chaos, reported the next day that he could sail in three more days. The three days had passed when the Commanding General of the Army, Major General Nelson A. Miles, arrived at Tampa. He was appalled:

> There are over 300 cars loaded with war material along the roads about Tampa. Stores are sent to the quartermaster at Tampa, but the invoices and bills of lading have not been received, so that officers are obliged to break open seals and hunt from car to car to ascertain whether they contain clothing, grain, balloon material, horse equipments, ammunition, siege guns, commissary stores, etc.[1]

And that wasn't the worst of it. Port Tampa had been

built to accommodate only small steamers for Key West and Cuba. There was no real pier, only a tongue of land alongside of which a narrow channel had been dredged. Only two vessels could be loaded at once and most of the loading had to be done by stevedores who were forced to carry the supplies on their backs from the freight cars across fifty feet of sand and up a steep ramp. Working under such terrible conditions in the fierce heat so exhausted the stevedores that they often dropped and slept where they fell. Even worse, the developer of the port, Morton F. Plant, had built only a single-track railway to Tampa nine miles away and he added to the log jam by selling seats on excursion trains that ran up and down the already overburdened line.

On June 6 Shafter—who set up a packing case as a desk right on the pier—ordered his regimental commanders to load their troops aboard the transports. There was only one trouble. The ships could hold only from eighteen to twenty thousand men, not the twenty-five thousand waiting to embark. For a while that seemed academic since the single railroad track was so jammed that no troops got to the dock anyway. Many of them sat in closed freight cars and broiled under the Florida sun without food or water.

This was just the kind of situation in which an improviser like Teddy Roosevelt functioned best. When he found out by accident that the transport *Yucatan* had been assigned to his Rough Riders and to two other units, he simply put his men aboard and left the other units to fend for themselves. He neglected to report, however, that one of the other units ended up on a newer and more comfortable ship.

Eventually the army got aboard ship and the fleet began straggling down the bay, only to get the dismaying order from the War Department: "Wait until you get further orders before you sail." Shafter called back the fleet and for six days it sat motionless in the burning summer sun while the Navy sought to hunt down a Spanish flotilla that turned out to be non-existent, the "Phantom Fleet." William Dinwiddie of the Washington *Star* wrote:

> This fearful activity, this stupendous energy evidenced by an army suddenly electrified into motion was all for naught and for nearly five whole days the army lay idly at rest, waiting patiently. . . . It was a frightful ordeal for the army . . . one in which the men suffered mental depression and physical devitalization, largely shared by the ranking officers, who feared that, under the torrid suns and in the superheated and illy ventilated holds, where the masses of the army lay gasping, an outbreak of fever was imminent. Fevers did appear, but fortunately they were all malarial, and the dread typhus did not make its appearance.

Finally, on June 14, the fleet steamed out of Tampa Bay and made its leisurely way to Cuba, moving slowly along the Cuban coast so that the Spanish officers had no difficulty following its progress. Admiral Sampson wanted Shafter to land his men at both entrances of Santiago harbor and take by storm Morro Castle and the other shore positions. Although Shafter was much to be criticized for his later generalship, he was not that foolish. He had no taste for a glorious victory (and even victory was by no means certain) bought at the cost of unnecessary bloodshed. So he decided to land at Daiquirí and Siboney, fifteen or so miles from Santiago.

It was the right decision, for there was no better place to land, but if the Spanish had been more confident, they almost certainly could have defeated the American army, for the Yankees had to come ashore in open boats through heavy surf. Behind the beach was a well-fortified limestone bluff that commanded the ocean front for twenty miles. Had the Spaniards met the invaders there, it is hard to see how the landing could have been accomplished. Indeed, Shafter might not even have attempted the landing if it had been opposed, but he learned from Cuban rebels that there were only a few Spaniards defending the beaches.

At nine o'clock on the morning of June 22 Shafter put his troops into open boats and for twenty minutes the naval armada pounded the landing area, wreaking great destruction on everything but the target blockhouse. It didn't matter, for there weren't any Spaniards in the area. And that first day six thousand Americans disembarked without having a shot fired against them. They had expected attack, for they were vulnerable, but no attack came. The Americans were, however, greeted by cheering Cuban rebels in rags. At first the Americans happily shared their food and tobacco with them, but the Cubans soon became a nuisance and John Black Atkins of the Manchester (England) *Guardian* wrote that the Americans, even before they had engaged the Spaniards, became disgusted with the Cubans they had come to free: "'Why,' [the Americans] asked in effect, 'should we fight for men like these? They are no better than the Spaniards.' And it escaped the notice of nearly all, that mean and savage ways were to be expected in those who had long been treated with meanness and savagery."

The first land battle of the Spanish-American War took place early on the morning of June 24. Major General Joseph Wheeler, an old Confederate general, threw his dismounted cavalry against strong Spanish positions at Las Guásimas. He knew the positions were only lightly defended and he wanted to take them before the Spaniards changed their mind, for here again was a position from which the Spaniards might well have defeated the Americans if they fought with the courage and ability they were to demonstrate at Santiago later. A sustained resistance there would have kept the Americans on the scorching coast until yellow fever arrived, would have kept open the road by which six thousand Spanish reinforcements could have arrived from Guantánamo only forty miles distant, and would have deprived the Americans of the well-watered plain near Sevilla, the only good place for a camp between Santiago and the landing beaches.

At first the battle didn't go well because the Spaniards put up a determined stand. But American reinforcements eventually carried the day as Wheeler, who last saw battle against the North in the Civil War more than thirty years before, shouted, "We've got the Yankees on the run. . . ." Teddy Roosevelt's Rough Riders fought well in the difficult terrain and oppressive heat, as did a Negro unit, the Tenth Regular Cavalry. (There were several black units in the American army and all fought with courage and distinction.)

The Americans pressed forward toward Santiago, handicapped by poor communications. The single road was so narrow (the sides so steep it could not be widened) that a man on horseback could not pass a wagon, so vehicular traffic had to be one-way, causing frequent blockages. For six days the Americans waited for supplies, without sending out patrols, without cutting new roads through the jungles. They simply received no orders, except that the aggressive Wheeler was told not to start another engagement.

The Spaniards had few advantages, for food was scarce, hardly enough to last a siege of any length. But they were in a good defensive position and the Spanish commanders prepared the ground well with trenches and breastworks. They pointed their guns at the only two openings from the jungle. For some reason the Americans did not make other trails, so the Spaniards knew where to expect the attacks.

The attacks began on July 1, twin assaults on the village of El Caney and San Juan Hill, the latter one of the most famous battles in American history. Shafter sent nearly 7,000 men against the mere 520 Spaniards who defended the village and the neighboring stone fort, El Viso. The Americans used old field artillery. (The American army did not even know of the existence of vastly better artillery already in use in Europe.) The Americans hit El Caney hard. Though vastly outnumbered, the Spaniards put up tough resistance and took a heavy toll of Americans.

A lieutenant in the Twenty-fifth Infantry, a Negro regiment, wrote this account:

> The dead, dying and wounded are being taken past to the rear; the wounded and their attendants are telling the Twenty-fifth: "Give them hell, boys; they've been doing us dirt all morning."
>
> A member of the Second Massachusetts, carrying several canteens, and going to the rear for water, says to our soldiers: "The buggers are hidden behind rocks, in weeds and in under-brush, and we just simply can't locate them; they are shooting our men all to pieces."
>
> The procession is, indeed, terrible! Men with arms in slings; men with bandaged legs and bloody faces; men stripped to the waist, with a crimson bandage around the chest or shoulder; men staggering along unaided; men in litters, some groaning,

some silent, with hats or blood-stained handkerchiefs over their faces; some dead, some dying! . . .

The Spaniards were hard to locate because they were using smokeless powder while the Americans were using that old black powder which gave away their position with every shot.

Finally the Spaniards were simply overwhelmed by the sheer weight of numbers and firepower. But they had given a magnificent account of themselves. Although they lost 235 killed and wounded and 120 taken prisoner, they had inflicted 441 American casualties, including 81 dead. It was a glorious battle save for one detail. El Caney had no strategic value. The men on both sides died in vain, for its possession did not bear on the main battle one way or the other.

The main battle was for San Juan Hill, the battle that made the Rough Riders a legend and Teddy Roosevelt President. Lieutenant General Arsenio Linares Pombo assigned only twelve hundred Spaniards to block the eighty-four hundred Americans but they were well dug in and the Americans short of artillery and, even more critical, of direction. The corpulent General Shafter was sick from over-exertion in the terrible heat and, many critics have charged, incompetent, so the battle fought itself. It was a nightmare. There was only one good road the Americans could use and the Spaniards knew it. This was bad enough but the Americans marked their precise position along the road by floating an observation balloon directly above the advancing troops. It was a perfect target marker for Spanish artillery until the balloon itself was hit and collapsed. Fortunately, the Americans later discovered a side road, so some of them escaped the shelling.

While the Americans could not yet see the enemy, the Spaniards were pouring in a deadly fire. The Americans were blocked and they finally decided they could no longer stay where they were; they had to advance or retreat and retreat would have meant defeat. So the Americans pressed forward. Roosevelt rode his horse in front of his regiment, fully exposed to enemy fire, but he was not seriously hit. He decided it was too dangerous to remain at the foot of the hill so he ordered one of those famous Rough Rider charges. Later he wrote:

By this time we were all in the spirit of the thing and greatly excited by the charge, the men cheering and running forward between shots. . . . I . . . galloped toward the hill, passing the shouting, cheering, firing men and went up the lane, splashing through a small stream; when I got abreast of the ranch buildings on top of Kettle Hill, I turned and went up the slope. Being on horseback I was, of course, able to get ahead of the men on foot, excepting my orderly, Henry Bardshar, who had run ahead very fast in order to get better shots at the Spaniards, who were now running out of the ranch buildings. . . . Some forty yards from the top I ran into a wire fence and jumped off Little Texas, turning him loose. He had been scraped by a couple of bullets, one of which nicked my elbow, and I never expeted to see him again. As I ran up the hill, Bardshar stopped to shoot, and two Spaniards fell as he emptied his magazine. These were the only Spaniards I actually saw fall to aimed shots by any one of my men, with the exception of two guerillas in trees.

Almost immediately afterward the hill was covered by the troops, both Rough Riders and the colored troops of the Ninth, and some men of the First. . . .

No sooner were we on the crest than the Spaniards from the line of hills in our front, where they were strongly intrenched, opened a very heavy fire upon us with their rifles. They also

opened upon us with one or two pieces of artillery, using time
fuses which burned very accurately, the shells exploding right
over our heads.

Then came the famous charge up San Juan Hill proper,
a charge that the foreign military attachés accompanying the
army said could not possibly succeed. This account was
written much later by Richard Harding Davis, perhaps the
most famous war correspondent in American history:

> I have seen many illustrations and pictures of this charge on
> the San Juan hills, but none of them seem to show it just as I
> remember it. In the picture-papers the men are running up
> hill swiftly and gallantly, in regular formation, rank after rank,
> with flags flying, their eyes aflame, and their hair streaming,
> their bayonets fixed, in long, brilliant lines, an invincible, over-
> powering weight of numbers. Instead of which I think the
> thing which impressed one the most, when our men started
> from cover, was that they were so few. It seemed as if someone
> had made an awful and terrible mistake. One's instinct was to
> call them to come back.

The great novelist Stephen Crane was there too: "Yes, they
were going up the hill, up the hill. It was the best moment
of anybody's life. . . . up went the regiments with no music
save that ceaseless fierce crashing of rifles."
Again Davis:

> They had no glittering bayonets, they were not massed in
> regular array. There were a few men in advance, bunched
> together, and creeping up a steep, sunny hill, the tops of which
> roared and flashed with flame. The men held their guns pressed
> against their breasts and stepped heavily as they climbed.
> Behind these first few, spreading out like a fan, were single
> lines of men, slipping and scrambling in the smooth grass,
> moving forward with difficulty, as though they were wading

waist high through water, moving slowly, carefully, with strenuous effort. It was much more wonderful than any swinging charge could have been. They walked to greet death at every step, many of them, as they advanced, sinking suddenly or pitching forward and disappearing in the high grass, but the others waded on, stubbornly, forming a thin blue line that kept creeping higher and higher up the hill. It was inevitable as the rising tide. It was a miracle of self-sacrifice, a triumph of bull-dog courage, which one watched breathless with wonder. The fire of the Spanish riflemen, who still stuck bravely to their posts, doubled and trebled in fierceness, the crests of the hills crackled and burst in amazed roars, and rippled with waves of tiny flame. But the blue line crept steadily up and on, and then, near the top, the broken fragments gathered together with a sudden burst of speed, the Spaniards appeared for a moment outlined against the sky and poised for instant flight, fired a last volley and fled before the swift-moving wave that leaped and sprang up after them.

In a Hollywood movie that would have been the end of the battle, but this was a real war. The Americans were atop the hill, but the air was still thick with Spanish bullets. There was little celebration, for more than a thousand Americans had been killed or wounded, there were no reserves, and many feared that disaster was imminent. But there was one benefit to the Battle of San Juan Hill, as described by Frank Freidel in his fine *The Splendid Little War.*

The immediate result of the battle among the survivors had been to help erase lines of section and color. Frank Knox [to be Navy Secretary during World War II] wrote home that he had become separated from the Rough Riders, "but I joined a troop of the Tenth Cavalry, colored, and for a time fought with them shoulder to shoulder, and in justice to the colored race I must say that I never saw braver men anywhere. Some of those who rushed up the hill will live in my memory forever."

Lieutenant [John J.] Pershing [Commander of the American Expeditionary Force in World War I] felt that a new unity had come out of the trial by battle: "White regiments, black regiments, regulars and Rough Riders, representing the young manhood of the North and the South, fought shoulder to shoulder, unmindful of race or color, unmindful of whether commanded by an ex-Confederate or not, and mindful only of their common duty as Americans."[2]

Two days after the charge up San Juan Hill, Teddy Roosevelt wrote, "We are within measurable distance of a terrible military disaster." But the Americans dug in as best they could in the rocky soil and hung on. The Spaniards pounded them heavily with artillery and the relentless tropical sun took its toll. Behind the lines surgeons worked until they dropped, but could treat only a fraction of the seriously wounded men, most of whom lay under hot sun, drenching rain, and through the chill nights without attention.

Shafter sent fresh troops up forward and it soon became apparent, after the men began to recover from the shock and exhaustion of the assault, that the Americans would hold. But the casualties had been terrible: 143 killed and 1,010 wounded in addition to those at El Caney. Nonetheless, the Spaniards were trapped in Santiago with insufficient food and water. They had chosen to fight in the wrong place at the wrong time. And Shafter, even though some of his generals wanted to pull back and rest the troops, decided to demand Santiago's surrender. He declared that he would shell the city if it did not surrender and he suggested that women, children, and foreigners leave before 10 o'clock the next morning, the Fourth of July.

But on that third day of July 1898 events took place that meant the virtual end of the war. The Spanish fleet attempted to escape from Santiago Harbor. No one expected it; indeed Admiral Sampson had sent two ships off to Guantánamo to be refueled and had gone off to Siboney on the *New York,* accompanied by two other ships. Some of the remaining American ships had unhooked several of their engines to economize on coal. This, of course, severely cut their speed and was a useless economy because there was plenty of coal. But it didn't seem risky on that dull Sunday morning. So the surprise was complete when the Spanish fleet suddenly emerged from the entrance to the harbor.

This sudden foray might have worked except that the bottoms of the Spanish vessels were foul, greatly cutting their speed; most of their ammunition was defective; and the vessels were decked with inflammable wood that should have been torn out during the weeks at anchor. Thus, even though the Americans were taken completely by surprise, they still had all the advantages. The six Spanish ships were simply no match for the American battlewagons *Oregon, Iowa,* and *Texas,* the cruiser *Brooklyn,* and the armed yachts *Vixen* and *Gloucester.* The Spanish fired rapidly, but neither their aim nor their ammunition was any good and the big American guns were just too much for them. Admiral Sampson, who rushed back at the first sound of firing, arrived just in time to see the end of the battle. It had been an unequal one. The Americans suffered only one killed and one seriously wounded while the brave Spaniards lost 323 killed and 151 wounded and most of the rest of the 2,227 men were captured. A few got ashore and made their way to Spanish lines.

Santiago refused to surrender and, after a few days of inconclusive talks, the Americans began a land and naval bombardment. It began on July 10 and continued into the 11th. Many of the Americans were impatient to storm the city and Roosevelt accused Shafter of "incompetency and timidity," but Shafter did not want needless casualties. However, cases of the feared yellow fever were beginning to appear, for the American Army had not taken even the most rudimentary sanitation measures. And then tropical rains came. General Miles arrived from Washington and told the Spaniards that he had enough reinforcements to take the city and that their gallant defense of Santiago more than satisfied the honor of Spanish arms. Finally, on July 17, Santiago surrendered. After 382 years the Spanish flag was hauled down for the last time. There was good cause for rejoicing, for as the Americans entered the city, they saw entrenchments that would have cost many lives to seize. As it was, only 379 Americans were lost in battle in the war, although more than 5,000 died from other causes, mainly disease.

The surrender of Santiago meant, in effect, the end of the war. General Miles took an expedition to Puerto Rico, making the first landings on July 25, but there was little opposition and by August 13 an armistice had been signed.

Before ending this account of the Spanish-American War, it is necessary to return briefly to the Philippines, where it began. Dewey had defeated the Spanish navy but he could not effectively seize the shore without an army. President McKinley decided to send one, but in the meantime there was the question of the insurgents. Dewey allowed the insurgent leader, Emilio Aguinaldo, to return to the islands, where he soon had a strong following. He assumed that the United States would eventually turn the Philippines over to him. Dewey continued friendly relations with him while refusing any military help.

Aguinaldo's strength grew steadily and on July 1 he proclaimed himself President of the revolutionary government. But Aguinaldo was soon to learn that the Americans had not come to free the Philippines from Spain. An American army under Major General Wesley Merritt began arriving on July 17 and on August 13 captured Manila. The insurgents were discouraged from participating. The battle had been planned with the Spanish so that there would be plenty of gunfire to satisfy Spanish honor, but no casualties. Some insurgents got into the battle, which led to some genuine fighting between Spaniards and Americans, but the casualties were light.

Upon instructions from Washington, Dewey and Merritt resisted insurgent demands that there be a joint occupation of Manila pending a peace conference. Thus began one of the ironies of history. The Americans had entered the war to free Cubans from Spanish rule, only to end by assuming rule over another colonial people, the Filipinos. Most of the American people apparently approved this contradictory policy, believing it was the duty of the United States to assume the burden of governing the Philippines.

President McKinley explained it all to a group of ministers visiting him at the White House. This is how H. Wayne Morgan described the scene:

> . . . With uncharacteristic self-revelation he told a group of ministers how he had reached his decision. "I have been criticized a good deal about the Philippines, but don't deserve

it," he said. He explained that the islands had come as "a gift from the Gods" and outlined his dilemma and alternatives during the summer and fall of 1898. He had frankly thought at first of retaining only part of the islands. He sought help from all parties but got little support. He was a deeply religious man. After much prayer and thought, it came to him one evening that he had four choices: (1) he could not return the islands to Spain, "that would be cowardly and dishonorable"; (2) he could not turn them over to another power, for "that would be bad business and discreditable"; (3) he could not leave them to themselves, for anarchy and bloodshed would follow in the wake of native ignorance and inability to govern; and (4) so "there was nothing left for us to do but to take them all, and to educate the Filipinos, and uplift and civilize and Christianize them, and by God's grace do the very best we could by them, as our fellowmen for whom Christ also died."[3]

McKinley was no doubt sincere, as were many others who agreed with him, but there was at least one other alternative. The United States could have established a protectorate and set a specific or general date for the Philippines' eventual independence. But that was not to be and so now the United States was involved in the Pacific in a major way. During the heat of the war Congress had agreed to annex Hawaii and Americans had seized the island of Guam. This involvement in the Pacific has influenced America profoundly to this day.

The irony was compounded when, in February 1899, a Filipino revolt broke out. Now American soldiers were being used to put down natives and the revolution lasted for three bloody years, a struggle more costly than the Spanish-American War itself. It took 70,000 American troops to crush the revolution and a disillusioned American public learned that some United States soldiers used the same tortures against Filipino patriots that the Spaniards had used against the Cubans. But when the revolution was eventually put down, the United States began a benevolent rule of the Philippines. Aguinaldo himself became a friend of the United States and the Philippines were given their independence soon after the end of World War II.

The loose ends were tied up in a peace treaty in Paris in December. The United States got Puerto Rico, the Philippines, Guam, and the right (which it several times invoked) to intervene in the domestic affairs of a theoretically independent Cuba. At home many of the sick and wounded recovered slowly. Yet before long the Spanish-American War became in the American imagination, to use John Hay's words, a "splendid little war," a sort of happy adventure instead of the bloody struggle it was in fact. It was a struggle that changed the course of American history, for the United States was now indisputably a great world power with colonial possessions in both the Caribbean and the Pacific. No longer could the United States maintain its innocent belief that it could, as George Washington had urged, stay aloof from the tensions of the rest of the world. It was now inescapably entangled with the world and would be for centuries to come.

Part III
DOLLAR DIPLOMACY

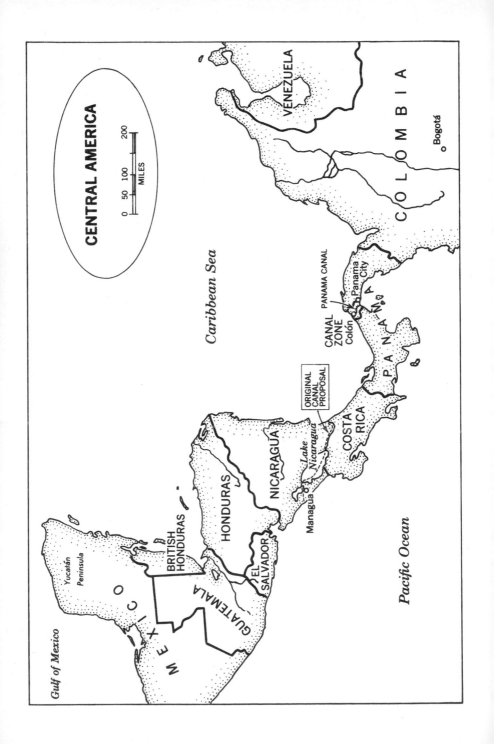

DOLLAR DIPLOMACY

Chapter Eight

OUTSIDE THE NATIONAL ARCHIVES building in Washington is carved the legend "What Is Past Is Prologue." Nowhere is that more true than in America's relations with what we have come to call our Good Neighbors to the south, Latin America. The great crises of the 1960s in Cuba and the Dominican Republic were born in that curious period in the first third of this century when the United States practiced "Dollar Diplomacy."

Before examining the turbulent events of that period which saw the United States send troops to Cuba, Mexico, Nicaragua, Haiti, and the Dominican Republic, it is necessary to know something about the Caribbean in the early years of this century. Surprisingly, considering the passage of time, American intervention, and substantial U.S. economic aid since World War II, conditions there were much as they are now, although more exaggerated then than now. Then, as now, there was widespread poverty of the most appalling kind; the land was owned by a relatively few families who controlled not only the wealth of the nations but their politics as well. The social chasm between the upper classes and those below was wide and deep and, except for the military, there was little or no way to cross it. The poor were repressed not only by the rich but also by government officials at all levels.

These Caribbean nations all had republican forms of government and splendid constitutions filled with noble words, but this was just empty show, for the masses of the people had no experience with nor training for democracy, and their leaders, who usually sought power for its own sake and to fatten their purses, were not about to change things. There were, to be sure, political parties and elections but not as we know them. One party was generally called "conservative" and the other "liberal" but usually the only difference between them was the name, for political, social, or economic issues seldom separated the parties. The names were convenient but meaningless symbols.

When elections were held, they were usually meaningless too, for power was seized by force and the party in power almost always won the elections, which were marked by fraud and coercion. Often the weaker party did not even contest the election, for if it did so too strenuously, its leading members were often thrown in jail or out of the country. There were courts and legislatures, too, but they followed the same pattern. The party in power—or often a single dictator—told them what to do and they did it—or else.

Even this gives a picture of greater stability than existed. The parties were usually only loose coalitions of leaders who seldom scrupled to betray a comrade. Further, the parties (or the country itself) were frequently fragmented by local leaders who tried to use their local strength to bargain their way into positions of national power and riches. And, to add to the chaos, rulers of the neighboring countries often backed one power-seeker or another, attempting that way to bolster their own rule and prevent a neighboring country from being used as a base for revolution.

That's not all. Although the army was the single most important factor in keeping a dictator or party in power, they were not armies in any modern sense. They were almost random bands of ignorant, barefoot peasants usually drafted against their will, poorly trained if at all, and led by officers often corrupt and almost invariably untrained. Thus, even though the army was important, it was hardly more impressive than the bands recruited by revolutionaries. Further, army officers could often be bribed to join a revolution, bringing their rag-tag soldiers with them.

In short, during the first third of the century things were much as they are now in the Caribbean: periods of chaos alternating with shorter or longer periods of relative calm (but little progress) under this or that dictator. This chaos was one of the prime factors leading to American intervention, but there were others as well. The Spanish-American War had just ended and the United States was feeling its oats as a world power. Thus, it was more devoted to the Monroe Doctrine than ever before. Too, there was growing sentiment for a canal across the narrow isthmus of Central America and determination to protect it from all threats real and imaginary.

Strategic concern over the Panama Canal was to dominate the thinking of successive administrations for decades to come. And Teddy Roosevelt's decisions regarding the canal set the tone of American policy for years thereafter.

Briefly, this was the situation. Roosevelt, as we saw in the section on the Spanish-American War, was a jingo, a passionate believer in a big navy and in America's playing the role of a major power. It follows then that Roosevelt was one of the biggest boosters of an isthmian canal.

For years it had been assumed that any American-built canal would go through Nicaragua, taking advantage of natural waterways and lower mountains, but the Frenchman Ferdinand de Lesseps, builder of the Suez Canal, who was put in charge of the project, chose Panama. The French effort failed, partly because of graft and extravagance and partly because of terrible epidemics of yellow fever. The French company went bankrupt in 1899. But speculators bought up the stock and hoped either to get American financing for another attempt or to sell outright to the American government the property, the equipment, and the little work so far accomplished.

However, the United States seemed to be set on the Nicaraguan route, despite the tireless lobbying of men with great financial interests in the Panama route. Then, at the last moment, Roosevelt got his Canal Commission to recommend the Panama route and promptly began negotiations with Colombia, of which Panama was then a part, for a canal concession. A convention was agreed upon in early 1903. The United States Senate ratified it in March but then the Colombian Congress, as was its right, rejected it. This may well have been a foolish act, but the nation had just ended a civil war and passions were such that the long-term advantages of the canal could not overcome the political heat of the moment.

This outraged Roosevelt and, although the circumstances

are not clear, he obviously decided he was going to have his canal even if he had to seize Panama. Although Panama had never been firmly controlled by the central government at Bogotá, it was legally part of Colombia and in 1846 the United States by treaty had guaranteed Colombian sovereignty. A revolution was brewing in Panama, but Roosevelt always insisted that the United States gave the rebels no encouragement. The lobbyists who had vast stakes in a Panama canal also argued that they gave the rebels no help, but there is considerable skepticism about this.

Whether or not the rebels were helped to start the revolution, there is no doubt about the help they got once the revolution broke out. The rebels had begun to seize the isthmus when a Colombian warship landed 400 troops at Colón. If these troops had been able to cross the isthmus, that no doubt would have been the end of the revolution, but an American warship, the U.S.S. *Nashville,* acting on orders, blocked the Colombian troops and the revolution succeeded.

Roosevelt would soon have his canal, for a Frenchman with a big financial stake in the Panama route, Philippe Bunau-Varilla, now turned up as the Panamanian emissary to Washington and signed a treaty with Secretary of State John Hay without giving the new government in Panama a chance to look at it. Panama ratified it nonetheless, for the treaty recognized Panama's independence. It also gave the new nation $10 million in cash with an additional $250,000 to be paid each year. In return the United States was given a ten-mile-wide Canal Zone in which it could act "as if it were sovereign." More than half a century later, in 1963, this treaty was the root cause of riots in the

Canal Zone that imperiled U.S.-Panamanian relations and brought the bitter dispute into the United Nations Security Council.

But in 1903, Roosevelt, to use his own words, "took the Canal Zone." And he was proud of it, writing to his old friend Henry Cabot Lodge in 1909, "The vital work, getting Panama as an independent republic, on which all else hinged, was done by me without the aid or advice of anyone, save in so far as they carried out my instructions; and without the knowledge of anyone."[1] To this day Roosevelt has been much criticized. The eminent historian Samuel Flagg Bemis, even though he agreed that an isthmian canal was necessary, put it this way:

> This . . . does not justify the methods by which Theodore Roosevelt "took" the Canal Zone. It was an intervention by force which did a great injustice to a sister republic. It was unnecessary. It profited hugely a private foreign interest that was actively lobbying in Washington, namely the French New Panama Canal Company. An Isthmian canal under United States ownership and control could have been secured, alternately from Nicaragua, or unexceptionally from Colombia, with a little more time and patient diplomacy. It was an act for which reparation has since been paid, and we may hope that the rancor that it caused lies wholly buried today in the grave of the rough-riding statesman who was responsible for it.[2]

Chapter Nine

IF THEODORE ROOSEVELT'S ACTION in connection with Panama set the tone for United States policy in the Caribbean, his action in connection with the Dominican Republic established the legalistic basis, for it was on the "Roosevelt Corollary" to the Monroe Doctrine that the United States based its military interventions in Nicaragua, Haiti, and the Dominican Republic. (See Appendix IV.) This story begins in Venezuela.

As in most Latin American countries, conditions there were unsettled at the turn of the century and Venezuela found itself unable to pay its foreign creditors, most importantly those in Germany and Great Britain. After some bickering the two European nations, through their ministers in Caracas, on December 7, 1902 demanded immediate settlement of their claims. On December 9 German and British warships seized several small Venezuelan craft, sinking a couple of them. And on the 13th they bombarded a couple of forts.

General Cipriano Castro, Venezuela's new ruler, at first wanted to arrest all British and German nationals in the country but was talked out of it by the American Minister, Herbert W. Bowen. Then Castro decided to suggest arbitration of the claims. The United States passed this on to London and Berlin, where the suggestion was evidently coolly received. But the two countries soon changed their minds when they became aware of the hostile response in the United States to their use of force in Venezuela. This hostility surprised even Roosevelt, who nonetheless did not want to be "put in the position of preventing the collection of an honest debt."[1] Yet he began to share the concern of the press about British and German infringement on the Monroe Doctrine. The alarmed European nations then asked Roosevelt to arbitrate, but he persuaded them to turn the matter over to the Permanent Court at the Hague.

In the meantime Britain and Germany, joined now by Italy, blockaded the coast of Venezuela. The United States in general and Roosevelt in particular did not like this and Roosevelt sent Admiral Dewey to the vicinity with the bulk of the Atlantic Fleet to put pressure on the Europeans. There is some uncertainty as to the exact sequence of events, but after Venezuela agreed to put aside 30 percent of its customs receipts at Puerto Cabello and La Guaira to pay any judgments that came out of the arbitration, the European powers lifted the blockade. A year later the Hague Court tribunal of three judges ruled that the intervening powers should have preferential treatment in the settlement of the claims against Venezuela.

This confronted Roosevelt with a predicament. On the one hand Britain and Germany had specifically recognized the Monroe Doctrine. On the other hand, the Hague ruling would make it more likely that European nations would intervene in Latin America so their claims would have first preference. Out of this predicament came the Roosevelt Corollary. Roosevelt's thinking first became public in a letter he had his friend Elihu Root read at a dinner in New York on May 20, 1904 to celebrate the anniversary of Cuba's independence. In part the letter said:

. . . It is not true that the United States has any land hunger or entertains any projects as regards other nations, save such as are for their welfare.

All that we desire is to see all neighboring countries stable, orderly, and prosperous. Any country whose people conduct themselves well can count upon our hearty friendliness. If a nation shows that it knows how to act with decency in industrial and political matters, if it keeps order and pays its obligations, then it need fear no interference from the United States. Brutal wrongdoing, or an impotence which results in a general loosening of the ties of civilized society, may finally require intervention by some civilized nation, and in the Western Hemisphere the United States cannot ignore this duty; but it remains true that our interests, and those of our southern neighbors, are in reality identical. All that we ask is that they shall govern themselves well, and be prosperous and orderly. Where this is the case they will find only helpfulness from us.[2]

Considerable criticism greeted this statement and a few days later Roosevelt, in another letter to Root, elaborated his view: "If we are willing to let Germany or England act as the policeman of the Caribbean, then we can afford not to intervene when gross wrong-doing occurs. But if we intend to say 'Hands off' to the powers of Europe, then sooner or later we must keep order ourselves."[3]

This was a crucial point in American history. Defenders of Roosevelt and succeeding Presidents who ordered military interventions are well represented by the distinguished historian earlier cited, Samuel Flagg Bemis. In response to suggestions by other historians that Roosevelt should have let foreign investors fend for themselves, Bemis wrote:

. . . the other great powers would not renounce the right of intervention to secure justice, including contract debts; it had

proven impossible in Venezuela a year previously for the United
States to leave alien investors to shift for themselves. The
European powers had intervened, and the Hague Court had
just put an impressive sanction of international law on the
justice of their use of force. If Roosevelt had stood aside in
1904, another intervention would almost certainly have followed and the control of the United States over the Panama
Canal might have been checkmated at the very start of con-
struction. Certainly the danger of this was sufficiently imminent to cause grave concern. Roosevelt was acting upon the
traditional motive of security for the Continental Republic as
he and his compatriots sensed it at the time. Not until the
menace of European intervention had temporarily disappeared
as a result of the First World War could a President of the
United States safely think of liquidating the protective imperialism that had been established in the vital Caribbean area
at the beginning of the century; not until then could there
be a reasonable expectation, during the period between the
two great wars, that the non-American powers would refrain
from intervention in the New World to secure justice denied
to their nationals.[4]

The case then at point was the Dominican Republic, a
tiny, impoverished nation that would haunt the United
States more than once in this century. In April 1904 the
American Minister reported—although Rome denied it—that
the Italian navy was about to intervene to secure the rights
of Italian nationals. The Dominican Republic—torn by alternating revolutions and dictators—owed about $32 million
to French, Belgian, German, Spanish, and Italian creditors.
The financial-political tangle was complicated beyond words
but eventually in the fall of 1904 an agent appointed by
the United States (with Dominican agreement) began collecting customs revenue. The various creditors began clamor-

ing for the support of their governments. This is the way
Roosevelt saw it: ". . . [he] had to look forward to a foreign intervention or take the responsibility for intervention
by the United States. He had little choice other than to
intervene to secure justice for all the foreign creditors."[5]

Roosevelt publicly repudiated any idea of annexing the
Dominican Republic, as some suggested—even some Dominicans. What he—and the shaky Dominican government
—wanted was for the United States to appoint an agent
who would attempt to put the island republic's finances in
order. This was arranged by treaty in 1907 and the agent
paid out to the creditors pro rata forty-five percent of the
receipts after expenses, and turned the rest over to the
Dominican government so it would have funds to operate.
This financial and political intervention foreshadowed the
military intervention that would follow within a few years.
It was justified by the President in a message (the Roosevelt
Corollary) sent to the Senate on February 15, 1905, the
substance of which we saw in his two letters to Elihu Root.

Although many historians defend the decisions to intervene by Roosevelt and his immediate successors, there are
critics also. They argue that the United States then, as in
the decades after World War II, was too ready to judge
how other nations should order their domestic affairs.
Although there was, to be sure, frequent chaos in the
Caribbean states, perhaps arrogance is not too strong a word
to characterize Roosevelt's statement: "Brutal wrong-doing,
or an impotence which results in a general loosening of the
ties of civilized society, may finally require intervention by
some civilized nation, and in the Western Hemisphere the
United States cannot ignore this duty; . . ."

Roosevelt also frequently referred to the need for foreign investors to receive justice, but presumably these businessmen knew the risks they were taking and some critics have wondered why the United States concerned itself with the collection of private debts. It is this criticism that caused the birth of the term "Dollar Diplomacy." This criticism does have some basis, for many of the financial claims against the Caribbean nations were dubious indeed. This question is discussed by Dana G. Munro in his standard work on the subject, *Intervention and Dollar Diplomacy 1900–1921*. In his almost overwhelmingly detailed study Munro writes:

> The collection of pecuniary claims by force often led to gross injustice. Some foreigners who did business in the Caribbean found it easy to take advantage of officials whose inexperience in the workings of international finance made it difficult for them to distinguish between sound and unsound proposals, and whose judgment could be influenced by bribery or promises of participation in future profits. Goods were frequently sold to the local governments at outrageous prices, and unconscionable terms were exacted for small loans to meet urgent necessities. Concessions obtained through misrepresentation or corruption gave the promoters extraordinary advantages in grants of public property, monopolistic privileges, and exemptions from taxation. It was of course transactions of this type that were most likely to be repudiated when there was a change of government. It was often difficult to judge whether a given contract was so vitiated in its origin or so outrageous in its provisions as to make it unworthy of diplomatic support, because the evidence was apt to be unreliable and colored by partisan prejudice, and benefits obtained by the foreigner always had to be set off against the risks involved. Far too frequently, however, foreign governments sup-

ported claims without inquiring into the character and conduct of the claimants and without considering whether their demands might not be fraudulent or exaggerated. They tended to ignore considerations of fair play in their determination to teach the local authorities that they must respect their nationals simply because they were Germans, Italians, or Frenchmen.[6]

But while such claims were all too often indefensible and while the United States government did often try to advance the private interests of American investors, it now seems clear that the basic motive for U.S. diplomacy in the Caribbean was a concern not for dollars but for national security. Roosevelt and his successors genuinely feared foreign intervention in this vital area and would have feared it no matter what the reason. It just so happened that the most likely reason for such intervention was the fiscal chaos of the Caribbean states.

The basic question is: was American intervention necessary for national security? There is no doubt that the Panama Canal, and the approaches to it, were vital to American military, political, and commercial interests. Although fears for the safety of the Canal were no doubt exaggerated, it is normal, perhaps even wise, to err somewhat on the side of caution in matters of national security. Nonetheless, after the Spanish-American War the United States was paramount in the Caribbean and there was simply no European nation willing or able to challenge it. The United States could have kept any European power from intervening or restricted any interventions so they would not have been a threat to the Panama Canal. And if the United States was concerned about the Caribbean nations' satisfying the claims of foreign creditors, it could have achieved this by diplomatic means, for even without intervention, the United States had powerful, even decisive influence.

The American ability to restrict European intervention was demonstrated during that same period when Roosevelt was willing to permit France to use force against Venezuela and operate the customhouses as long as France solemnly pledged itself not to undertake any "permanent occupation" of the country. This no doubt could have been done elsewhere in the Caribbean. But this was not how Roosevelt saw it, nor his successors, and it must be conceded that present-day writers have the advantage of hindsight; they can see how badly American intervention turned out.

Chapter Ten

THE FIRST MAJOR AMERICAN military intervention took place in Cuba in 1906. This was somewhat different from the interventions that were to follow in nearby countries, for it grew directly out of the circumstances of the Spanish-American War. Although there had been a century or more of American sentiment for the annexation of Cuba, the war of 1898 was fought, as we saw, primarily out of a national impulse to free the cruelly repressed Cubans from Spain. Thus it was not surprising that the American Congress accepted without debate the famous Teller Amendment to the April 20, 1898 joint resolution for intervention to free Cuba: "That the United States hereby disclaims any disposition or intention to exercise sovereignty, jurisdiction, or control over the said island except for the pacification thereof, and asserts its determination, when that is accomplished, to leave the government and control of the island to its people."

Although many American imperialists no doubt regretted that unequivocal language, it did represent the will of the people. Therefore a victorious United States, although it could keep the Philippines, Puerto Rico, and Guam, had to set Cuba free. But it did not quite do that. Although Cuba was nominally independent, the United States insisted that the historic Platt Amendment be embedded not only in the Cuban constitution but in a *perpetual* treaty between the two nations that could be modified only with the consent of both.

By terms of the Platt Amendment the Cuban government agreed "that the United States may exercise the right to intervene for the preservation of Cuban independence, the maintenance of a government adequate for the protection of life, property and individual liberty. . . ." The amendment also gave the United States the right to obtain naval stations "to maintain the independence of Cuba, and to protect the people thereof, as well as for its own defense. . . ." (See Appendix V.) Here again, in this last provision, we see American concern for protecting the vital Caribbean area.

The Cuban constitutional convention was not eager to accept the Platt Amendment, for it seemed to them to be a clear infringement on their sovereignty. Nor was the con-

vention eager to surrender its sovereign rights to territory
to be used for American bases and, indeed, the American
naval station at Guantánamo has often been a bitter issue
between the nations.

Secretary of War Root, the chief architect of American
policy in Cuba, attempted to quiet the Cuban fears by telling a delegation to Washington:

> . . . that the main purpose of the amendment was to pre-
> serve, not to impair, Cuba's independence; and he was quoted
> as saying that intervention would occur only to prevent a
> foreign attack or when a veritable state of anarchy existed
> within the republic. . . . The Secretary's arguments were rein-
> forced by a letter from Senator Platt stating that the amend-
> ment had been carefully worded to avoid any possible idea
> that it would establish a protectorate or otherwise impair
> sovereignty and independence. Unfortunately, Root made no
> record of these conversations, and later administrations at
> Washington sometimes interpreted the Platt Amendment in
> a way that was hardly consistent with the assurances he had
> given.[1]

Whatever the assurances, the language of the amendment
makes it unmistakable that Cuba's sovereignty was limited.
Nonetheless, the constitutional convention accepted it; there
was little choice, for the American army was still in Cuba.
Yet even though the Platt Amendment gave the United
States unquestioned rights in Cuba, it may not have been
to American advantage to have insisted on the amendment.
This view is suggested by another eminent historian, Dexter
Perkins:

> . . . It is arguable, indeed, that in the decades that followed,
> the United States got the worst of both worlds. It did not

control the situation; but neither could it be indifferent to it. The flow of American capital naturally created a special interest of importance; a reciprocal agreement admitting Cuban sugar to the American market on terms of special advantage cemented this interest; and Cuba became, in the eyes of the critic of American foreign policy, an economic province of the United States.[2]

This is sometimes overlooked by American writers who see only the advantage to the United States of intervening in Cuba either to serve American interests or out of genuine concern for Cuba. However, the existence of the Platt Amendment enabled contending Cuban parties to use American intervention—or the possibility of it—as a political weapon and that is exactly what happened in 1906.

But before examining that situation, it is important to note that the United States, between the end of the war in 1898 and the election of a Cuban president in December 1901, undertook a wide range of projects to benefit the Cuban people. This wide range has been described by Leland Jenks in his *Our Cuban Colony:*

> The cleaning of streets and sewers, the establishment of systematic sanitation under Major Gorgas, the repair of public buildings, more public works than had been undertaken in a generation of Spanish rule, the modernizing of Havana with the Prado and Malecón, the inauguration of a school system under the auspices of Alexis Frye and Matthew Hanna, the suppression of yellow fever as the result of experiments made by Reed, Lazear, Carroll and Agramonte in verification of the theory of the Cuban, Dr. Carlos Finlay, the honest collection of taxes and administration of justice, the reorganization of the University, the separation of church and state, prison reform, the introduction of the writ of habeas corpus, the mer-

cantile register, reorganization of the judiciary, the provision
for railway regulation, and the organization of municipal self-
government—these events . . . make up a striking record of
solid accomplishment.[3]

This was indeed a striking record but there was one vital
thing the United States had not given Cuba: genuine self-
government. Politicians of all stripes had in the back of
their minds the hope that if things went bad for them,
perhaps they could get the United States to intervene on
their behalf. The first President, Tomás Estrada Palma, began promisingly, for he was an honest and efficient man
who tried to rule in the general interest. But the basic
weakness of Cuban society could not long be denied. Although the merchants and the landowners were prosperous,
the great mass of the Cuban people was poverty-stricken,
illiterate, and, like their leaders, totally lacking in democratic experience.

Estrada Palma was wholly unable to persuade the Congress to pass vital election legislation and, as 1905 neared,
when his successor was to be chosen, political agitation developed in which both sides, Estrada Palma's Conservatives
and the opposition Liberals, resorted to fraud and violence.
In these circumstances the government had the upper hand
and won easily in both local and national elections.

Shortly after mid-1906, when Estrada Palma was reinaug-
urated, a revolution broke out. It wasn't much of a revolution but the government wasn't much of a government
either and although there was little real fighting, the nation
was paralyzed. Some leaders, who did not want American
intervention, tried to arrange a truce, but the efforts collapsed. Estrada Palma was evidently convinced that the

United States would intervene on his behalf so he made no real effort to settle the dispute or put down the revolution by force.

But intervention was the last thing the United States wanted and the State Department did everything possible to discourage Estrada Palma's reliance on American intervention. Yet he persisted, so President Roosevelt sent the new Secretary of War William Howard Taft and Assistant Secretary of State Robert Bacon to Havana in September to see if they could work something out. They got the assent of the Liberals to a compromise but Estrada Palma scorned it as being against his personal decorum and the dignity of his government. Last-minute attempts to put together another compromise failed and on the 28th Estrada Palma carried out the simple stratagem that would ensure American intervention. He resigned and so did the Vice President. Since Estrada Palma had already accepted the resignations of the Cabinet ministers in line to succeed him, there was no effective government in Cuba.

That night Taft sent a Marine guard to prevent any looting of the national treasury and the next day, September 29, he proclaimed himself Provisional Governor of Cuba. Roosevelt was furious:

> I am so angry with that infernal little Cuban republic that I would like to wipe its people off the face of the earth. All that we wanted from them was that they behave themselves and be prosperous and happy so that we would not have to interfere. And now, lo and behold, they have started an utterly pointless and unjustifiable revolution, and got things in such a snarl that we have no alternative but to intervene.

It's impossible to say whether the intervention was avoidable, although some scholars have suggested that if Taft, who virtually ignored Estrada Palma during his first few days in Havana, had been more diplomatic with the sensitive President, a compromise might have been worked out.

At first 2,000 Marines were sent ashore. Later they were relieved by an Army force of 5,600 men. They were stationed in the larger towns, leaving the countryside to the Cuban rural guard. The American intervention lasted until early 1909. Although United States rule has been criticized for not genuinely attempting to stop corruption and for allowing a multitude of questionable appointments to government jobs, by and large it accomplished its ends. Under Charles E. Magoon the United States carried out a vast program of public works, put Cuba's tangled finances in order, and, most important, improved the electoral laws and carried out an honest election in November 1908.

American troops pulled out after General José Miguel Gómez was inaugurated on January 28, 1909. It was the last military intervention in Cuba although the United States frequently intervened politically to a greater or less degree until the Platt Amendment was abrogated voluntarily by the United States in 1934. United States economic dominance in Cuba continued to grow and the American Ambassador in Havana was often regarded as the most important man on the island. Even though the 1906 intervention was genuinely undertaken to restore order in Cuba, there were, of course, many Cubans who believed that whatever the reason, any intervention was a violation of their sovereignty. This feeling has been a legacy of the Platt Amendment.

Chapter Eleven

ALTHOUGH THERE HAS BEEN some lasting controversy over
the American intervention in Cuba in 1906, much more has
swirled around the dispatch of U.S. Marines to Nicaragua,
Haiti, and the Dominican Republic. The first, and longest,
of these interventions—the one in Nicaragua—stemmed in
part from local conditions. Tension among the five small
Central American nations has been a way of life for the
century and a half they have been independent since Spanish
rule collapsed in Mexico in 1821. For a while the five states
—Costa Rica, El Salvador, Honduras, Guatemala, and Nicaragua—were united in the Federal Republic of Central
America, but that soon fell apart because of squabbling
among the various leaders, which has continued to our
time; witness the conflict in 1969 when El Salvador briefly
invaded Honduras.

Early in the century, as now, only one of the five states,
Costa Rica, enjoyed any real measure of prosperity. That
was no doubt because most of the people were small farmers of European descent who owned their own land. Thus
conditions existed for a prosperous state, both politically
and economically. But in Guatemala, the most populous
nation, most of the people were Indians who spoke only
their own languages and were almost completely excluded
from political life. Most of them scraped a bare living by
working in near-slavery on coffee plantations owned by
foreigners or rich natives. In the other three countries—
Nicaragua, Honduras, and El Salvador—most of the people
were *mestizos,* of mixed Indian and white blood, also mostly

illiterate and living under cruel conditions, although not quite so bad as in Guatemala.

Except for Costa Rica, which often was somehow able to stay aloof from the quarrels, the Central American states continually intervened in each other's affairs, aiding in revolutions or engaging in open warfare. For decades the United States had generally ignored these squabbling little nations, but after 1903 Roosevelt, now concerned with the strategic importance of the Caribbean, began to take an interest in the area. Careful to avoid any seeming compulsion or dictation, the United States worked with Mexico to encourage peaceful settlement of the recurring Central American disputes. But their success, wherever it existed, was temporary.

By 1907 the chief troublemaker was the dictator of Nicaragua, José Santos Zelaya, who had ruled with an iron hand since 1893. He invaded Honduras in March, and using machine guns for the first time in Central America, inflicted terrible casualties on the Hondurans and the large force from El Salvador sent to help. Zelaya set up a puppet government and a general war seemed imminent because none of the other Central American governments wanted him to control Honduras.

The situation was complicated beyond description and a pessimistic Secretary of State Elihu Root wrote that there was no way to establish peace except through a long period of armed intervention "that we cannot undertake." Root was not as eager to intervene as some of his successors. For a while things seemed to take a turn for the better when the five states agreed to meet in Washington on November 14, 1907 under the sponsorship of the United States and Mexico. They soon arrived at a General Treaty of Peace and Amity by which the five agreed that all disputes among them would be settled by a Permanent Central American Court to be quartered in a building paid for by the American financier Andrew Carnegie in Cartago, Costa Rica. But not surprisingly the agreement soon broke down, primarily because of the rival determination of Zelaya and the Guatemalan dictator, Manuel Estrada Cabrera, to control the governments of El Salvador and Honduras. And the court turned out to be substantially ineffective.

By 1909 William Howard Taft had succeeded Roosevelt, who, to his eventual sorrow, had abided by his pledge not to seek re-election. Taft seemed well qualified to deal with Latin America, for he had had experience in Panama and Cuba and his long residence in the Philippines as Governor seemed to demonstrate his success in dealing with people of Spanish culture. But he left Latin-American policy almost entirely to his Secretary of State, Philander C. Knox. Knox was an eminent lawyer, but seemed totally unable to understand the florid, sensitive Latin temperament. He himself wrote to Taft on March 14, 1911 that he found it hard to cultivate "the delicate entente with the Latins which has been nourished and maintained largely in the past upon champagne and other alcoholic preservatives." And within the State Department Knox left Latin America largely to his new Assistant Secretary, Huntington Wilson, an able and experienced career diplomat. But he too lacked the essential quality of sympathy with the Latin temperament.

In its basic philosophy the Taft Administration differed little from Roosevelt's. It, too, was concerned about European intervention in the strategic Caribbean and believed such interference could best be forestalled by promoting stability in both government and finance. Perhaps Taft was somewhat more concerned than Roosevelt about protecting American lives and property. In one way, however, there was a substantial difference. "Where Root had made every effort to avoid any appearance of domination or coercion, Knox showed less concern for the amenities of diplomatic intercourse and a greater readiness to consider the use of force when diplomatic methods failed."[1] Here Taft, as well as his successor, Woodrow Wilson, was prepared to go beyond diplomacy.

Taft was also more convinced that the way to Caribbean stability was through financial reform and he was eager to have Caribbean debts in the hands of New York bankers rather than in European hands. It was this aspect of his policy that gave rise to the term "Dollar Diplomacy." This, as we saw earlier, was an overstatement. "The purpose of dollar diplomacy was to promote the political objectives of the United States, not to benefit private financial interests."[2]

The United States began to move toward more active intervention in 1909 when the policy of cooperation between it and Mexico began to collapse. Mexico was willing to give advice to the Caribbean lands, but it would not go beyond the use of moral influence. So the Taft Administration, not without some pleasure at having more freedom of action, began to go it alone.

About this time the Nicaraguan dictator, Zelaya, and the United States began to quarrel over claims some American citizens had against Nicaragua. These claims were settled, but this did little to improve relations between the two nations, for the United States was convinced in early 1909 that Zelaya was continuing to dominate Central America by meddling in the domestic affairs of neighboring states. But he also had troubles at home and in October a revolution against him broke out. The United States has been accused of fomenting the revolution, but it now seems clear that Washington had no connection with the uprising in its early stages, although Americans in Nicaragua may have given encouragement.

Soon, however, the United States abandoned its formal neutrality when Zelaya shot two American citizens, Lee Roy Cannon and Leonard Groce, who were captured while allegedly attempting to blow up a troop ship. Zelaya argued that Nicaraguan law authorized the death penalty, but the State Department countered that the two Americans were regularly commissioned officers in the revolutionary army and thus should have been treated as prisoners of war.

The United States responded sharply to their execution with a note the like of which is seldom seen in diplomatic intercourse. On December 1, the note handed to the Nicaraguan chargé d'affaires in Washington, breaking off diplomatic relations, included this kind of language: "Since the Washington conventions of 1907, it is notorious that President Zelaya has almost continuously kept Central America in tension and turmoil . . ." It was "equally a matter of common knowledge" that his government had done away with republican government in Nicaragua . . . "a blot on the history of Nicaragua."

Then the United States included a passage that clearly encouraged the Nicaraguans to overthrow Zelaya. It said both factions would be held accountable for the protection of American life and property, but that the United States would hold off on demanding a stiff punitive indemnity for the execution of Cannon and Groce until it could be determined whether the United States would be dealing with a regime "entirely dissociated from the present intolerable conditions and worthy to be trusted to make impossible a recurrence of such acts." In short, if the government isn't changed, Nicaragua will be forced to pay a heavy indemnity.

Taft also took a hard line on December 7, 1909 in his annual message to Congress. This alarmed Mexico. Not only was it suspicious of American intervention in Central America but it regarded Zelaya as a welcome counterweight to the Guatemalan dictator, Manuel Estrada Cabrera, who had given Mexico much trouble. Now Mexico attempted to revive Mexican-American cooperation but was coolly rebuffed by the State Department.

Mexico persisted, however, and got Zelaya to promise to resign in favor of José Madriz. A respected member of Zelaya's party, he had nonetheless opposed the dictator. However, he had recently accepted an appointment from Zelaya as the Nicaraguan member of the Central American Court. Zelaya resigned on December 16 and the Nicaraguan Congress elected Madriz provisional President. But the United States refused to recognize the new government, terming it merely a continuation of the Zelaya regime.

Madriz immediately called for talks between the government and the rebels. The rebels agreed and the United States offered a warship for the meeting place, but the rebel negotiator was drowned on his way to Managua and the talks never took place, as the changing military situation made one side, then the other, reluctant to negotiate.

The United States was hoping for a rebel victory, but this hope was all but shattered when the rebel army was almost wiped out on February 22, 1910. The United States didn't know what to do. It did not see how it could intervene in the revolution openly and it did not want to intervene surreptitiously. So it just waited, although in April when Britain said it would recognize the Madriz regime unless the United States objected, Washington asked London to hold off.

Things took a better turn—from the point of view of the United States—in May. The government forces attempted to take Bluefields, a town on the Caribbean coast that was the last remaining rebel stronghold. The attempt would probably have succeeded but American naval commanders blocked it, primarily by not allowing the Nicaraguan warship, *Máximo Jerez,* to blockade the port, which was cut off on the land side by government troops.

This temporary respite did not seem to promise much hope to the rebels, for all reports from Nicaragua indicated the government would still triumph. But the failure at Bluefields and the refusal of the United States to recognize Madriz encouraged his enemies. Surprisingly the rebel forces defeated government troops in August and suddenly the Madriz regime collapsed. Managua was entered on August 28.

General Juan J. Estrada, a rebel leader, became the provisional President. He was given, by the State Department, the precise language to use in requesting American recognition. "Estrada was to give assurances that he would hold elections within six months and that he would contract a loan secured by the customs. He should also promise to prosecute the murderers of Cannon and Groce and to pay a reasonable indemnity, and he was to ask the United States to send a commission to deal with any matter that might require a formal agreement between the two governments."[3]

The United States was striking a hard bargain. At first neither Estrada nor the other revolutionary leaders wanted to go along. Madriz, not conforming to a time-honored Latin American custom, had surprisingly left a good deal of money in the treasury, so money was not a pressing problem. Perhaps more important, they did not want to risk being defeated in elections only six months away, nor were they eager to turn the nation over to American financial control. But they really had no choice. The support of the United States was essential to their survival, so they agreed.

It is hardly surprising that a political tug-of-war began almost immediately among the former rebels, and the United States began to fear that the still-strong Zelayista party might take advantage of the situation to regain power. The United States used its influence to see that Estrada was elected President by a constitutional convention; the United States had become convinced that a popular election simply would not work. Estrada had to agree not to run for re-election and a personal friend of his, Adolfo Díaz, was chosen as Vice President.

Everything seemed to be going well from the American point of view and the new government was formally recognized when it was inaugurated on January 1, 1911. But then the new American Minister to Nicaragua, Elliott Northcott, made the horrifying discovery that an overwhelming majority of the Nicaraguans were antagonistic to the United States. Estrada, who felt he was dependent upon American support, wanted to go along with the agreement, but this made him increasingly unpopular.

By March, Estrada was so alarmed that he wanted the United States to set up a virtual protectorate, to supervise elections, and, if need be, put down any further revolutions. The United States did what it could to patch up the deteriorating situation, but Nicaragua's basic instability was too great. Estrada dissolved the constituent assembly, but the new one was, if anything, even less cooperative. The friction spread to the American Legation, where the senior officers differed over whom to support. As a last desperate move, Estrada arrested his chief opponent, Minister of War General Luis Mena, and tried to arm his own supporters. But the army refused to go along, the American Minister intervened to save Mena's life, and Estrada, deciding the situation was hopeless, fled the country.

Vice President Díaz succeeded Estrada, but he soon also fell out with Mena, who had the support of the army. As the political situation deteriorated even further, the United States continued to be more concerned with the financial system, according to its belief that financial stability was the key to everything. Díaz agreed to a treaty under which Nicaragua would negotiate a loan with American bankers to pay its debts and develop the country. The loan would be repaid by customs duties administered by a Collector General approved by the American President.

But this treaty, and a similar one for Honduras, were not immediately acted on by the American Senate, so some New York bankers advanced money to Nicaragua on the assumption that the treaty would eventually be ratified. The political situation grew even more tangled and then, in May, the Foreign Relations Committee of the American Senate declined to recommend that the treaties be approved by the entire Senate.

On October 7, 1911 Mena was elected President by the

constituent assembly for a term to start fifteen months later. In July 1912 another revolution broke out, led by the president-elect. Since Mena had the support of most of the army, he had the upper hand. When many of Zelaya's followers joined him, the situation became desperate.

Díaz asked that the United States "guarantee with its forces security for the property of American citizens in Nicaragua and that it extend its protection to all the inhabitants of the Republic. . . ." The American Minister in early August 1912 called ashore 100 sailors from the U.S.S. *Annapolis* to serve as a legation guard. Simultaneously, the State Department arranged to have more men sent to Nicaragua.

The situation grew still worse later in the month. The rebels pressed their campaign, disregarded the efforts of Costa Rica and El Salvador to mediate, and seized the important town of León on the Pacific coast, massacring the government garrison. Major Smedley Butler pushed inland to Managua with 350 Marines but the rebels still controlled much of the country. As more American troops began to arrive, other Central American nations began to get alarmed. They did not want the Zelayistas to regain control of Nicaragua, but they were also deeply suspicious of American control.

The United States brushed aside such concern and on September 4 sent to the new American Minister, George T. Weitzel, a strong statement supporting the government. He was authorized to make it public at his discretion and he did so on September 13. The statement said that American policy was to keep communications open, protect the life and property of U.S. citizens, and station an adequate guard at the legation in Managua. It said further:

. . . In discountenancing Zelaya, whose regime of barbarity and corruption was ended by the Nicaraguan nation after a bloody war, the Government of the United States opposed not only the individual but the system, and this government could not countenance any movement to restore the same destructive regime. . . . Under the Washington conventions, the United States has a moral mandate to exert its influence for the preservation of the general peace of Central America, which is seriously menaced by the present uprising. [Unable to protect American life and property, the Nicaraguan government had asked the United States to protect not only Americans but all inhabitants and the United States intended to protect its citizens and to] contribute its influence in all appropriate ways to the restoration of lawful and orderly government in order that Nicaragua may resume its program of reforms unhampered by the vicious elements who would restore the methods of Zelaya.

The revolt of General Mena in flagrant violation of his solemn promises to his own government and to the American Minister . . . and his attempt to overturn the Government of his country for purely selfish purposes and without even the pretense of contending for a principle, make the present rebellion in origin the most inexcusable in the annals of Central America.[4]

And in case the American position was not quite clear, the statement added that the "uncivilized and savage" conduct of the rebels gave the revolt "the attributes of the abhorrent and intolerable Zelaya regime." However, it must be pointed out that as bloody as the revolution was, it was entirely in the Latin-American tradition and there was little difference between the two sides in this as in most other disputes.

Although there was little doubt as to the side which the United States favored, Weitzel was horrified to find out that

Admiral Southerland, in charge of the Marines, was actually telling rebel leaders at León that the American forces would be strictly neutral. An anguished President Díaz cabled Washington that his position was hopeless. And Weitzel became so enraged that he recommended that the rebel leaders be captured, tried, and hanged by the Americans.

With the publication of the American statement and the arrival of more troops, the rebel movement began to collapse and on September 24 General Mena himself surrendered to the Americans. For quite a while too sick to give the revolution much direction, Mena had received a promise of personal protection. Some rebels still held on atop two entrenched hills overlooking the railroad between Managua and Granada. Weitzel wanted Admiral Southerland to take the hills but he, understandably, did not want to do the government's fighting for it. However, Washington told him to act. He waited a few days until the government forces made a futile attempt and then sent Marines up the hills. They suffered four dead and seven wounded but took the hills on October 4. There was street fighting in León when the Marines occupied the city. Three more Americans were killed, but by October 8 the revolution was over. Soon the bulk of the American expeditionary force departed but one hundred Marines stayed as a legation guard, a symbol of United States determination to regulate Nicaraguan affairs and, more important, a symbol all through Latin America of North American imperialism.

Washington undoubtedly thought that its policy had succeeded and it moved to solidify the situation. Weitzel decided that the best way to achieve this was to take a hand in Nicaragua's politics and with his support Adolfo Díaz was elected, unopposed, to a four-year term as President. The opposition had decided there was no point in even contesting the election.

How successful was the intervention? Samuel Flagg Bemis summed it up this way:

> Thus fortified the government kept up payments on the old loans by the London bankers and the new loans of the New York bankers. Meanwhile, continued political agitation, crime, periodic revolts, disease, grasshopper plagues, and earthquakes worried, robbed, harassed, ravaged, devoured and shook the already impoverished country and its people. The intervention of the United States was barely adequate to maintain elected governments in power and thus keep the pledged finances in order; it was not enough to regenerate Nicaragua as effective protectorate had done in Cuba. Light as the intervention was, it was sufficient to arouse the animosity of other Latin American countries to whom Nicaraguan dissidents made their appeal. A full protectorate would not have been more hateful, and could have benefitted the people much more.[5]

The judicious Bemis said further that "Intervention in Nicaragua and the occupation of that republic were certainly high-handed, uncalled for by any immediate exigency of foreign policy or national security, and actually contrary to the principles of the Washington conventions of 1907." And by, in effect, turning over Nicaragua's finances to Wall Street bankers the United States gave credence to the slogan that was heard the world over, that of "Dollar Diplomacy," even though, as we have seen, the basic motivation was to prevent foreign intervention, however remote that might have been, in the area of the Panama Canal.

Dexter Perkins wrote that the Marines kept "in power an unpopular regime." And Dana G. Munro, whose monumental work has been a major source for this book, wrote:

> In Nicaragua, the continued presence of the legation guard was interpreted to mean that no revolution would be tolerated. This meant that the conservatives would stay in power, though everyone, including the State Department, knew they were a minority party. The arguments advanced in defense of this policy: the assertion that the liberals included a large proportion of the "ignorant mob," and that most of their leaders represented the evil *zelayista* tradition, were perhaps put forward in all sincerity by officials who had little contact with any except the conservatives, but they made little sense to anyone who had friends in both parties. The support of a minority government was inconsistent with the principles that governed American policy in the Caribbean, but for more than ten years no Secretary of State wanted to assume responsibility for the revolution that would almost certainly follow the legation guard's withdrawal.[6]

This criticism of American foreign policy of more than a half century ago has often been applied in recent years, concerning not only Latin America but the rest of the world as well—particularly Vietnam.

During the first thirteen years of the American intervention, there were few if any basic changes in Nicaragua, although the United States did supervise the elections that insured the seating of friendly candidates, trained a national constabulary, and kept the tangled finances of Nicaragua fairly orderly.

In 1925 the United States dared to withdraw its small contingent of Marines. Almost immediately a revolution erupted and a new government was elected. But this government was forced out of power by the United States and Adolfo Díaz was again installed as President. Again a revolution and again Marines were landed, with Secretary of State Frank B. Kellogg seeing a specter of Communism in Nicaragua, a foreshadowing of American concerns after World War II.

This time, however, the opposition to the United States occupation did not collapse almost immediately. Guerilla warfare was carried on by the revolutionaries. Their most important leader was a young exile, Augusto C. Sandino, who returned to Nicaragua in July 1926. He got hold of a quantity of arms secretly supplied by Mexico and with his supporters slipped north to the mountains. In time he cleared out the government (Conservative) forces and took control of Jinotega, the coffee center. However, by mid-1927 most of the rebels had surrendered and a cable was sent to Kellogg that began, "The Civil War in Nicaragua is now definitely ended."[7]

But the United States had not taken into account the young Sandino. On July 16, in response to an ultimatum from Marine Captain G. D. Hatfield, commandant of the strongly fortified garrison at Ocotal, Sandino attacked, and after fifteen hours of continuous battle occupied the entire town except for the Marine barracks. The Americans responded by sending war planes over the town and reportedly two or three hundred Nicaraguans were killed. As word of the battle filtered out, Sandino became a hero all through Latin America.

The United States tried to keep the American press out of Nicaragua and, with occasional exceptions, succeeded. Thus, until Carleton Beals of *The Nation* worked his way on foot and horseback to Sandino's mountain stronghold of El Chipote, there was little disposition to dispute the American

characterization of Sandino as an "outlaw" and "bandit."
Then Beals' stories appeared and Sandino became a romantic
figure all over the world.

Through *The Nation* Sandino replied to a surrender ultimatum made by Admiral D. F. Sellers, declaring that "The
only way this struggle can be ended is by the immediate
withdrawal of the invading forces from our territory."
Sandino also called for a non-political provisional President
and the supervision of elections, not by Marines but by
representatives of various Latin-American nations. Earlier he
had pledged that he would lay down his arms as soon as
the Marines left, that he would never again participate in
civil war, and that he would never accept any government
office. Still through *The Nation,* Sandino also appealed to the
United States Senate, where there had long been opposition
to American interventionism. He protested the "continued
barbarism . . . such as the recent total destruction of Quilali,"
one of ninety towns that Beals reported had been destroyed,
mostly by air attacks.

Sandino held out in the mountains until the Marines left
in January 1933. He immediately kept his pledge and laid
down his arms. He and his followers were granted virgin
lands on the Coco River. "There they cleared the jungle,
built houses, planted crops and started industries. Though
provocative raids, killing peaceful citizens, were made by
the National Guard, headed by General Anastasio
Somoza . . . , Sandino refused to retaliate, telling his followers he preferred to leave the country rather than engage
in civil strife."

A year later President Juan B. Sacasa invited Sandino to
Managua. He dined at the National Palace, but after dinner

he and two aides were dragged from their car by members of
Somoza's National Guard. They, and a small boy who happened along, were shot. Beals wrote: "The orders for the
seizure of Sandino had been given at a meeting of Somoza
and his staff a few hours earlier. Though the names of the
assassins were well known, and they gleefully displayed their
trophies, the gold teeth, and trinkets of the victim, around
Managua, no effort was made to punish them." Obviously
Somoza feared that Sandino might stand in his way.

Although most critics of the Nicaraguan intervention have
agreed that it was well intentioned (some, however, have
called it willful imperialism), they point to the results. Three
years after the assassination of Sandino, Somoza drove Sacasa
out of the National Palace and shortly thereafter installed
himself. He established a cruel and repressive dictatorship,
with the Somoza family drawing to itself enormous riches
while most of the Nicaraguan people continued in stark
poverty. Somoza had obtained his power when he was
appointed by the U.S. Marines as one of the leaders of the
constabulary. He passed his power on to his sons, and the
Somoza family has continued its totalitarian rule to this
writing, "doing as Washington bade and receiving the
generous loans which make easy the life of a Central American
despot."[8]

Chapter Twelve

ALTHOUGH NO PRESIDENT IN American history is so closely identified with peace as Woodrow Wilson, the fact is that Wilson three times ordered armed interventions in Latin America: Mexico in 1914, Haiti in 1915, and the Dominican Republic in 1916. The Mexican intervention was brief—only a matter of months—but it established the tone of Wilson's philosophy regarding Latin America.

Earlier in the century the United States had attempted to get Mexico to cooperate in trying to maintain stability in Central America, primarily so it would not appear to Latin America that the *norteamericanos* were forcing their own way. But soon the Mexican-American cooperation had broken down because the two countries could not agree on common policies, at least in part because Mexico, too, was suspicious of its northern neighbor. Contributing to the Mexican-American difficulties was the fact that Mexico was also subject to the basic weaknesses that plagued the smaller states to the south.

In Mexico, too, American intervention was preceded by a revolution. But necessary to an understanding of the intervention is a knowledge of the background. Briefly, Mexico was the only Latin-American nation other than Cuba in which Americans had made enormous financial investments. Foreign investments in Mexico totaled more than those of Mexican nationals and more than half the foreign investments were American. There were also more than 40,000 Americans living and working in Mexico. Thus the United States was primarily concerned with stability so that American lives and property would be safe. Accordingly, Washington for decades had looked with favor on the somewhat benevolent dictator Porfirio Díaz, who had ruled with an iron hand since 1876. But beneath the deceptive surface of stability churned the natural forces of great social revolution, a condition that still exists in much of Latin America.

The lid blew in 1911 and a revolution put into office the decent Francisco I. Madero. President Taft immediately recognized the new government and, when Madero complained to him that insurgents were obtaining arms north of the border, Taft persuaded Congress to pass a joint resolution permitting the President to regulate the supply of arms to any American country where there was domestic violence. This formalized what the United States had already been doing. The power to regulate arms gave to the United States, of course, the power to make or break revolutions in most of Latin America, a power Wilson, when he succeeded Taft, was not hesitant to use.

Taft used his power to help Madero but nonetheless the new Mexican President was not able to control the almost irresistible turbulence set free by the 1911 revolution. The American Ambassador to Mexico, Henry Lane Wilson, wanted Taft to put troops and warships at his disposal should he feel them necessary to protect Americans and other foreigners. Taft did not want to do this, for he knew from his Philippine experience how costly and how futile intervention could be. Taft just hoped that things would not entirely collapse while he was still in office. He almost made it, but not quite. In Taft's waning days, Madero was overthrown by one of his own generals, Victoriano Huerta.

Huerta proclaimed himself Provisional President on February 18, 1913 and swore "on a scapulary of the Virgin

of Guadalupe, and also on a medal of the Sacred Heart of
Jesus, and again by the memory of his mother who had once
worn these sacred images on her breast, that he would permit
no one to attempt the life of Señor Madero."[1] Ten days
later Madero and his Vice President were shot—according to
Huerta's authorities, while trying to escape.

Despite this ugly situation, many important nations
promptly recognized the Huerta government, basing recognition on the traditional criteria: undeniable authority within
the land and a pledge to fulfill international obligations.
According to recognized international practice, recognition
did not imply approval of a new government, merely diplomatic acceptance. It had only to do with the government's
effective control of the country and was not concerned with
its constitutionality. The decision then was up to Taft, even
though he had only a few days left in office. His Ambassador,
Wilson, recommended that Washington regard the deaths of
the President and Vice President as a closed matter, that
Washington recognize Huerta in return for prompt settlement of all important issues between the two nations.
Primarily, of course, this concerned the safety of American
lives and property. Huerta had promised Ambassador Wilson
such safety as soon as he was recognized. But the deaths of
the two Mexican leaders had so outraged American public
opinion that Taft decided to leave the question to the incoming Wilson Administration.

The Assistant Secretary of State in charge of Latin American affairs, Huntington Wilson, agreed with Ambassador
Wilson that President Wilson should promptly recognize
Huerta. But the President said no; recognition would be
immoral. This, at the very beginning of his administration,

emphasized a characteristic of Wilson that has been much remarked on by historians—his profound moral sense. At first this seems most appealing, for almost everyone would like to see more morality in international politics. But on second thought, a question is raised: can one always judge accurately in moral terms the domestic affairs of another nation?

This is a vital question, which not only profoundly affected American foreign policy toward Central America but even more profoundly influenced American foreign policy after World War II. The question is well discussed by Samuel Flagg Bemis in his important *The Latin-American Policy of the United States*. Referring to the Huerta situation, Bemis wrote:

> . . . Was it now for other governments, however shocked and revolted, to insist that regimes must succeed each other in Mexico by peaceful and orderly constitutional process? If so, must each and every revolution in the New World, or the whole world over, await a diplomatic verdict as to its propriety? And where would revolutions find unbiased diplomatic judges? Certainly not in the case of Panama. If revolutions in Mexico and Central America alone were to be held up for diplomatic judgment, while recognized elsewhere, then would not this be diplomatic intervention by the United States . . . ?
>
> Right here, when he searches for the will of the people outside his own land, the Wilsonian is overwhelmed, or certainly ultimately to be overwhelmed, by a tangle of difficulties in applying his policy of judgment on revolutions against other constitutions than his own. In many Latin American countries, not to mention the rest of the world, governments have been republican only in form and letter. Once ensconced in constitutional authority, a government, that is to say a strong man, by control of electoral machinery, the police and

the army, can extend his power under color of the constitution. To deny the right of revolution against such a regime would be to frustrate real self-government. . . . At best the tasks and responsibilities of sitting in judgment on revolutions, even if judgment could be politically unbiased, extend to infinite gradations, degrees, circumstances, difficulties, diplomacies, and inconsistencies. That is why traditional international practice has avoided the danger of dogma in dealing with this problem. That is why, since Wilson's time, the United States has jettisoned his nonrecognition policy.[2]

(After World War II, of course, the United States resumed the Wilsonian practice of moral judgment in the nonrecognition of the People's Republic of China and other Communist nations. Many present-day critics, using the same arguments employed by Bemis in regard to a situation more than half a century ago, have declared that this was a serious mistake that has actually hurt the United States by establishing and continuing, sometimes for decades, a condition of hostility and international tension. But this question of morality in foreign affairs is not one easily settled, for is one to say flatly that moral considerations should never figure in international relations?)

Sound or not, the policy of non-recognition was adopted by Wilson and on March 11, 1913, just nine days after his inauguration, he made public a "Declaration of Policy with Regard to Latin America." (See Appendix VI.) By the terms of this declaration the United States would oppose governments established in violation of the constitution and against the popular will. And he decided to unseat Huerta. First, he surreptitiously allowed arms to get to Huerta's opponents, including Pancho Villa, who would later make raids into

American territory. Then, on February 3, 1914, Wilson removed the embargo on arms shipments. This open support of Huerta's enemies encouraged them and enraged the Mexican President. The tension between the neighboring countries grew.

The tension led to an explosive incident. American warships were patrolling the Mexican coast and in early April a party of sailors went ashore at Tampico to buy some supplies for the U.S.S. *Dolphin*. A Mexican junior officer arrested them and paraded them through the streets. The American commander demanded their release and they were set free by a higher Mexican officer who expressed his nation's regrets. Huerta himself joined in the apology. But the United States regarded that as insufficient. The American naval commander, backed up by Wilson, demanded a twenty-one-gun salute to the United States flag. This was too much for Huerta and he refused. The United States never did get that salute.

As the situation grew even more tense, Wilson asked Congress on April 20 to approve his proposal that he be empowered to use the armed forces to obtain respect for the United States. He got it on April 22, but on the 21st he had already acted in anticipation of Congressional approval. On the 21st the Navy, killing a number of Mexicans, seized the port of Vera Cruz to prevent the landing of a shipment of arms arriving on a German merchant ship.

Wilson did not like to occupy Mexican territory but felt himself unable to withdraw until the shaky Huerta regime was toppled. He was rescued from his dilemma by Argentina, Brazil, and Chile, who volunteered to act as joint mediators. Wilson readily accepted and so did Huerta, who soon resigned. He fled into exile and eventually died a poor man.

Wilson had succeeded in toppling Huerta and the American forces evacuated Vera Cruz on November 23, 1914, but things did not improve greatly. Chaos again prevailed in Mexico and rival hordes led by Carranza and the legendary Villa and Zapata swept in and out of Mexico City. Eventually, Villa conducted a series of savage and bloody raids on United States territory and an American force under General John J. Pershing chased him vainly across northern Mexico. But the approach of American intervention in World War I caused Wilson to be eager to drop the matter. He hardly wanted a war with Mexico—and war was very near—while fighting the war against Germany that was only weeks away. So when Venustiano Carranza, the winning revolutionary, established himself as President, Wilson on March 3, 1917 quickly recognized the new government.

How has Wilson's Mexican policy been assessed? Perhaps most historians would share the view of Samuel Flagg Bemis:

> Woodrow Wilson's Mexican policy, based on his principle of not recognizing an usurper's overthrow of constitutional government, can hardly be called an unqualified success. He intervened diplomatically to save the Mexican people from a new dictator. This novel action, the product of idealism and inexperience, involved him against his will in limited military interventions, and it very nearly brought the United States into an unnecessary war with Mexico at an extraordinarily critical moment of its history. He opened full wide the sluiceways of a revolution that distressed and ravaged the people beyond measure. Hundreds of American citizens lost their lives in the ensuing violence. Most of the survivors left the country, abandoning their homes and property. In subsequent decades, hundreds of millions of legitimately invested American capital was lost. Destruction of property of the Mexican *cientificos*

[scientists] naturally turned against the United States the survivors of that elite, the most intelligent and able fraction of the population. The intervention in the port of Vera Cruz and the northern states alienated the remainder. For a long time afterward neither the suffering people of Mexico nor their successive governments were sincere friends of the United States.[3]

Chapter Thirteen

ONCE THE FIRST WORLD WAR broke out in Europe, President Wilson's thoughts were mainly directed across the Atlantic. Nonetheless, he could not ignore the continued turmoil to the south. Even before the situation in Mexico was resolved, troubles began to erupt in Haiti. This was of particular concern to Washington, for German influence in the former French colony was almost as strong as that of the French. And with American sympathies clearly on the Allied side, Wilson was obviously worried about any German presence in the Caribbean. Particularly Washington was worried about the possibility of Germany's getting a coaling station in Haiti that would allow the German navy to operate in Caribbean waters. Although the fear was probably exaggerated, it was true that Germans owned the most important public utilities in Haiti and that German ships handled most of the black republic's trade. More significant, Germans financed most of the revolutions that wracked Haiti.

Again, before discussing Wilson's intervention, it is necessary to get some picture of the situation. Even by Caribbean standards the situation was bad. The story goes way back to the end of the 18th century. Haiti was one of the few French colonies in Latin America. On the western third of the great island of Hispaniola (the Dominican Republic was to the east), a few white planters and French officials ruled hundreds of thousands of black slaves. Torn by the French Revolution, the mother country was unable to retain effective control of Haiti and, when a slave revolt broke out in 1791, the resultant savage fighting saw the virtual extermination of the whites. The black governments that followed independence in 1804 were deeply suspicious of the outside world and there was little contact. But by the time of our story both Frenchmen and Germans, some of whom were married to Haitians, were active in the economy.

The population was about 95 percent black peasants who spoke a *patois*—a mixture of French and various African dialects. Their religion was the mysterious *voodoo,* still practiced in much of the country. But while the blacks were overwhelmingly dominant in numbers, the country was largely ruled by the mulattoes, who considered themselves the *élite,* and called themselves that. The elite spoke French, practiced Catholicism, kept in some touch with French culture. The most fortunate of them even studied in Paris. From the beginning of Haiti's independent history the chief political issue was: who should rule—blacks or mulattoes? There was bitter feeling between them mostly because of the elite's conviction that they were vastly superior. Nonetheless, neither side could rule effectively without at least some support from the other.

Early in the century Haiti resembled the other Caribbean lands in that it was a dictatorship, republican in form, but really ruled through force and terror. In the first years of the century one dictator followed another, their reigns sometimes lasting only a few months. Violence and bribery took the place of elections, although sometimes elections were held as a matter of form, with soldiers lined up in ranks voting over and over again as instructed by their officers. One time when a President, Tancrède Auguste, died suddenly in May 1913, the contenders could not even wait for his funeral to end. It was interrupted by a gun battle between the followers of rival generals.

Chaotic as the situation was before, it became even worse after Auguste's death. The nation was in an almost constant state of revolution. Madison Smith, Wilson's minister to Haiti's capital, Port-au-Prince, described the situation this way:

> Practically no method of obtaining more than a bare living is open to the Haitian except through a government position. Politicians, who are at any time willing to inaugurate a revolution, are abundant, and with a comparatively small sum of money can obtain an army and take the field against the Government. In this emergency the man with the money appears—almost invariably a German merchant who looks upon the financing of a revolution as a straight business proposition. The revolutionary gives his paper for not less than double the amount borrowed, and when the revolution succeeds the merchant receives his money again with 100 percent or more interest. As most revolutions succeed, there is little risk in such loans and they are easily obtained.[1]

The reason why revolutions almost invariably succeeded

is simply explained. With even generals paid only ten to twenty dollars a month and privates getting only fifty cents, some of which was taken by their officers, there was little morale and as little training and discipline. Since the peasants recruited by the revolutionaries got paid much more and were allowed to plunder, their armies were, if not better trained and disciplined, at least more enthusiastic.

As in the rest of the Caribbean, the United States got involved when Haiti's finances collapsed and Washington again feared European intervention. With one shaky dictatorship succeeding another, there seemed little chance that Haiti could fulfill its financial obligations in Europe and the United States. When one dictatorship collapsed in January 1914, both American and German warships landed troops to maintain order and British and French warships were on their way.

The original leader of the revolt was deposed before he could reach the capital and a new revolutionary, Oreste Zamor, marched into Port-au-Prince and, following the time-honored script, was elected President by the Congress, influenced no doubt by the fact that Zamor's motley army was very much in evidence.

Needless to say, financial difficulties were increasing and President Wilson let Haiti know, in effect, that if the new government wanted American support to keep it in power, it might want to ask the United States to administer the customs. Zamor and his Cabinet angrily denounced such a plan; they accused the United States of trying to establish a protectorate over Haiti. Also the French and German governments opposed any unilateral American action.

While the situation simmered, Zamor kept borrowing

small amounts from German merchants on usurious terms. He fell deeper in debt and Washington got increasingly worried about German control of Haiti. Both Germany and France wanted to participate in any customs arrangement, but with the outbreak of war in Europe the United States could safely ignore them. However, the war further aggravated the situation in Haiti. Credits for the coffee crop were impossible to obtain and German and French funds were diverted from Haiti.

Zamor still refused to discuss the American customs plan; maybe he was too busy trying to stay in power, for now he was under severe attack from still another revolutionary. When it became apparent, however, that he was about to be overthrown, he appealed for American help, saying he would accept the customs plan. Washington ordered two warships and eight hundred men to Port-au-Prince but it was too late. Zamor fled the capital in October 1914.

For a while Washington wanted to restore Zamor to power, but the situation was too chaotic. The United States wanted to carry out a plan similar to the one it was enforcing on the other part of the island, the Dominican Republic. It wanted the party chiefs to establish a provisional government that would hold free elections for a constitutional government. But the new American Minister, Arthur Bailly-Blanchard, convinced Washington that there were no real political parties in Haiti, merely quarreling factions that raised rival mercenary armies, and that the populace was simply too indifferent and too ignorant to participate in an election. So that plan was given up.

The new dictator, Davilmar Théodore, was approached. He, too, turned down the American customs plan and made a more limited counter-proposal. But even this was turned down by his followers, who were irate about any measure of American control. As usual, the situation continued to deteriorate. The National Bank refused to give Théodore any more money so he printed his own. The bank would not accept it, so Théodore responded by seizing $65,000 in gold from its vaults.

By now the situation was complicated beyond belief and Théodore found power slipping out of his hands. Now General Vilbrun Guillaume Sam took over and, again following the script, was elected President on March 4, 1915, the third President in six months. While the most intricate diplomatic and financial maneuverings were going on, there was still another revolution. This time French marines intervened, but the revolution continued and on July 27 there was a successful uprising right in the capital city.

A horrible chain of events was the last straw. President Sam sought refuge in the French Legation but reportedly gave orders for a massacre of political prisoners held in the jail at Port-au-Prince. Some 170 persons, many of them from the city's more prominent families, were killed in cold blood. After the slaughter, the commander of the prison sought shelter in the Dominican Legation, but relatives of the slain smashed their way in and killed him. By the next day organized mobs of the elite ranged through the streets. They invaded the French Legation, dragged Sam out from under a bed, and tore him to pieces in the streets.

Just as this was happening, the U.S.S. *Washington* sailed into the harbor. Following orders, Admiral Caperton landed Marines and sailors to restore order. The captains of British and French warships in the harbor honored his request that they not land troops, accepting the American admiral's assurance that he would protect all foreign interests. With the total collapse of government in Haiti the United States could now do whatever it wanted to, but it was not quite sure what that was. Secretary of State Robert Lansing wrote to Wilson on August 3 that the situation was "distressing and very perplexing. I am not at all sure what we ought to do or what we can legally do." He thought that perhaps intervention could be justified on humanitarian grounds. Wilson was just as perplexed and he replied that he feared "we do not have the legal authority to do what we apparently ought to do . . .; I suppose there is nothing for it but to take the bull by the horns and restore order."

Washington ordered Caperton to control Port-au-Prince and the surrounding food-producing area and to take over the principal customhouses. As he received reinforcements, Caperton took over the port cities, one by one. He collected the customs receipts that had been going to the local military leaders and deposited them in the National Bank subject to his control. This, of course, raised the suspicions of the Haitians, who all along had opposed any substantial degree of American control. In an attempt to allay such suspicion, the American admiral on August 9 issued a proclamation saying:

> I am directed by the United States Government to assure the Haitian people that the United States has no object in view except to insure, to establish, and to help maintain Haitian independence and the establishment of a stable and firm government by the Haitian people.
>
> Every assistance will be given to the Haitian people in their attempt to secure these ends. It is the intention to retain the

United States forces in Haiti only so long as will be necessary for this purpose.

Caperton reported to Washington that people of all classes were demanding the election of a President. Washington wanted to postpone this for a while—until it had decided what it wanted to do—but Caperton convinced the State Department that to do so would mean an undesirable use of force. Thus the Haitian Congress elected Sudre Dartiguenave, president of the Senate, as national President.

The United States intended to impose a treaty on the new Haitian government in return for recognition but Dartiguenave and his Cabinet said they would resign if the United States did not consider modifications. Washington yielded on this point, but the negotiations ended with a treaty that was changed only in minor points. In effect, the treaty gave the United States complete control in Haiti.

A good part of the Haitian population accepted this protectorate status without much hostility. The mulatto elite particularly felt that American rule was preferable to anarchy. One of their class was President and the Americans would keep the wild *caco* troops out of the capital. Also the upper classes welcomed American aid in developing the economy. At first there were good personal relations between the elite and the Americans, but when the wives of the American officers began to arrive, racial tensions arrived with them.

Many other Haitians did not welcome the intervention. They thought that Haiti was their country and that they should run it their own way without outside interference. In the interior many Haitians, particularly *cacos,* took up arms. Washington did not want armed clashes. Nevertheless, when Marine patrols attempted to open up communications with the interior in late September, they were attacked. There was considerable fighting in October and November and, alarmed by reports of heavy Haitian casualties, Washington ordered Caperton to end offensive operations. By February 1916 most of the resistance bands had been dispersed and the Haitian constabulary, led by Marine officers and sergeants, was in effective control of the countryside. Needless to say, there were two entirely different views of the resisters. To the Americans they were brigands; to most Haitians they were patriots.

For nineteen years Haiti was ruled by Americans. This was not just rule at the top. It went several levels down into the various government departments, so that white Americans were conspicuous rulers all through that black nation. The rule was less effective than it might have been because there was no overall control: authority was divided between the State and Navy Departments. Often, however, the dominant figure was the Marine brigade commander, since the Haitian *gendarmerie* was under his direct command.

The Americans achieved a great deal in the fields of public works, health, finance, and agriculture and the Garde d'Haïti, the constabulary, was well organized. But in one vital area there was little progress. Democracy was something that existed in form but not in fact. Nor were relations between the Haitian government and people on one side and the United States on the other always happy. In fact, there was more than a year of open armed rebellion.

The rebellion stemmed from the revival of an old law. When the American-led constabulary began to maintain order in the countryside, it became obvious to its Marine

leaders that roads were both a military and economic necessity. Since there was little or no money, the old corvée law,
almost forgotten, was revived. With the approval of the
Haitian government, peasants were required to help build
roads by contributing a few days' labor a year or paying a
tax. At first the peasants did not object; they seemed to
enjoy the food and entertainment provided by the constabulary. Soon, however, abuses began to develop. Many peasants
were forced to work longer than the law specified or at
places far from their homes. Often they were mistreated
and subjected to extortion, either by the *gendarmes* or by
local officials. And the American officers were often tactless
or arbitrary. Resentment began to boil up and eventually it
boiled over into armed insurrection. The leader was Charle-
magne Peralte, who in September 1918 had escaped from
prison, where he had been serving a term for banditry.

Thousands of his followers began operating in the sparsely
settled hills of eastern and northeastern Haiti. It became
clear almost at once that the Haitian constabulary could
not contain the outbreak and soon the 2,000-man Marine
force was sent into action. Fighting lasted for more than
a year, from March 1919 until about May 1920, with the
rebels even attacking Port-au-Prince twice. But the rebels
were no match for the well-armed Marines. Some two thousand Haitian rebels were killed before the uprisings were
suppressed.

As reports of this action began to filter back to the
United States, there were charges in Congress and in the
critical press of Marine atrocities:

> Most of the fighting, on the part of the Marines and the
> *gendarmerie,* was done by small patrols led in many cases by

non-commissioned officers or privates in the Marine Corps. Because of the expansion of the Marine Corps during the European war, and because many of the better elements in the corps were in Europe, some of these men in Haiti were inadequately trained and ill prepared for the difficult task of carrying on such operations in a hostile country, where they had little supervision or support by their superiors. Most of the Marines, and most of the constabulary, conducted themselves in a creditable way, but there were enough reports of cruelty to shock public opinion in the United States and to strengthen the hands of the anti-imperialist groups that were by this time beginning a campaign against a continuation of the occupation. There were undoubtedly a few cases where prisoners were shot without a trial. Two subsequent investigations, however, one by a naval court of inquiry and the other by a committee of the United States Senate, indicated that most of the atrocity charges could not be substantiated.[2]

About the time of the *caco* revolt, relations between the occupying authorities and Haitian officials began to deteriorate, largely because the Haitians began to realize the extent to which they had relinquished control of their own affairs. From their viewpoint, the Americans were assuming authority far beyond that specified in the treaty. For a time in 1919, when Dartiguenave was reluctant to press for legislation the United States wanted the Haitian Congress to pass, the American Minister suspended the salaries of the President, his cabinet, and the council of state. The State Department was distressed at this peremptory action, yet it did want Haiti to conform to its wishes.

Cooperation between the United States and Haiti improved noticeably when Louis Borno succeeded Dartiguenave in 1922 but, perhaps inevitably, discontent began to arise again and, when it became violent in 1929, President Hoover decided that the occupation should be ended as quickly as possible. Appointed to achieve this was Dana Munro, then a young State Department official, who later became one of the foremost scholars of this period and wrote the splendid book that is essential to an understanding of those years, *Intervention and Dollar Diplomacy in the Caribbean 1900–1921*. Munro has been termed by other historians "a wise minister," but even so it took five years to end the occupation, with Franklin D. Roosevelt giving the final orders in 1934.

As with Nicaragua, the best way to judge the ultimate results of the American occupation of Haiti is to examine briefly what has happened since. Although many students of the occupation have given the United States credit for establishing a measure of stability, for an extensive program of public works, and for untangling Haiti's disastrous finances, there are serious criticisms as well. Little was done about the corrupt courts and, more important, virtually nothing was done about the state of public education, which hardly existed. Most of the people were illiterate when the Marines arrived and they were still illiterate when the Marines left nineteen years later. Without improvement in education there could be no progress toward democracy.

At first the momentum started by American rule seemed to continue promisingly. Sténio Vincent, who took office in 1930, remained President until 1941. He ruled well, as did his successor, Elie Lescot, another mulatto, who ruled until 1946. By this time, however, the restive black majority wanted one of their own in the presidency. Responding to this, the Garde d'Haïti put Dumarsais Estimé into power. "It was now clear that the effective rulers of Haiti were the troops of the Garde d'Haïti trained by the Americans, and especially the five hundred men of the Palace Guard."[3]

Estimé was not as skillful as his predecessors and he found himself in conflict with the neighboring dictators of the Dominican Republic and Cuba. This apparently was not what led to his downfall, however. That came when he planned to perpetuate himself in office. So in 1950 the same Palace Guard that put him into office threw him out. He was succeeded by the strong man of the army, Colonel Paul Magloire, who was properly elected for a six-year term. He ruled vigorously and well. But when he, too, tried to remain in power beyond his legal limit, he was forced out by a general strike in December 1956.

The fundamental weakness of Haitian society became evident again when, within eight months, there were seven governments. Disorders spread and, in September 1957, François (Papa Doc) Duvalier was inaugurated as President following a questionable election. He has been in power to this writing, presiding over a poverty-stricken country with a rule that has seldom been equaled in this hemisphere for cruelty and brutality. For a number of years he was actively supported by the United States, which perhaps saw no alternative. This, along with real achievement, has to be taken into consideration in any final judgment of the American intervention in Haiti.

Chapter Fourteen

PERHAPS THE AMERICAN INTERVENTION in 1916 in the Dominican Republic is the most relevant of all for modern readers, because memories of that intervention were still alive in 1965 when United States Marines again landed in Santo Domingo. The first Dominican intervention was undertaken in circumstances similar to those in Nicaragua and Haiti. As we saw earlier, the United States under Theodore Roosevelt had established a customs receivership in the Dominican Republic in 1907. This was to bring order to the chaotic Dominican finances so that European nations would not intervene to protect the interests of their citizens.

At first this policy seemed to be succeeding splendidly and, during the Taft Administration, Secretary of State Philander C. Knox often cited the Dominican Republic as a demonstration of how American customs receiverships could benefit the unstable, poverty-stricken nations of the Caribbean. Indeed, on one occasion, in January 1911, Knox argued that the customs treaty provision authorizing the United States to protect the Dominican customs service, "unexercised and without any undue interference on the part of the United States, has cured almost century-old evils."

It is true that the customs receivership had helped the Dominican Republic, but so had the able administration of Ramón Cáceres. And when revolution again broke out in 1911, it did not mean that the customs program had failed, merely that it alone was not enough to bring stability and prosperity to the Dominican Republic. Again, it was not the fault of any particular program, but the eruption to the surface of the fundamental instability of the nation.

The disturbances that preceded intervention began in 1911 and reached their peak in November when Cáceres was assassinated. Cáceres' cabinet assumed control of the country but the real power lay with the army commander in Santo Domingo, Alfredo Victoria. Since he was too young to be president, he forced the congress to elect his uncle, Eladio Victoria. But the younger Victoria was not subtle in the exercise of the real power and he alienated the other leaders of his own party as well as those of the opposition. Thus, in January 1912, various leaders were at the heads of insurgent bands operating in a number of provinces. When the United States saw its favorite policy on the verge of collapse, President Taft on September 24 sent 750 Marines to Santo Domingo. That did not bring enough improvement to satisfy Washington so the United States forced President Victoria out of office, hoping a successor could bring the civil strife to an end.

Victoria resigned on November 26 and on November 30 the congress elected, as Provisional President, Adolfo Nouel, the Archbishop of Santo Domingo. The civil war ended for the time being and the Marines, who had been confined for two months in serious discomfort aboard their transports, were pulled out. But the respite did not last long. Most of the rival leaders did not really want peace, unless it was on their terms.

Shortly after his inauguration, Monsignor Nouel fell ill

from overwork and despair. He tried to resign on December 15, 1912 but the American Minister, W. W. Russell, persuaded him to withdraw his resignation.

The United States was now aware of a new dimension to the problem. It did not help the country much if the customs were collected honestly, only to have the money spent corruptly and foolishly. The country was now broke. A loan of $1,500,000 was not sufficient, and the conditions on which it was approved only increased Dominican suspicion of the United States.

Soon thereafter Wilson was inaugurated as President of the United States. He was opposed to the financial aspects of American policy in Latin America and in a famous speech at Mobile, Ala., on October 27, 1913, severely criticized the terms that investors demanded in lending money to Latin nations. Yet his policy was similar to Roosevelt's and Taft's, for he had the same concerns about United States security. To this was added his moral concern for constitutional government. He was dead set against the seemingly endless chain of revolutions and once declared that "I am going to teach the South American republics to elect good men."

It was in this context that Wilson viewed the situation in the Dominican Republic. It must be remembered that Wilson was also deeply involved with Mexico and Haiti and, most important, with the approaching war in Europe. Wilson had barely moved into the White House when it became evident that the discouraged Archbishop Nouel was about to resign in despair. Wilson cabled him directly, asking him to stay on, but the reply was noncommittal and before March ended the Archbishop resigned and sailed for Europe.

Again the United States had to cross its fingers and hope that a capable, and cooperative, president would emerge. It seemed to take less part than usual in the election of José Bordas Valdés as Provisional President. Although there was one brief attempt at revolt, his election seemed fairly popular. But he, like the Archbishop, had little control over provincial leaders. For a while the country was quiet, but then the strongest of the provincial leaders, Desiderio Arias, began to exert his strength. He got concessions from President Bordas that angered other leaders and soon another revolution was underway. On September 8 Horacio Vásquez, nominal leader of one of the two principal parties, proclaimed himself Provincial President.

Wilson did not like this one bit and Secretary of State William Jennings Bryan told the Legation in Santo Domingo to notify the revolutionaries that the United States would not recognize them even if they won and would withhold from them the government's share of customs receipts. And the United States made it plain in other ways that it was wholeheartedly backing the Bordas government. Seeing that their cause was hopeless, the rebels signed a peace treaty in October but with the understanding that the United States would supervise elections, to ensure their fairness, first for a constituent assembly and then for a permanent president.

The United States hastily rounded up twenty-nine agents in Puerto Rico to act as observers for the assembly election. The observers arrived just a few days before the election, but even though they had little time for preparation, the election went fairly well. No doubt to Bordas' dismay an opposition coalition won a majority in the assembly. However, the constituent assembly did little because Bordas' supporters, by remaining away, were able to prevent a quorum.

While another political difficulty was developing there was, as always, the problem of money. Bordas was not able to, or did not wish to, keep expenditures within income. By the beginning of 1914 the government was seriously in debt and on January 7 the congressmen threatened to "cause chaos" if their December salaries were not paid. The State Department authorized a $20,000 advance and did so again two days later when the American Minister said the government would fall if it did not.

The basic problem, of course, was political and another crisis was soon at hand. Other party leaders became hostile when it appeared that Bordas wanted to be elected permanent President. They did not expect a free election, for, among other reasons, the United States was making no preparations to ensure one. Again, although the United States was not sure what course to follow, it decided the best bet was to support Bordas. But Bordas precipitated a crisis by announcing suddenly on March 19 that the election would be held on April 1 and 2. He also removed the pro-Arias governors of four provinces. The purpose was obvious: he wanted to control the forthcoming election. This presented Washington with another dilemma. It wanted Bordas and yet it wanted free elections, even though it had made no adequate preparation for them, knowing that the promise of free elections had been the basis on which the opposition parties had put aside their weapons the previous October.

The American Minister, again acting hastily, rounded up

thirty Puerto Ricans already in the Dominican Republic and prepared to use them as observers. He never got the chance, for, in the few days before the elections, Arias' followers began a revolution in two cities. The election was postponed and the United States sought some kind of compromise. None seemed possible, but Washington was reluctant to resort to armed intervention. The United States already had its hands full. It was trying to persuade Haiti to accept a customs receivership, and Argentina, Brazil, and Chile were attempting to mediate the crisis with Mexico caused by the American occupation of Vera Cruz. An intervention then would help neither situation. And the Navy was having difficulty in providing enough ships for all the simultaneous trouble spots.

Bordas was now in serious trouble because the opposition had banded together and the rebels were getting arms from Haiti, across the border. This time the State Department acted with resolution. On July 29 Bryan cabled the American Legation that President Wilson had a peace plan and he asked all sides to lay down their arms. A general armistice agreement was signed on August 6 and a few days later a three-man commission arrived from the United States.

They laid down the law. The contending factions were to choose a Provisional President. If they did not, the United States would. The new government would hold an election closely watched by the United States. If the election was fair, the United States would support the new government and permit no further revolutions. If the vote was not free, another election would be held. The commissioners said there was to be no discussion of the Wilson plan; it was to be accepted—period. The tough words were backed up by a show of force. A contingent of Marines had arrived with the commission, although it remained aboard ship. And commanders of the numerous naval vessels in Dominican waters told local leaders that force would be used to stop further fighting.

By this time most of the Dominican leaders had had enough fighting and were ready for peace. By the end of August all the leaders except Arias had accepted the Wilson plan and Dr. Ramón Báez was chosen Provisional President. He was a physician who had not been very active in politics. His first problem was what to do about Arias. Bryan wanted Báez to ask the American Marines to arrest Arias. But Báez did not want American armed intervention and he reached an agreement with Arias by which the provincial leader recognized the Provisional President but in effect remained virtually independent.

In the meantime the presidential election campaign was on. The leaders of the two old parties, Juan Isidro Jiménez and Horacio Vásquez, were the principal candidates. The polling took place over three days beginning October 25, 1914. Two Americans, usually Navy men, were at each polling place. The vote was close, with Jiménez winning over Vásquez by 40,000 to 35,000. After some wrangling Jiménez was inaugurated on December 5, 1914.

As usual Washington hoped the worst was over and as usual it wasn't. Jiménez was barely in office when the State Department notified him it wanted additional powers for Americans. This was beyond what the United States had stated earlier and Jiménez, backed by the Congress, refused to go along. Washington was further disappointed by the performance of Jiménez. Old, and in poor health, he was not able to control the contending leaders who supported him in the election in exchange for important government positions. Most powerful was Arias, who not only had a large following in both houses of Congress, but as Minister of War controlled the army. This dissension within the government encouraged the opposition to make difficulties.

The United States tried to head off trouble by making it clear time and again that it would support Jiménez and would permit no revolution. But this situation was complicated by the growing hostility between the Dominican Congress and the United States. A further complication was the illness of Jiménez in the summer of 1915, with the government being left to the sharply divided Cabinet. And in July there were a couple of small insurrections.

In mid-1915 Bryan resigned as Secretary of State and was succeeded by Robert Lansing. Lansing agreed with those subordinates who believed that the United States should take a greater hand in Dominican affairs. In September, W. W. Russell, who had returned as American Minister, was told to push for a new treaty that would give the United States the same right to intervene in the Dominican Republic that it had under the Platt Amendment in Cuba.

Jiménez was horrified by the suggestion and did not even dare tell most of his Cabinet about it. He quickly sent a personal letter to Wilson explaining that even public discussion of the proposal would endanger his administration. Russell was then ordered to carry out his alternative instructions, by which the United States informed the Dominican government that it interpreted the Treaty of 1907 to give it the right to appoint a financial adviser with very wide

powers and, as well, a director of a much-expanded constabulary.

In November news of what amounted to an American
ultimatum leaked out and added to the anti-American feeling that had been growing since the July intervention in
Haiti. Jiménez, after consulting leaders of the opposition,
rejected the American plan on December 8, pointing out
that the Dominican people were unanimously opposed to
intervention. The American Minister feared that the opposition might start another revolution or that Jiménez might
resign, leading to the election of Arias, Washington's least
favorite person, as President. In January 1916 Russell
warned Washington that he feared trouble and he was
instructed to tell Jiménez that the United States would send
troops to put down any rebellion. This was not much help
to Jiménez, for there was such opposition to American
intervention that any government kept in power by it
would lose almost all popular support.

Beset by Arias on one side and Washington on the
other, President Jiménez decided that although there was
little he could do about Washington, perhaps he could do
something about Arias. On April 14, 1916 he called Arias'
chief lieutenants, the commander of the fortress at Santo
Domingo and the head of the Republican Guard, to his
country home and imprisoned them. The tactic backfired.
The fortress garrison remained loyal to Arias and the leaders
of the opposition rallied to him. The American Minister
and Archbishop Nouel, who had returned to the island,
tried to work out an agreement. No use. Jiménez tried on
May 5 to take the capital city with forces sent by provincial
governors loyal to him. But they lacked ammunition. He

turned to the Americans, who had sent two warships, which landed men to protect the American Legation and that of Haiti, where many foreigners had sought refuge. Jiménez asked the Americans to take the city but thought better of it a few hours later, withdrew his request, and resigned.

The American Minister and Admiral Caperton told Arias, who now controlled the capital, that the Americans would take the city by force if he did not surrender it immediately. He quickly withdrew into the interior. This was fortunate, for "If Caperton had carried out his threat to bombard Santo Domingo City, his action would have shocked all Latin America. Russell had warned the State Department that even the government's forces might turn against the Americans if the capital were attacked." [1] Although there was no resistance in Santo Domingo, the people were hostile and there was resistance elsewhere. Three Marines were killed in one engagement.

The State Department now hoped that the situation would take the course of the earlier one in Haiti, with American troops remaining until the government agreed with Washington's political and financial proposals. But it was more difficult here. The American Minister could not find anyone of stature who would guarantee before election as Provisional President that he would follow Washington's directions. The situation remained chaotic until July, when both Dominican parties and the Americans agreed to ask Archbishop Nouel to serve again as President. He turned them down flat. He had had enough the first time. Then, on July 25, the Congress elected Dr. Francisco Henríquez y Carbajal for a five-month term. Dr. Henríquez also declined to accept the entire American plan, but he was in a hopeless position. The Americans were now withholding both customs and internal revenue receipts and only the presence of U.S. troops kept the government in power.

Washington would not compromise with Henríquez. Further, it was concerned with his successor when the five-month term ended, for it still seemed that any new government would be dominated by Arias. Not only did Washington blame him for most of the troubles—although he was little different from other factional leaders in the past—but he was outspokenly pro-German. This, of course, in 1916, was not likely to endear him to Washington.

As the summer of 1916 wore on the situation got worse. Washington had assumed that withholding funds would force the Dominicans to give in. They did not, however, and the only result was that the United States was blamed for the intolerable economic situation. The population was growing increasingly restive and the American Minister unwisely chose that time to turn the screw a bit tighter. On October 24 the Marines attempted to capture a local leader in the suburbs of Santo Domingo and the struggle resulted in the death of a Marine captain and sergeant. The next day a Marine patrol was attacked and three Dominicans were killed in the fight.

By now Washington saw no way out of the growing dilemma except full-scale military occupation and on November 26 President Wilson gave his approval "with the deepest reluctance . . . convinced it is the least of the evils in sight in this very perplexing situation." On November 29 Captain H. S. Knapp, the new naval commander, proclaimed military occupation with himself as Military Governor.

When the provisional government told Knapp it was considering staying in office to help, he told them they might if they liked but that they would receive neither recognition nor salaries. Thus the Dominicans were denied the dignity of even a nominal government and naval officers took over all the executive departments and were in charge at every level. Even the Congress was suspended.

During the occupation, particularly in early 1917, there was some armed resistance by what the United States, as in Haiti and Nicaragua, called "bandits." Although some aspects of the American occupation have been praised, as we shall see, there was also serious criticism. "The harsh measures taken by some Marine officers during the fighting there, and a few atrocities committed by individual soldiers, gave the Dominican patriotic groups much material for propaganda when they began an organized movement to have the occupation withdrawn." [2] As reports of this nature began to filter back to the United States despite press censorship, there was a public outcry and, later, a Congressional investigation.

> . . . Grave abuses of power by the occupying forces were later uncovered by a congressional investigation in Washington; it revealed rough treatment of citizens, some cases of careless shooting, and more cases of incompetent handling of uncooperative nationals by both officers and men. A few editors who criticized the occupation officials were court-martialled. When a Dominican poet, Fabio Fiallo, was sentenced to jail for denunciation of the United States, indignation was wide-

spread and his case was trumpeted all over Latin America as an instance of American arrogance. Altogether, the American rule of the Dominicans seemed needlessly irritating, and both countries were relieved when it ended.[3]

But while serious criticism of the American occupation was clearly justified, there were achievements too. With the customs and internal revenue spent more wisely, a wide program of public works was made possible. Much was accomplished in public health and, most important, there were vast changes in the Dominican public school system. Buildings were erected, additional teachers were recruited, they were paid much better, and the student enrollment in eight years was raised from 12,000 to more than 100,000. Here, if perhaps nowhere else, the Dominicans approved of the American occupation.

Hostility against the Americans, always present, began to increase toward the end of 1919 and Dominican leaders began a campaign to force an end to the occupation. The campaign was carried on throughout Latin America and the United States. The State Department became alarmed at the growing criticism of the United States at home and abroad and wanted to begin steps to end the occupation, but the Navy, which had complete control, continued to insist that a long occupation was necessary for it to complete its work. It was not until November 1920, when Wilson's second term was almost over, that the State Department was able to get permission to move toward ending the occupation.

It is not surprising that Washington still wanted "reforms" and was prepared to insist that a new Dominican government ratify all that had been done by the military government and accept continued restrictions on national sovereignty. Such proposals were flatly rejected by the Dominicans, who wanted nothing less than complete independence. Hostility between the Dominicans and the Americans on one hand and strained relations between the Navy and State Departments on the other made progress more difficult and little was achieved until 1922. Then President Warren G. Harding sent the able diplomat Sumner Welles, later to gain fame as Franklin D. Roosevelt's Under Secretary of State, to the Dominican Republic. He worked out the withdrawal and arranged for the popular election in which Horacio Vásquez was chosen President. He was inaugurated in 1924 and the Marines left.

Again, the best way to evaluate the American occupation is to examine briefly what has happened since. As in Nicaragua and Haiti, the American intervention, despite undeniable physical accomplishments, did little to foster the real growth of democracy. As in Haiti, momentum from the occupation lasted for some years and it seemed at first that the Dominican Republic was finally to have an era of peace and prosperity. But eventually, perhaps inevitably, the nation's fundamental weaknesses could no longer be denied.

Although Vásquez was fairly competent, he, too, could not resist seeking illegal re-election. As usual a revolution followed, in 1930, and again as in Haiti it was the American-trained and equipped constabulary that dominated the situation. Its leader was Rafael Leonidas Trujillo Molina, a name that has become perhaps the most infamous in Latin-American history. Trujillo brought prosperity and stability to the Dominican Republic but at a frightful cost.

"The republic's serenity has been won by a long-drawn-out purge as thorough as any devised by Stalin or Hitler. Critics of the Benefactor of the Fatherland have been shot in lonely side streets or jailed without trial, or have escaped into exile." [4] It is widely believed, although proof has never been obtained, that Trujillo had his political opponents murdered in Mexico, Puerto Rico, even in the United States. His personal fortune—he had a virtual monopoly on just about every segment of the Dominican economy —was estimated to be in the hundreds of millions and his many relatives were also fantastically rich. He was not reluctant to spend his money to gain favors, particularly in the United States, and many prominent Americans, including Senators and Representatives, were his guests in Ciudad Trujillo, as Santo Domingo had been renamed. Most of them came back to the United States singing Trujillo's praises.

By 1960 it became clear that Trujillo had gone too far. Reports began to multiply of widespread jailings by the secret police, of murder and torture. All through Latin America and the United States, where the government had long looked on indulgently, there was an outcry against Trujillo. But that will be discussed further when we consider the second American intervention, in 1965, which grew out of Trujillo's dictatorship. One of the two chief goals of the first intervention by the United States was to establish an effective constabulary. It was that constabulary, led by the American-trained Trujillo, that enabled the "Benefactor" to take power and rule for three decades with brutality and corruption unsurpassed even in the history of Latin-American dictatorships.

Chapter Fifteen
Epilogue to Dollar Diplomacy

THE AMERICAN MILITARY INTERVENTIONS in Latin America early in this century plus the much more frequent political and financial interference in the domestic affairs of Latin nations inevitably led to widespread suspicion of the United States. From this grew the universal longing to somehow regulate the northern giant. Out of this longing developed the doctrine of non-intervention, a new principle of international law. It developed gradually over decades and was resisted, although politely and with increasingly less vigor, by the United States, until it too was finally ready to concur.

The signal that the United States was about ready to accept the revolutionary principle of non-intervention came on April 14, 1933, when President Franklin D. Roosevelt, shortly after his first inauguration, made the famous Good Neighbor speech. But three years were to pass before the United States finally accepted non-intervention. This historic moment came at the special Inter-American Conference for the Maintenance of Peace, proposed by President Roosevelt, at Buenos Aires in December 1936. The first session was attended by Roosevelt himself. Fresh from the triumph of his landslide re-election, the President arrived in Argentina aboard a battleship to a tumultuous reception. On December 23 the Conference signed two documents: a treaty for the Maintenance, Preservation and Re-establishment of Peace, and an Additional Protocol Relative to Non-Intervention.[1] According to the protocol, the countries declared "inadmissible the intervention of any one of them, directly or indirectly, and for whatever reason, in the internal or external affairs of any other of the Parties."

Thus the United States, only two years after it ended its last military intervention, accepted the principle of nonintervention. Nonetheless, there seemed to some scholars still to be a loophole. The protocol forbade intervention by "any one" country, raising the possibility that joint intervention might be permissible. This, too, will be discussed when we consider the Dominican intervention of 1965.

What then is the final judgment on the American military interventions in Latin America during the first third of this century? First, it must be recognized that the interventions were well meaning, intended for the benefit of the peoples involved as well as for the security of the United States. But many critics of American policy then and now have wondered about the American tendency to believe that it knows better than another nation how that nation should order its domestic affairs. Undeniably there is an American tendency to believe that the American way is the only way, or if not the only way, certainly the best. But in the specific case of "Dollar Diplomacy," perhaps it would be hard to improve on the judgment of Sumner Welles, one of the architects of the second Roosevelt's Good Neighbor Policy:

. . . No aspect of our earlier inter-American policy has done more harm than this to the welfare of the entire hemisphere. The intervention policy not only aroused the suspicion that the United States was bent upon a course of continental imperialism, but has provoked resentments and antagonisms that are still latent now, many years after the adoption of the Good Neighbor Policy. It has done equal harm by retarding the political self-reliance of many of the peoples of these republics. It has all too often checked the growth of a national democracy, forged to meet the individual needs of such people. . . .

Democracy will never be firmly established in any part of the Americas as a result of alien intervention or coercion. It will continue to grow stronger as industrialization increases, as living standards are correspondingly raised, as freedom of information and of expression becomes more secure, and the solidarity of the American Republics becomes more firmly crystallized.[2]

Part IV
INTERVENTION IN LEBANON

INTERVENTION IN LEBANON

Chapter Sixteen

LIKE ALL THE INTERVENTIONS already discussed, the curious one in Lebanon had antecedents long before the event. Most important was the growth of nationalism among the Arabs. Nationalism did not spring up suddenly, but only after the end of the Second World War, when Britain and France began to relinquish their long-time power in the Middle East, was it able to flower. It was heightened by the creation of the State of Israel. Nationalism alone had not been enough to unite the Arabs, who had a long tradition of squabbling among themselves. But the universal and bitter opposition to Israel seemed an even greater unifying force than the Moslem faith. This nationalism served as a vehicle for the pan-Arab enthusiasm of Gamal Abdel Nasser, who took power in Egypt in 1952, almost certainly with the help of the United States Central Intelligence Agency (CIA) in overthrowing the feudal King Farouk.

As British and French power lessened, the United States became increasingly interested, partly because of the vast and vital supply of oil in the Middle East but equally because it feared the growth of Russian influence in the area.

This, briefly, is the chain of events: The early Eisenhower years saw the completion of Secretary of State John Foster Dulles's program for creating a ring of alliances around the Communist world. In 1954 the United States formed the South East Asia Treaty Organization (SEATO), later to play a key role in the increasing American participation in the Vietnamese civil war. And in early 1955 Dulles constructed the Baghdad Pact (Middle East Treaty Organization—METO) with Britain, Turkey, Iran, Iraq, and Pakistan participating. The United States, although not directly a member, was associated with it by a number of bilateral pacts.

Although METO was meant to strengthen American security, it was immediately confronted by some serious problems. The United States regarded the ring of alliances as defensive but Russia and China regarded them as hostile "encirclement," in line with Lenin's prediction of such encirclement by the capitalist nations. Russia promptly declared that the Baghdad Pact was directed against her. On the other hand, the anti-imperialist but non-Communist Arab nations thought that the Baghdad Pact was intended to preserve in power the conservative, feudal, pro-Western monarchies in Iraq, Jordan, and Saudi Arabia. Consequently, the Baghdad Pact contributed to the already great ferment in the volatile Middle East and made Syria and then Egypt receptive to Russian overtures.

Although the United States was committed to Israel, it hoped also to woo the Arab states, even, if possible, to enlist them on the American side in the Cold War. Nasser wanted arms from the West and the United States agreed to sell them but the Communists undercut the American price. John Foster Dulles ventured into this tangle by making a counter-move. He offered to finance a large part of the great Aswan High Dam that Nasser envisioned as his lasting monument, his pyramid. Nasser eagerly accepted, but now Dulles found himself in hot water at home. The strong pro-Israel sentiment in the United States turned against Dulles, and when Nasser ended his recognition of the Chiang Kai-shek regime on Formosa in favor of Mao Tse-tung's Communist government on the mainland, the strong pro-Chiang China Lobby also turned on the Secretary of State.

To make matters worse for Dulles, Egypt decided to purchase its arms from the Communists and the Soviet Union offered to pay for the Aswan Dam. Dulles thought the Soviets were bluffing, that they simply could not afford such an expense. He now decided he could strike a severe blow at Nasser by suddenly, in July 1956, withdrawing the American offer to finance the dam. His decision was evidently based on his famous pronouncement of the month before that neutrality was "an immoral and short-sighted conception." Dulles had decided to switch from wooing Nasser to opposing him.

It was now Nasser's move and he stunned the West by nationalizing the Suez Canal, the great supply line through which passed much of the oil vital to Western Europe. This made Nasser a hero all through the Arab world but it also set the stage for one of the great dramas of the fall of 1956, the attack on the Suez Canal by Britain, France, and Israel.

Britain and France, in their last imperial gasp, decided that Nasser had to be crushed. They found a ready ally in Israel, which saw Nasser as a permanent danger to its survival. On October 29, 1956 Israeli armored columns struck at the Sinai Peninsula and two days later British and French planes began to hit Egypt. In another few days the Canal would have been taken and possibly Nasser would have been toppled, but to the horror of Britain and France Eisenhower came out publicly and flatly against the invasion. Eisenhower and Dulles, no friends of Nasser, simply believed that the invasion was wrong. They may also have been influenced by the fact that the United States was criticizing the Soviet Union for its bloody intervention that same autumn in the rebellion in Hungary. Nikita Khrushchev, perhaps trying to balance the widespread condemnation of his having sent Russian tanks to Budapest, chimed in by rattling Russia's nuclear rockets and the United Nations as a whole was horrified. Britain and France lost their nerve, and Egypt was saved at the very last minute.

Now, for the moment at least, American prestige in the Middle East—except, of course, in Israel—was high, for despite the Russian warnings, it was clear that the United States more than any other nation was responsible for ending the Suez invasion. But this soaring prestige did not last long. Dulles feared that the humiliation of the British and French had caused a power vacuum in the Middle East and that the Russians would hurry to fill it, for, afford it or not, Khrushchev was to carry out his offer to finance the Aswan Dam.

To fill that supposed vacuum the Administration persuaded Congress in early 1957 to pass a blank-check resolution authorizing what came to be known as the Eisen-

hower Doctrine. The resolution empowered the United
States to give economic and even military aid "to secure
and protect the territorial integrity and political independence
of such nations, requesting such aid, against overt armed
aggression from any nation controlled by International
Communism."

What was the response in the Middle East? The Baghdad
Pact members welcomed the Eisenhower Doctrine and the
pro-Western Arab states of Lebanon and Iraq accepted aid.
But they were the only members of the Arab League to do
so. The others—particularly the more militant nations—were
intensely opposed to the Doctrine. They detected no power
vacuum; they saw no Communist menace. What they saw
was a further attempt by the United States to shore up
feudal governments that they wanted overturned.

The Eisenhower Doctrine, therefore, did not win any
new allies for the United States, nor drive any Arab states
toward Russia. What it did was fan the flames of pan-
Arabism and on February 1, 1958 pan-Arabism reached its
high point with the short-lived political union of Egypt
and Syria into the United Arab Republic. This union inspired pan-Arab sentiment to an even higher pitch and the
tone of the Arab radio stations, normally shrill, became
even more violent. Finally the UAR called for the overthrow
of conservative governments wherever they existed in the
Arab world. This ferment took hold in feudal Iraq and even
in stable, sophisticated Lebanon.

By May 1958 a formidable rebellion had broken out in
Lebanon composed of leftists, pan-Arabs, Moslems generally,

and neutralists who were aroused by the government's endorsement of the Eisenhower Doctrine, its pro-Western policies, its Christian Maronite [Lebanese Catholic] and non-Moslem orientation, and the intention of President Camille Chamoun to retain office beyond his stipulated term.[1]

Lebanon is unique in the Arab world. Although it is predominantly an Arab state, it is the only one with a substantial Arab Christian population. In 1958 the Christians were a slight majority though the Moslems were quickly catching up. The political offices were divided by agreement, with Christians serving as president, foreign minister, and commander-in-chief of the army and Moslems as prime minister and speaker of the house. The President in 1958, Camille Chamoun, was pro-Western and it has often been reported that he was working with the CIA to establish Lebanon as a bulwark against Nasser's pan-Arab "positive neutralism." In return he expected the United States to help him stay in power, which required that the Lebanese constitution be amended so he could succeed himself.

By May Lebanon was in turmoil and Chamoun blamed Nasser for the trouble. On May 22 Chamoun called for an urgent meeting of the UN Security Council, accusing the newly formed United Arab Republic of interfering in Lebanon's domestic affairs. Lebanon told the Security Council that the UAR was guilty of:

> . . . the infiltration of armed bands from Syria into Lebanon, the destruction of Lebanese life and property by such bands, the participation of United Arab Republic nationals in acts of terrorism and rebellion against the established authorities in Lebanon, the supply of arms from Syria to individuals and bands in Lebanon rebelling against the established authorities,

and the waging of a violent radio and press campaign in the United Arab Republic calling for strikes, demonstrations and the overthrow of the established authorities in Lebanon, and through other provocative acts.[2]

The Security Council met and the UAR denied the charges, arguing that the disturbances in Lebanon were caused by Chamoun's illegal attempt to succeed himself. On June 11 the Council decided to "dispatch urgently an observation group to proceed to Lebanon so as to ensure that there is no illegal infiltration of personnel or supply of arms or other materiel across the Lebanese borders; . . ."[3]

The observation group consisted of three men of excellent reputation: former President Galo Plaza of Ecuador, Major General Odd Bull of Norway, and Rajeshwar Dayal of India. The UN group made its first report from Beirut on July 1. It did not confirm the Lebanese charges that men and arms were being infiltrated from Syria. The UN group did see bands of rebels with weapons of all kinds originating from many countries, but the group said: "It has not been possible to establish from where these arms were acquired. Nor was it possible to establish if any of the armed men observed had infiltrated from outside; there is little doubt, however, that the vast majority was in any case composed of Lebanese."[4]

Both Lebanon and the United States questioned the validity of the report. It was true, as the UN group affirmed, that the rebels prevented access to some areas and that it would be difficult to determine who were Syrians and who were Lebanese in a country where the frontier was not clearly demarcated and where people from each side carrying arms had always crossed freely. And it was certainly true that the UAR, from both Syria and Egypt, was directing inflammatory broadcasts at Lebanon, but it also seems beyond question that the struggle was civil in nature, with most of the participants Lebanese, whether or not some men and arms crossed into Lebanon from Syria.

Rebel support was widespread, not only in the countryside but from such respectable Lebanese as former President Bi-shara el-Khouri and Patriarch Paul Meouchy. And the army commander, General Fuad Chehab, refused Chamoun's demands that the rebellion be put down by government troops. He regarded the army as the only cohesive force in the nation and he was afraid that it would disintegrate if directed against the rebels, since many soldiers supported the rebels and he himself believed they had legitimate grievances. Therefore, Chehab used troops only to patrol the streets and prevent clashes between Christians and Moslems.

By early July it seemed that the United States might not intervene, although it had been considering intervention for some weeks. The UN reports minimizing UAR intervention made it difficult for the United States to justify sending troops on the basis of outside intervention. But Chamoun, who now never even ventured near a window in the presidential palace for fear of assassination, was in a panic. He wanted United States troops. Still Eisenhower held off, until shocking news arrived from neighboring Iraq. In Baghdad, home of the Middle East Treaty Organization, revolution had broken out on July 14 and the king, the crown prince, and the prime minister were massacred.

Eisenhower and Dulles decided the United States could

wait no longer, that revolutionary forces were on the verge of sweeping across the entire Arab world. The revolution in Iraq, led by Abdul Karim Kassim, was indeed brutal, but the feudal kingdom had for generations allowed its people to languish in neglect and corruption, while revolutionary forces were building up there as elsewhere in the world.

Eisenhower called in congressional leaders, who were cool to American intervention. They saw the turmoil in Lebanon as a civil war and saw no evidence of Communist participation to justify invoking the Eisenhower Doctrine. But Eisenhower cited another provision of the Doctrine, which stated that the independence of the Middle East countries was vital to peace and the national interest of the United States. So without much protest in the United States Eisenhower dispatched 14,000 Marines to Lebanon, a force about twice the size of that tiny nation's army. A few days later Britain sent troops to Jordan to support the rule of King Hussein.

In a message to Congress on July 15, Eisenhower said that the first contingents of Marines were already in Lebanon. He declared that "United States forces are being sent to Lebanon to protect American lives and by their presence to assist the Government of Lebanon in the preservation of Lebanon's territorial integrity and independence, which have been deemed vital to United States national interests and world peace." (See Appendix VII.)

Eisenhower's message also challenged the UN interpretation of events:

> About two months ago a violent insurrection broke out in Lebanon, particularly along the border with Syria, which with

Egypt, forms the United Arab Republic. This revolt was encouraged and strongly backed by the official Cairo, Damascus, and Soviet radios, which broadcast to Lebanon in the Arabic language. The insurrection was further supported by sizable amounts of arms, ammunition, and money and by personnel infiltrated from Syria to fight against the lawful authorities. The avowed purpose of these activities was to overthrow the legally constituted Government of Lebanon and to install by violence a government which would subordinate the independence of Lebanon to the policies of the United Arab Republic.

And Eisenhower made a connection between the American intervention in Lebanon and the revolution in Iraq:

We share with the Government of Lebanon the view that these events in Iraq demonstrate a ruthlessness of aggressive purpose which tiny Lebanon cannot combat without further evidence of support from other friendly nations.

It was a curious intervention. According to a New York Times reporter on the scene in Beirut, the first contingents of Marines were received by the populace "like a circus coming to town." As they waded ashore in full battle dress, Lebanese waved at them cheerfully and, reportedly, tried to sell them souvenirs. The Marines moved inland and occupied the international airport just outside Beirut. As they reached full strength, they took positions around the capital, but during their four-month stay hardly a shot was fired. One Marine captain told a Newsweek correspondent that "All we do is sit for a couple of days, then move to another place to sit some more."

The Marines were sent to Lebanon to bolster the government of President Chamoun but they scrupulously refrained from any participation in the civil war. Indeed, their presence seemed to handicap rather than help Chamoun. Many influential Lebanese who had not supported the rebels protested the American intervention and a New York *Times* political analyst on the scene wrote that the Marines "served in a curious way to weaken friends of the United States and strengthen the Lebanese Opposition, which continues both its armed insurrection and its economic strike. . . . It is the Lebanese Government, which called for entry of United States forces, that is subject to the greatest pressures to make compromises."[5]

Shortly after the American troops landed, Eisenhower sent to Beirut the experienced diplomatic trouble-shooter Robert Murphy, then a deputy under secretary of state. He found Chamoun, who had not left the presidential palace for weeks, completely out of touch with the situation and beyond saving. Murphy then became a mediator, not a partisan, and was pleased when various factions agreed on General Chehab as successor to Chamoun. Chehab was elected by the Lebanese Parliament by 48 to 8 on July 31, just a couple of weeks after the first American troops landed.

Gradually, the fighting died down, although there were sporadic outbreaks, and on September 24 President Chehab announced that a former rebel leader, Rashid Karami, had been appointed premier. At the United Nations the Arab states agreed to a compromise resolution in the General Assembly by which foreign troops were to be withdrawn from Lebanon and Jordan and under which the Arab nations pledged not to interfere in the domestic affairs of their neighbors. The last American Marines left on October 25 and on December 10 Premier Karami said that Lebanon had returned to its traditional policy of neutrality and that it was no longer bound by the terms of the Eisenhower Doctrine.

What can be said about the American intervention in Lebanon? For one thing, it was superficial compared to the interventions discussed earlier and those that were to follow in Vietnam and the Dominican Republic. Also there was comparatively little protest within the United States; certainly far, far less than would have followed such an action ten, or even five, years later. Clearly the people and the Congress were still prepared to accept with only scattered criticism even such extreme actions by their government. The skepticism that was to greet many of the foreign policy moves of Presidents Kennedy, Johnson, and Nixon had yet to develop.

Despite the intervention, President Chamoun was not able to retain power and Lebanon soon thereafter moved out of the Western camp to a position of neutrality, although it has remained friendly. But both these developments were probably inevitable in view of the Arab nationalism sweeping the Middle East. Eisenhower's intervention probably had little effect on either development, nor did it severely damage American-Lebanese relations. However, it did open the United States to much criticism even by friendly nations, who wondered aloud why the United States felt itself required to intervene in a civil war against the revolutionary forces that were surfacing all over the world. And the intervention did antagonize the most militant Arab states and turn them more toward the Soviet Union, but perhaps American support of Israel would have done that anyway.

Defenders of Eisenhower's intervention argue that it prevented Lebanon and Jordan from being swallowed up by the revolution that began in Iraq. That may well be so, although it is impossible of proof one way or the other. The substance of the criticism of the intervention is well summarized by these extracts from an article by the well-known analyst Vera Micheles Dean that appeared in the *Foreign Policy Bulletin* of August 15, 1958:

> The United States, because of its emphasis on defense of the non-Communist world against the Communist powers, the U.S.S.R. and Communist China, has put itself in the position of seeming to defend the *status quo* in areas of the world where the continuance of present conditions or present relations with the West are increasingly regarded as intolerable. . . . It has thus dissipated, critics declare, the store of good will and admiration formerly inspired by its traditional anticolonial policy and revived by its policy toward Britain and France during the Suez crisis of 1956.
>
> The United States has made a mistake in talking about the "vacuum" in the Middle East, which is obviously inhabited by populations that for years have been struggling to escape first from the domination of the Ottoman Empire and then from British and French rule under League of Nations mandate during the interwar years. The use of this term arouses resentment among Arab nationalists.
>
> The United States and Britain have acted in the Middle East on the assumption that the U.S.S.R., although admittedly also a great power—and one which is geographically far closer to the area than the Western nations—must be and can be "kept out." This assumption Middle Eastern experts consider as entirely unrealistic. . . .[6]

Although the armed intervention in Lebanon was more superficial than those that preceded it and those that were to follow, it does demonstrate that Eisenhower, no less than every other American president since World War II, was willing to commit troops abroad if he thought events in some foreign land threatened national security. But critics argue that it is difficult to see how American security was threatened in tiny and far-distant Lebanon and that such interventions put the United States on the losing side—the side of the counter-revolutionaries in a revolutionary age.

Part V
AGAIN THE DOMINICAN REPUBLIC

AGAIN THE DOMINICAN REPUBLIC

Chapter Seventeen

ALTHOUGH THE SECOND American armed intervention in the Dominican Republic took place a half century after the first, the two were directly related. The first intervention was followed by the seizure of power by Rafael Trujillo. He had stood high in favor with the Marine officers who established the Guardia Nacional to enforce law and order in the chaotic little nation. Trujillo had soon seized control of the guard and within six years of the Americans' departure in 1924, he was unchallenged master of the land. He began a thirty-year reign of terror so brutal as to be beyond comprehension. For most of that time he had the tacit, often active, support of the United States government. Trujillo knew the value of American support and spent lavishly to ensure it. Visiting Senators and Representatives were entertained royally and it was an open secret that Trujillo made handsome bribes to Americans at influential levels.

But in the last few years of his life, Trujillo's excesses extended beyond his own land and when he tried to have Venezuela's President Rómulo Betancourt assassinated, he went too far for the other Latin nations. Betancourt had supported Dominican liberals who wanted to overthrow Trujillo. The liberals were also backed by the new leader of Cuba, Fidel Castro, who sponsored an invasion of the Dominican Republic by exiles on June 14, 1959.

Trujillo responded with a wave of repression so cruel— even by his own barbaric standards—that he lost the long-time support of the Dominican Catholic Church. Outside the country the Organization of American States (OAS) met and unanimously imposed sanctions. And despite the efforts of his supporters in the United States, Washington broke diplomatic relations in August 1960.

The dictator's end was not far off. It came on a lonely country road on the night of May 30, 1961. Trujillo and his chauffeur were hurrying through the night when their car was overtaken by another with four armed men inside. They fired through the windows with pistol, carbine, and shotgun. The dictator's limousine lurched to a stop, Trujillo staggered out and was cut down for good by another fusillade. His life was over but not the reign of terror, for his son, Ramfis, and his brothers traced down the plotters, torturing and then killing eighteen of the twenty. Of the four assassins only two survived, Luis Amiama Tío and Antonio Imbert Barreras, who was to play a major role during the months when American troops occupied the capital city of Santo Domingo. Although the killers were hailed as heroes, it is not certain whether they were motivated by a patriotic conviction that the tyrant could be removed only by death or by personal considerations of fear, jealousy, and hatred.

Ramfis Trujillo ran the country behind the facade of Joaquín Balaguer, who had been his father's puppet President.

But Ramfis had neither his father's ability nor his determination and, even more important, there was a new American President. John F. Kennedy was determined that American support would go to democracies in Latin America and not to the dictatorships routinely supported by Washington in the past. He sent a study team to Santo Domingo, but was convinced by their report that anti-Communist liberals were not yet strong enough to form a government. So Kennedy decided to support Balaguer and use United States influence to lead Balaguer toward democracy.

The situation was, of course, chaotic after three decades of one-man rule, but the anti-Trujillo forces would support Balaguer only if Ramfis Trujillo followed his uncles into exile. He was fed up anyway with the chore of running a nation and was eager to return to his play-boy existence in Europe, well financed by the funds the Trujillos had been extracting from the family-dominated national economy. However, just before leaving he telephoned his uncles in Bermuda and advised them to come back and take over. They in turn called their supporters in the Dominican armed forces and it appeared that Balaguer would be overthrown in a pro-Trujillo coup. But Kennedy supported Balaguer by sending eight ships, with eighteen hundred Marines aboard, which anchored just offshore. Now the military rediscovered their loyalty to Balaguer, and the Trujillo uncles, who had come back to Santo Domingo, returned to exile.

American support, however, was not enough to keep Balaguer in power and he was soon toppled by widespread riots, and fled into exile. Kennedy poured American resources into the Dominican Republic and during 1962 the "American presence in the Dominican Republic . . . com-

pletely dominated the politics and the economy of the un-
happy island."[1] John Bartlow Martin, a political writer and
close associate of UN Ambassador Adlai Stevenson, was
sent to Santo Domingo as Ambassador. His primary concern was to prevent a Communist takeover, although he
recognized that there were very few Communists in the
Dominican Republic and that the main threat to the nation
was posed by the right-wing military. Nonetheless, American policy was largely determined as a deterrent to Communism. Needless to say, the old rich families and the
generals forever harped on the "Communist menace."

The new president was Rafael Bonnelly, the head of the
police under Trujillo, and there were three main parties
contending for control: the conservative Unión Cívica
Nacional (UCN) with largely upper- and middle-class
support; the Fourteenth of June Movement, a nationalist
group with some revolutionary elements; and the Partido
Revolucionario Dominicano (PRD), a liberal, reformist
party headed by the exiled writer Juan Bosch and popular
with the lower classes. There were also about a hundred
"well-trained, fully-committed, and fully-disciplined"[2] Communists. Although they received minor amounts of money
and arms from abroad, they were divided into three quarreling groups: one Moscow-oriented, another Peking-oriented,
the third including members of the Fourteenth of June
Movement.

The military leaders, in the Latin-American tradition, kept
arguing that mass repression would solve the Dominican
problems. "Despite the fact that there was no organized
Communist or leftist guerilla movement and that the
military continually pressed for purges, coups, reprisals,

and mass arrests, the programs which the United States launched made the Communists the exclusive target and the military the chief beneficiaries."[3]

Notwithstanding the powerful American presence, political unrest continued and there were threats of insurrection from both the right and the left. But the United States was able to keep Bonnelly in office until the elections of December 20, 1962. They were won handily by the returned exile Juan Bosch, a writer and political scientist, who got 62 percent of the vote, largely on the strength of his promise of social reform, something badly needed after three decades of Trujillo. A close friend of many leading Latin-American democratic reformers, Bosch was attacked during the campaign by the UCN as a supporter of Trujillo, an unlikely charge since he had been exiled for twenty-four years and had carried on anti-Trujillo work during much of that time. Then the conservative UCN attacked him for being friendly toward Communism, although he had long been an anti-Communist and had cleaned them out of his PRD when he returned to Santo Domingo in late 1961.

Whatever reservations the Kennedy Administration might have had about Bosch were submerged and Vice President Lyndon B. Johnson went to the inauguration on February 27, 1963 as Kennedy's representative and was photographed embracing the handsome Bosch. The Dominicans rejoiced, for now they had the first democratic government since immediately (and briefly) after the first American intervention ended in 1924. But this new experiment in democracy was not to be long-lived. Bosch did begin a program of social reform, but it was an uneven program. Some of his cabinet appointments were questionable, as were some of his policies, and, perhaps most important, he angered the rich conservatives and the military.

Then, inevitably, Bosch came under attack on the grounds that he was harboring or protecting Communists. Although no proof was ever offered by anyone that Dr. Bosch actually favored Communists or had brought any of them into his Government on any level, the opposition press, radio and television, the military hierarchy and the leaders of rightist groups began a powerful and well-financed campaign to make it appear that Dr. Bosch was at best a dupe of the Communists. He was blamed for not exiling Communists or suspected Communists and for allowing other Communists to re-enter the Dominican Republic. But it was forgotten that Bosch—as a democratic social reformer—was also the target of furious attacks from Fidel Castro's Cuba.

The argument of this independent-minded President was that a democratic society had to take a risk with its enemies and try to defeat them politically—through improving democratic institutions and living standards—instead of applying police methods that in a country as sensitive as the Dominican Republic could easily become reminiscent of the Trujillo rule. In any event, as Bosch pointed out, the rightist Council of State Government that had preceded his own regime was quite generous in letting Communists organize and freely enter the country.[4]

Not only were the rightists and the military aligned against Bosch, but many of the American officials were too. They thought that Bosch was not ready enough to follow American advice and that he was not tough enough on the Communists, although, as noted earlier, there weren't many militant Communists in the country. And the many United States military attachés were plainly sympathetic with the Dominican military.

Bosch's political end came on September 25, 1963, only

seven months after he took office. He was overthrown by an army coup led by Colonel Elías Wessín y Wessín, whom Bosch had tried to oust for attempting an earlier coup. Although the Kennedy Administration had not been very impressed by Bosch and although it had made little effort to keep him in power, it was upset, for it genuinely supported the concept of a democratic reform government. Thus it quickly broke diplomatic relations and cut off military and economic aid. But when Ambassador Martin returned to Washington, Kennedy said to him, "I take it we don't want Bosch back." "No," Martin replied, "he isn't a President."[5] That might well have been so, for Bosch had demonstrated some weaknesses as President. Yet seven months did not seem a fair test in a country that had been in chaos. And he had been democratically elected by a substantial majority. Neither of these considerations seemed to trouble the United States then or later.

Events in the Dominican Republic might have taken a different turn if President Kennedy had not been assassinated in Dallas less than two months later. Within three weeks of his taking office, Lyndon Johnson resumed diplomatic relations with the Dominican Republic, now headed by Donald Reid Cabral, who ruled in collaboration with the military. Johnson also appointed, as Assistant Secretary of State for Latin-American affairs, Thomas Mann, who had been in charge of Latin-American policy under President Eisenhower. Mann was one of Washington's leading hard-line anti-Communists, a believer in the development of Latin America by private investment, and a supporter of right-wing military juntas because they were tough on Communists.

But even though Reid Cabral tried industriously to promote progress in the Dominican Republic, he, too, was unable to cling to that uneasy seat of power. He was opposed, on the one hand, by Bosch supporters who wanted the President and constitutional government restored and, on the other, by the military. Reid Cabral had lost military support when he tried to cut the bloated armed forces budget, which accounted for thirty-eight percent of the national budget.

These two movements surfaced in rapid succession on Saturday, April 24, 1965. That day residents of Santo Domingo heard over a small commercial radio station that the Reid Cabral government had been overthrown, and they responded with joy. But the announcement was premature. It was not until several hours later that a group of military and civilian rebels captured Radio Santo Domingo, the government radio station. They took to the air to announce that a revolution to return Bosch to power had begun. At the same time the military rebels seized two barracks near the capital city. And in the city itself cheering crowds clashed with police.

At first the American Embassy, and thus Washington, did not think much was up. It was reported that loyalist troops had recaptured Radio Santo Domingo and that President Reid Cabral had issued an ultimatum, ordering the rebels to surrender by five that afternoon or be crushed by loyalist troops. But the Embassy was poorly informed, as it proved to be throughout the first weeks of the crisis. Even though it had a big political staff, a Central Intelligence Agency (CIA) unit, and military attachés presumably in constant touch with the Dominican military, the Embassy was totally surprised. The Ambassador, W. Tapley Bennett

Jr., had left the day before for a visit to his family and to Washington and eleven of the thirteen members of the Military Assistance Advisory Group had gone to Panama for a routine conference. Though there had been reports that the military might try to overthrow Reid Cabral that weekend, the Embassy had dismissed them as nothing more than rumors.

The Chargé d'Affaires, William B. Connett Jr., who had been in Santo Domingo less than six months, reported to Washington that the revolution seemed to be fizzling. The rebels had not surrendered by five that afternoon, but Reid Cabral had announced that the situation was in hand and he extended the ultimatum until six the next morning. However, the revolution was just beginning. The rebels still held as hostages the army chief of staff, Brigadier General Marco Rivera Cuesta, and his deputy, Colonel Maximiliano Américo Ruiz Batista. And they were calling on sympathizers in other military units. Younger officers, supporters of Bosch and the constitution, were rising against the older officers who had been prominent under Trujillo.

Now the other side struck Reid Cabral. The "loyalist" officers refused his order to attack the rebels and they put pressure on him to resign. He agreed to do so by Sunday morning, the 25th, and the military planned to establish a junta that would hold elections later in the year. But the younger officers enraged the older by opposing a junta and pressing for the immediate restoration of constitutional government under Bosch, who was in exile in nearby San Juan, Puerto Rico.

In the meantime, the pro-Bosch rebels installed as Pro-

visional President José Rafael Molina Ureña. Under the 1963
constitution he was, as president of the Chamber of Depu-
ties, next in line for the presidency in the absence of the
president, the vice president, and the president of the Senate.
But Bosch, by telephone from San Juan, seemed fully in
command of the revolution and expected to return to
Santo Domingo in triumph that day or the next.

Bosch's optimism was at best premature. The loyalist
generals decided to strike back. Wessín y Wessín, now a
brigadier general, sent planes to bomb and strafe the Presidential Palace where Molina Ureña had established himself.
Other planes from the San Isidro Air Force Base hit one
of the rebel barracks. The situation was chaotic and growing
more so every minute. The rebels opened the armories to
civilians, who took everything from pistols to machine guns.
Soon rebel bands, both military and civilian, were firing at
the Wessín forces, and Wessín's planes were bombing and
strafing the streets. And filling stations were giving gaso-
line away for Molotov cocktails so the people could defend
themselves against the expected attacks by Wessín's tanks.

By this time the American Embassy decided that something was indeed up and it reached a conclusion absolutely
basic to the incredible situation that developed: that the
return of Bosch would mean Communism in the Dominican Republic in six months and the United States troops
might, and probably would, have to be used to support
Wessín's forces to stop the pro-Bosch rebellion. This conclusion has been documented beyond question by journalists
who have had access to government cables. Thus the United
States Embassy had decided to ally itself with the right-

wing military in opposition to those supporting the return of the democratically elected Bosch.

It is not entirely clear why the United States Embassy reached this conclusion. One reason might be that Ambassador Bennett and most of his staff shared the belief of the American government in general that Communism was an active threat in the Dominican Republic and in most of Latin America. This was so despite the fact that the Embassy knew there were only a few militant Communists and that they were weak and divided. The United States evidently feared—and this soon became evident—that even a few Communists could dominate a widespread rebellion. Further, Ambassador Bennett, during his thirteen months in Santo Domingo, had almost exclusively confined his contacts to the Reid Cabral government, to the business and land-owning groups, and to some of the military officers supporting Reid Cabral. He evidently had had little or no contact with either the democratic, constitutional people in Bosch's PRD or the more extreme groups, which made up the opposition. It does seem certain, however, that the Embassy immediately dismissed the revolutionaries as leftists, made no real attempts to have contact with them, and clearly made no attempt to see that the revolutionary movement retained its democratic character. Nor did the United States in the first days get in touch with Bosch, for whatever reason, even to seek information.

Washington was receptive to the Embassy's alarm about Bosch and immediately began to discuss the possibility of military intervention. This was before the character of the revolution had become at all clear and before there was any expressed fear for American lives in Santo Domingo. By Monday, April 26, the situation had become even more confused. The rebels controlled most of the city, although the loyalists held a couple of isolated strong points. The only slogans broadcast by the rebels over radio and television were pro-Constitution and pro-Bosch, yet the Embassy people listening began to feel that the broadcasts sounded like those from Cuba in the first few days after Castro took over Havana. Nonetheless, though there was still no visible evidence of Communist leadership in the revolution, the Embassy had already made its choice. American military attachés were at General Wessín's headquarters at San Isidro, relaying requests for assistance. And even while the Embassy was reporting that the revolution had to be stopped, the Johnson Administration in Washington was proclaiming strict neutrality.

Wessín forces, spearheaded by tanks, tried to force their way across the Duarte bridge and into the city proper, but they were stalled by military and civilian rebels armed with all kinds of weapons, including homemade Molotov cocktails. A stalemate seemed to be developing, although the loyalist forces were largely confined to the San Isidro base and a couple of other strongholds, while the rebels had the run of the city. The rest of the country, although, as journalists later reported, apparently sympathetic to the rebels, seemed to be waiting to see who won. After thirty years of Trujillo the Dominicans tended to be cautious, the actual rebels excepted, of course.

Some have argued that Bosch might have tilted the balance in his favor if he had immediately flown to the Dominican Republic. Both the civilian and military airfields in

Santo Domingo were under loyalist control, but it was suggested he could have flown to another city in the Dominican Republic and then driven to the capital. He refused to try. However, since journalists who were frantic to get to the island could find no way to do so until the American military provided transportation, Bosch probably could not have gotten there either.

In Washington the Johnson Administration was deeply concerned and was considering simultaneously both a quick evacuation of Americans and other foreigners who might be threatened and a full-scale military intervention. The American fleet in the Caribbean was alerted to move closer to the Dominican Republic, a routine precaution, but the Administration went beyond that and began to alert Marine and Army units in the United States. Soon the Administration decided on an evacuation and both sides in the civil war agreed not to interfere. Evacuees began to congregate at the Hotel Embajador in the western residential area of the city. Helicopters were to take them out to waiting American ships on Tuesday, the 27th.

By Tuesday the military situation was developing further. The Wessín forces still were unable to break into the city proper, but the Navy, thought to be with the rebels, joined the loyalists and began bombarding rebel positions. Some Navy men, particularly the elite frogman unit, were with the rebels but the bulk of the tiny Navy joined the air force in sticking with Wessín. The United States Embassy had been concerned about this and naval attachés had been trying to persuade the Dominican naval commander to at least remain neutral.

Meanwhile the evacuees were gathering at the Embajador,

miles from the fighting and less than a mile from the shore. Marine helicopters arrived with unarmed communications teams who set up not only at the hotel and the American Embassy but at General Wessín's headquarters as well.

At the hotel there was an incident that added to President Johnson's concern. A group of rebels—some civilian, some military—somehow materialized at the hotel and said they were looking for counter-revolutionaries. The situation was, of course, confused—as was almost everything in Santo Domingo those days—and there was an exchange of fire between the rebels and someone up on one of the balconies. It is uncertain who began the firing. Then the rebels lined people up against the lobby walls and, for some reason, fired several bursts of machine-gun fire into the ceiling before leaving. No one was hurt, but the Embassy must have sent a vivid report, for some time later President Johnson spoke about rebels running up and down the hotel corridors, firing wildly into rooms and closets. No such thing happened. President Johnson and other Americans were also to speak later of mass murders by the rebels and the bearing of severed heads on pikes through the city streets. This, too, was not so, but it was this kind of information on which Johnson was basing his decision to intervene.

That Tuesday Ambassador Bennett arrived from the United States and immediately cabled Washington requesting communications equipment for Wessín. He said such equipment could mean the difference between victory and defeat. But that afternoon it seemed that the rebel cause was fast fading. Wessín's tanks were beginning to make some progress and were firing at the rebels at point-blank range.

Even more ominous to the rebels was the news that an army regiment from San Cristóbal, fifteen miles away, had driven to Santo Domingo and was prepared to enter battle on the side of Wessín. It now seemed that the rebels were going to lose.

About four o'clock in the afternoon, eight or nine rebels appeared at the United States Embassy and asked to see Ambassador Bennett. They were shown into his private office, after first checking their weapons, and said that there had been enough bloodshed. According to Bennett's account, they asked him to mediate with Wessín. He said he had no authority to negotiate or mediate but would pass on to Wessín any proposals they cared to make.

They went off and came back in about an hour, a larger group now, including Provisional President Molina Ureña and Colonel Francisco Caamaño Deño, a young officer who now headed the rebel forces. Again they checked their weapons with the Marine guard and trooped into the Ambassador's spacious office. The accounts of the second meeting vary widely. Bennett says he repeated what he said earlier about not being able to mediate or negotiate. However, Caamaño insists that Bennett arrogantly told the rebels to surrender. Bennett denies this as well as the charge that he insulted the rebel leaders. Whatever happened, Caamaño evidently felt he had been insulted and stormed out of the meeting, proclaiming: "Let me tell you, we shall go on fighting no matter what happens."

The revolution had apparently collapsed and news to that effect was flashed around the world. But the news was wrong. Somehow the rebels regrouped during the late afternoon and night; by Wednesday morning they were fighting with more determination than ever. Those who argue that the Communists played a major role in the revolution say that only determined Communists could have pulled the rebels together. And the Embassy reported that leftists and Communists were in the rebel command. However, neither the Embassy nor the CIA was able to name any such persons. There were, of course, Communists in the revolution, but according to all the evidence they were not influential at the command level, where the rebel leaders were clearly identifiable.

By Wednesday the rebels had reorganized their defense and almost all of Santo Domingo was under their control, including the utilities, the power plant, the telephone exchange, and just about everything else. And the rebels had captured at least twelve tanks. Meanwhile a junta had been formed at San Isidro. Because Wessín was hated by the rebels and was unpopular with many other Dominicans as well, his name was kept out of it. A little-known air-force colonel, Pedro Bartolomé Benoit, was picked as its president, although Wessín was still clearly the force behind it. "This junta, of course, was a government on paper only. It functioned at the San Isidro Air Force Base but it had no control over the Dominican capital and presumably none over the rest of the country, where military commands and the people at large seemed to be awaiting the outcome of the struggle in Santo Domingo before choosing sides."[6]

The United States decided it would be too much of a political risk to recognize the junta as the Dominican government, but it proceeded to deal with it as if it were. The junta decreed martial law over the city, although it was powerless to enforce it, and it began to broadcast orders to the rebels to surrender or be destroyed. This was a fairly imaginative act since the rebels were on the offensive.

The Embassy's optimism of twenty-four hours earlier had turned to bleak pessimism and Bennett, in cables to Washington, was talking about the possibility of a military intervention. Even before the junta formally requested intervention, Marines had landed on the beach near the port of Haina to scout it for amphibious operations.

By mid-afternoon on Wednesday, the 28th, Benoit had sent to Bennett a formal note, saying "We ask you for a temporary intervention and for assistance in restoring order." This was the basis on which the intervention was to be made, with the United States asserting that the "authorities" had requested such an intervention. These "authorities," however, controlled only the air base and a couple of other strong points. The rest of the city and the public facilities were controlled by the rebels.

After getting the note, Bennett telephoned President Johnson, telling him that the situation was out of hand. Somehow Johnson got the idea that while Bennett was on the phone he and his secretary were crouched under their desks seeking refuge from heavy machine-gun fire. However the President got this impression, it was one more example of the inaccurate, exaggerated, and melodramatic intelligence upon which the Administration based its decision to intervene. But Embassy officials later confirmed that the building had never been fired on by machine guns. Nor were there any bullet marks on the Embassy walls despite the frequent sniper fire in the area.

Chapter Eighteen

ON WEDNESDAY AFTERNOON, April 28, President Johnson made the decision he had been considering for some days: American Marines would again land in the Dominican Republic. Later that day Johnson went on television to tell the nation that

> The United States Government has been informed by military authorities in the Dominican Republic that American lives are in danger. These authorities are no longer able to guarantee their safety and they reported that the assistance of military personnel is now needed for that purpose. I've ordered the Secretary of Defense to put the necessary American troops ashore in order to give protection to hundreds of Americans who are still in the Dominican Republic and to escort them safely back to this country. . . . Four hundred Marines have already landed. (See Appendix VIII.)

There was no mention of Communism, although the evidence is incontrovertible that a fear of even the possibility of "another Cuba" was the overriding reason for the intervention. That is not to say, however, that there was not genuine concern about the lives of Americans in Santo Domingo.

The United States hastened to get OAS (Organization of American States) approval and Ambassador Adlai Stevenson informed the UN Security Council that American troops had gone to the Dominican Republic to "protect American citizens." But much of the rest of the world was not convinced and the American landings were harshly criticized at home and abroad. The focus of this criticism was the UN Security Council, which met frequently on the issue for weeks. The United States tried—vainly—to keep the UN completely out of the crisis, recognizing that most UN members were strongly opposed to the American intervention.

And although the United States went to the OAS, it did so only after it had already begun the intervention. The OAS finally supported the action of the United States, but without enthusiasm, and several of the most important Latin countries (Argentina, Chile, and Mexico) were among those against the United States intervention, which was, after all, a violation of the non-intervention treaty signed by the United States in 1936. But perhaps the United States believed that by getting OAS approval, even after the fact, it was not guilty of unilateral intervention.

By Thursday, the 29th, American Marines were pouring ashore. Despite the fact that the United States was publicly neutral, the Marines immediately began to supply the Wessín forces at San Isidro. They were out of food and their water and power supply had been cut off by the rebels. More significant, American troops interposed themselves between the rebels and the loyalists. There seemed little doubt that the loyalists, out of supplies and dispirited, were saved by the American intervention.

The American press began to descend on Santo Domingo and the Embassy immediately tried to convince them of the Communist character of the rebellion. The correspondents were given a list of fifty-three Communists and fellow travelers allegedly active in the revolution. This list became famous, to the acute embarrassment of the Johnson Administration, for it soon turned out that the list weakened rather than strengthened the United States argument. The

Embassy didn't know that any of them had actually appeared in high-level positions in the rebel command but suggested that probably they had succeeded in concealing their influence. Then it turned out that some of the people on the list were not Communists at all, and that several of them weren't even in the country when the revolution broke out. "In general then, the list was more of a catalogue of the names of Communists and pro-Communists than a compilation of leftist extremists who might have been active among the rebels."[1] Most of the "evidence" of Communist influence on the revolution was even less concrete than that.

To add impact to his report, Ambassador Bennett told the newsmen of rebel atrocities:

> Mr. Bennett told us that rebels had severed the heads of Wessín's soldiers and policemen they had killed and had paraded the heads on pikes in downtown Santo Domingo. With indignation the Ambassador went on to tell us of mass executions by the rebels of their enemies. He said Colonel Caamaño had personally executed a Colonel Calderón, who had been aide-de-camp to ousted President Reid Cabral. He reminisced over his pleasant acquaintanceship with Colonel Calderón and expressed his revulsion over the alleged killing of Calderón in cold blood by the rebel chief.[2]

The correspondents, not conceiving that an Ambassador would tell such stories without verification, sent reports of these "atrocities" only to find out later that the rebels had done none of these things. There were some mass executions, to be sure, but an OAS investigation determined that they were done by junta forces and not by the rebels.

In Washington President Johnson was taking a similar

line. He again went before a nationwide television audience but this time, May 2, he advanced another reason for the American intervention. (See Appendix VIII.) He declared that intervention was necessary because "a band of Communist conspirators" was taking control of what had begun as a "popular democratic revolution." His arguments were perplexing. On the one hand, reputable American correspondents on the scene were reporting that the United States forces were actively aiding Wessín's forces, yet Johnson declared that "The form and nature of a free Dominican government, I assure you, is solely a matter for the Dominican Republic. . . . And neither we nor any other nation in this hemisphere can or should take it upon itself to ever interfere with the affairs of your country, or any other country."

On Friday the rebels were still gaining, having captured the last of Wessín's enclaves in rebel territory. But before they could attempt a final assault on San Isidro, American troops engaged the rebels in combat and in heavy fighting captured the Duarte bridge and several blocks on the rebel side. This was not the last time the United States troops would help the junta. Soon they established an international security zone that cut the rebel area in half and later the American military allowed junta forces to travel freely through American lines—even during a cease-fire—while blocking the rebels. And several times they allowed the junta to launch attacks while preventing the rebels from doing so. Perhaps not surprisingly the American military got on well with the Dominican generals, at the same time hardly bothering to hide their contempt for the rebels.

On Friday, April 30th, John Bartlow Martin was back in

Santo Domingo at President Johnson's urgent request. He, too, was soon convinced—in less than two days—that the revolution was Communist-dominated and he stuck to his belief even though correspondents spent days looking for such evidence and were unable to find it. Further, many opponents of the revolution told correspondents that although there were some Communists in the movement, they did not dominate it. And many thought that the United States was actually helping the Communists by antagonizing the democratic elements in the revolution.

Martin set about trying to establish a government acceptable to Washington. He turned to an old acquaintance, Antonio Imbert Barreras, one of Trujillo's assassins. Though for a brief period he had been hailed as a hero, Imbert did not have a good reputation. He was regarded by many as over-ambitious, unreliable, and unscrupulous. Yet Martin thought he would do for the time being and on May 7 Imbert was sworn in as the President of the Government of National Reconstruction. Earlier Colonel Caamaño had been sworn in as the Constitutional President, Bosch waiving his claim.

The situation, for a fortnight almost incomprehensible, became even more confused. The United States gave money to the Imbert regime to pay governmental salaries (although most of Santo Domingo was in rebel hands) at the same time that Imbert was attempting to violate the cease-fire that had so painfully been established. Dominicans who had welcomed the American troops were becoming openly critical of the United States support for the junta and anti-Americanism was rising. The press and the Embassy grew increasingly hostile because correspondents were filing stories that flatly contradicted what the American government was saying in Santo Domingo and Washington. There were frequent exchanges of fire between the American troops and the rebels, usually started by the angry rebels. Within the American government there was a furious policy struggle between the anti-Communist hard-liners and those who wanted to work out a compromise between the Dominican adversaries. Tad Szulc in his splendid *Dominican Diary* wrote that his New York *Times* colleague, Marty Arnold, may have offered the best explanation: "You know, I think that none of this is happening. I think that all this is one great insane asylum and all of us are the inmates."

Such an explanation was tempting, for the OAS and the UN and the Papal Nuncio were all involved in compromise efforts, each working separately. President Johnson had sent down more high-powered men: Presidential Assistant McGeorge Bundy; Thomas Mann, now Under Secretary of State; Assistant Secretary Jack Hood Vaughn; and Deputy Defense Secretary Cyrus Vance. Later Ellsworth Bunker went down as the head of an OAS mission.

Bundy seemed to have the best understanding of what the revolution was all about and he sought a civilian of stature who could become Provisional President until elections could be held. He settled on Silvestre Antonio Guzmán, a non-political man of reputation, a wealthy and skilled plantation owner who had served Bosch as Minister of Agriculture. As negotiations continued, the rebels accepted the idea because it would mean a constitutional solution to the impasse—what they had sought all along. When Bundy told Imbert it was about time for him to resign so civilians could run the government again, he was furious. He decided to try to present the Americans with a *fait accompli* and the junta forces moved against the rebels, with correspondents reporting that junta tanks were firing indiscriminately at rebel soldiers and civilians alike. It was now mid-May and the United States faced a peculiar situation. A high-ranking government official, McGeorge Bundy, was trying to arrange a civilian government, at the same time as the American military were helping the man who had been put into power by the Americans sabotage the negotiations. Hundreds were being killed and wounded—mainly innocent civilians—and the UN representative, José Antonio Mayobre of Venezuela, was trying desperately to get a temporary cease-fire so the dead and wounded could be collected from the streets.

Even while Bundy was trying to establish Guzmán, believing this to be the best way to end the civil war, opposing views in Washington, evidently those of Thomas Mann, were beginning to prevail. The hard-liners wanted to allow Imbert to finish off the rebels, with the possibility that he might be permitted to stay in power. However, after several days of stalling, Imbert agreed to a temporary truce for humanitarian reasons. This was on May 20. Also by now there had been many press reports indicating that the United States was directly or indirectly helping the Imbert forces, despite the proclaimed policy of neutrality, and these reports began to embarrass the Administration. Perhaps for that reason President Johnson instructed the American military commander not to permit Imbert to press his attacks on the rebels. The Administration hoped that a military stalemate would cause both sides to agree to concessions.

But just as Bundy was succeeding in establishing a provisional government under Guzmán, he got orders from Washington to drop the whole thing. What clearly had happened was that the tug-of-war among officials in Washington had developed to the point where the United States simply had no coherent policy on the Dominican Republic. Bundy went back to Washington sad and discouraged, after conveying his sincere regrets to Guzmán.

Now the situation was just about back where it had started and efforts to find a solution had to begin all over again. It took three months to reach a settlement, which was remarkably like the one that Bundy had first arranged in May, only to have it undercut by the internal struggle of policy-makers in Washington. This time another respected figure, Héctor García-Godoy, a career diplomat who had been Bosch's Foreign Minister, was named Provisional President, again with the ready acceptance of Colonel Caamaño and the rebels. Again Imbert opposed it with all his might until he had to give in when the United States refused to finance his government any further.

In short, then, more than three months were wasted by the United States in seeking to arrive at a solution that could have been reached late in May. Because of its Hamlet-like hesitations and inability to evolve a consistent policy, the Johnson Administration appears to have lost a golden opportunity to enforce during the spring a settlement on terms acceptable to a majority of Dominicans.

Instead, the three wasted months led to additional losses

in Dominican and American lives—the death toll among Dominicans in the civil war stands officially at 2,850 and among U.S. troops at 28—to a far-reaching breakdown in the country's economic life and, worst of all, to a dangerous increase in Communist strength there.

If the United States policies from the first landing on April 28 to the settlement on September 3 were designed, as claimed by Washington, to forestall Communist domination over the Dominican Republic, then this effort has not really succeeded in the long run.

Information from intelligence sources, U.S. newsmen and other competent observers, reveals that between May and September there has been a considerable radicalization among Dominicans. The Moscow-line Communist party was reorganized in August and had time to plan new strategy. The Peking-oriented Communist faction has gained in strength and purpose. The Castro-type 14th of June Movement has increased its influence far beyond what it enjoyed at the time Mr. Bundy was negotiating for a settlement.

Weapons in the former rebel zone, the bulk of which could have been recovered in May or June, have been hidden in Santo Domingo and cached away in the countryside for "the next phase." Sentiment against the Imbert junta rose spectacularly because of its brutalities; and it rose in proportion against the United States for having so long supported its puppet.[3]

Under García-Godoy, American private investment funds again began to flow into the Dominican Republic, the investors obviously confident that the United States would protect their interests. The United States government poured foreign aid into the nation, more than twice as much on a per capita basis as went to any other Latin-American nation. And elections were held on June 1, 1966. Juan Bosch ran again and his opponent was Joaquín Balaguer, the former collaborator with the Trujillos. The United States threw the full weight of its powerful support to Balaguer, yet Bosch was the favorite. Balaguer won, however, getting about 56 percent of the vote. Although American support no doubt helped Balaguer, many feel that Bosch himself was the reason he lost. Dominicans, like most other Latin Americans, place a high value on *machismo* (masculine courage), and Bosch was so afraid of an attempt on his life that he never left his home during the campaign. He evidently thought he would have no trouble winning. He was wrong.

Since then—up to this writing—little has been heard from the Dominican Republic. Its major economic and social problems still remain, aggravated by a staggering birth rate among the poor. There is still great political tugging and hauling and it is yet too soon to say whether or not any lasting measure of stability has been achieved.

As to the intervention itself, what is the evaluation? The short-term assessment is clear. Many would agree with Adlai Stevenson, who was known to have said privately just before his death in July 1965 that the intervention was a "massive blunder." The world at large and many Americans have asked why the United States intervened in a revolution on the side of a right-wing military junta against democratic reformers who sought to restore to power a properly elected President. It revived all through Latin America the old fears of United States intervention and called into question through the world the basic motives of the United States. Even so judicious a man as UN Secretary-General U Thant later compared the American intervention with the Russian invasion of Czechoslovakia in 1968. Perhaps its greatest effect at the time was to heighten the criticism of President Johnson's foreign policy. There was in the first months of 1965 growing criticism by liberals, intellectuals, and students of the American escalation of the war in Vietnam. Then the Dominican intervention caused many who had tended to support President Johnson on Vietnam to question whether the Administration had a rational foreign policy.

There were, of course, defenders of the intervention. They argued that the intervention prevented the Dominican Republic from becoming "another Cuba." But there has never been any substantial evidence that the Communists had any significant influence on the revolution and the irony is that the intervention strengthened the appeal of Communism not only in the Dominican Republic itself but elsewhere in Latin America. Beyond that there is the more controversial question: Do nations, in Latin America or elsewhere, have the right to Communist governments if that is what they want even if it offends the United States?

But if the short-term assessment is clear, the long-term is not. It is simply too soon to say whether anti-Americanism caused by the intervention has simmered away. It is too soon to know how the intervention has affected the political structure of the Dominican Republic, and it is too soon to know what lasting effect the intervention has had on the OAS, which only reluctantly went along with it. But it is clear that any long-term goals the United States had for the Dominican Republic could have been achieved—more quickly and less expensively—without intervening on the side of the unpopular, ultra-conservative, and often brutal military junta.

EPILOGUE

IF IT IS IMPOSSIBLE to write with complete certitude about
even the recent past, it is certainly impossible to look very
far into the future. But it is plain that America has been
an interventionist nation, and some would argue that the
sense of manifest destiny has continued up to our time to
exert a great influence on our foreign policy. Some reputable
writers have gone so far as to say that the United States
has had the desire, perhaps unconscious, to establish a new
kind of empire, a sort of Pax Americana. That may or may
not be so, but it is indisputable that the American presence, military and civilian, is felt powerfully the world over,
that the United States has intervened in the affairs of other
nations, overtly or covertly, on many occasions in the past
quarter century.

How much change there has been in this American
willingness to intervene remains to be seen, but obviously
the widespread domestic protests against interventions in
the Dominican Republic and Vietnam have had great influence. Almost always in the past domestic protests against
American interventions have taken place, which have ranged
from strong protest against the Mexican War to tepid protest against the Lebanon expedition. But never has the pro-

test been as bitter and as widespread as against the Vietnam War.

Plainly this dissent will influence the thinking of any American administration in the near future. Many people will welcome any inhibition put on American readiness to intervene in other countries, but others will argue that these protests may have paralyzed, perhaps for decades, the ability of a President in the future to intervene when such intervention is indeed justifiable. And even those who have protested against the Vietnam War might favor intervention elsewhere under different circumstances. Once again we must recognize that there are no invariable rules for international conduct. Perhaps the best that can be hoped for is that this nation—and any other, such as the Soviet Union, with the power to intervene—will adopt the principle that intervention is profoundly undesirable and that it should be undertaken only as an absolutely last resort and only after the facts have been conscientiously examined. But when, in each case, one asks: what are the facts (for they are not always easy to ascertain), what do they add up to, and what is a last resort, again, there can be no invariable answer. In each instance the administration and the people would have to make up their minds. Perhaps the various administrations over the past century and a quarter were convinced that there was no alternative to intervention. Perhaps then we are now no better off as to intervention than we were in Polk's time, but maybe we could be. If the United States were not so quick to think that it knew how other nations should order their affairs, if we could change our national attitude to one of non-intervention rather than intervention, perhaps this nation and those with which we deal might be better off.

Appendices 1–8:

DOCUMENTS

APPENDIX I

The Monroe Doctrine

IN 1823 THE GOVERNMENT of the still-young United States feared that Spain, with the support of other European nations, might try to reconquer its former colonies in the New World. Great Britain suggested that the United States and Britain take a joint stand against such a possibility but President James Monroe, following the advice of Secretary of State John Quincy Adams, decided that the United States would act alone. He enunciated his famous doctrine —perhaps the basic document of American foreign policy— as part of his annual message to Congress on December 2, 1823.

. . . At the proposal of the Russian Imperial Government, made through the minister of the Emperor residing here, a full power and instructions have been transmitted to the minister of the United States at St. Petersburg to arrange by amicable negotiation the respective rights and interests of the two nations on the northwest coast of this continent. A similar proposal had been made by His Imperial Majesty to the Government of Great Britain, which has likewise been acceded to. The Government of the United States has been desirous, by this friendly proceeding, of manifesting the great value which they have invariably attached to the friendship of the Emperor and their solicitude to cultivate the best understanding with his Government. In the discussions to which this interest has given rise and in the arrangements by which they may terminate, the occasion has been judged proper for asserting, as a principle in which the rights and interests of the United States are involved, that the American continents, by the free and independent condition which they have assumed and maintain, are henceforth not to be considered as subjects for future colonization by any European powers. . . .

It was stated at the commencement of the last session that a great effort was then making in Spain and Portugal to improve the condition of the people of those countries, and that it appeared to be conducted with extraordinary moderation. It need scarcely be remarked that the result has been so far very different from what was then anticipated. Of events in that quarter of the globe, with which we have so much intercourse and from which we derive our origin, we have always been anxious and interested spectators. The citizens of the United States cherish sentiments the most friendly in favor of liberty and happiness of their fellow-men on that side of the Atlantic. In the wars of the European powers in matters relating to themselves we have never taken any part, nor does it comport with our policy to do so. It is only when our rights are invaded or seriously menaced that we resent injuries or make preparation for our defense. With the movements in this hemisphere we are of necessity more immediately con-

nected, and by causes which must be obvious to all enlightened and impartial observers. The political system of
the allied powers is essentially different in this respect
from that of America. This difference proceeds from that
which exists in their respective Governments; and to the
defense of our own, which has been achieved by the loss
of so much blood and treasure, and matured by the wisdom of their most enlightened citizens, and under which
we have enjoyed unexampled felicity, this whole nation is
devoted. We owe it, therefore, to candor and to the amicable relations existing between the United States and those
powers to declare that we should consider any attempt on
their part to extend their system to any portion of this
hemisphere as dangerous to our peace and safety. With the
existing colonies or dependencies of any European power
we have not interfered and shall not interfere. But with
the Governments who have declared their independence
and maintained it, and whose independence we have, on
great consideration and on just principles, acknowledged,
we could not view any interposition for the purpose of
oppressing them, or controlling in any other manner their
destiny, by any European power in any other light than as
the manifestation of an unfriendly disposition toward the
United States. In the war between those new Governments
and Spain we declared our neutrality at the time of their
recognition, and to this we have adhered, and shall continue to adhere, provided no change shall occur which, in
the judgment of the competent authorities of this Government, shall make a corresponding change on the part of
the United States indispensable to their security.

The late events in Spain and Portugal show that Europe

is still unsettled. Of this important fact no stronger proof can be adduced than that the allied powers should have thought it proper, on any principle satisfactory to themselves, to have interposed by force in the internal concerns of Spain. To what extent such interposition may be carried, on the same principle, is a question in which all independent powers whose governments differ from theirs are interested, even those most remote, and surely none more so than the United States. Our policy in regard to Europe, which was adopted at an early stage of the wars which have so long agitated that quarter of the globe, nevertheless remains the same, which is, not to interfere in the internal concerns of any of its powers; to consider the government *de facto* as the legitimate government for us; to cultivate friendly relations with it, and to preserve those relations by a frank, firm, and manly policy, meeting in all instances the just claims of every power, submitting to injuries from none.

But in regard to those continents circumstances are eminently and conspicuously different. It is impossible that the allied powers should extend their political system to any portion of either continent without endangering our peace and happiness; nor can anyone believe that our southern brethren, if left to themselves, would adopt it of their own accord. It is equally impossible, therefore, that we should behold such interposition in any form with indifference. If we look to the comparative strength and resources of Spain and those new Governments, and their distance from each other, it must be obvious that she can never subdue them. It is still the true policy of the United States to leave the parties to themselves, in the hope that other powers will pursue the same course. . . .

APPENDIX II

Polk's Message on War with Mexico

EVEN BEFORE PRESIDENT JAMES K. POLK received news of the clash between American and Mexican troops, he had decided that he would soon ask Congress for a declaration of war. But he was spared that possible embarrassment when he learned on May 9, 1846 that such a clash had taken place. He sent his war message to Congress on May 11.

To the Senate and House of Representatives:

The existing state of the relations between the United States and Mexico renders it proper that I should bring the subject to the consideration of Congress. . . .

In my message at the commencement of the present session I informed you that upon the earnest appeal both of the Congress and the convention of Texas I had ordered an efficient military force to take a position "between the Nueces and the Del Norte." This had become necessary to meet a threatened invasion of Texas by the Mexican forces, for which extensive military preparations had been made. The invasion was threatened solely because Texas had determined, in accordance with a solemn resolution of the Congress of the United States, to annex herself to our Union, and under these circumstances it was plainly our duty to extend our protection over her citizens and soil.

This force was concentrated at Corpus Christi, and remained there until after I had received such information from Mexico as rendered it probable, if not certain, that the Mexican Government would refuse to receive our envoy. Meantime Texas, by the final action of our Congress, had become an integral part of our Union. The Congress of Texas, by its act of December 19, 1836, had declared the Rio del Norte to be the boundary of that Republic. Its jurisdiction had been extended and exercised beyond the Nueces. The country between that river and the Del Norte had been represented in the Congress and in the convention of Texas, had thus taken part in the act of annexation itself, and is now included within one of our Congressional districts. Our own Congress had, moreover, with great unanimity, by the act approved December 31, 1845, recognized the country beyond the Nueces as a part of our territory by including it within our own revenue system, and a revenue officer to reside within that district has been appointed by and with the advice and consent of the Senate. It became, therefore, of urgent necessity to provide for the defense of that portion of our country. Accordingly, on the 13th of January last, instructions were issued to the general in command of these troops to occupy the left bank of the Del Norte. This river, which is the southwestern boundary of the state of Texas, is an exposed frontier. From this quarter invasion was threatened; upon it and in its immediate vicinity, in the judgment of high military experience, are the proper stations for the protecting forces of the Government. . . .

The movement of the troops to the Del Norte was made by the commanding general under positive instructions to abstain from all aggressive acts toward Mexico or Mexican citizens and to regard the relations between that Republic and the United States as peaceful unless she should declare war or commit acts of hostility indicative of a state of war. He was specially directed to protect private property and respect personal rights.

The Army moved from Corpus Christi on the 11th of March, and on the 28th of that month arrived on the left bank of the Del Norte opposite to Matamoras, where it encamped on a commanding position, which has since been strengthened by the erection of fieldworks. . . .

The Mexican forces at Matamoras assumed a belligerent attitude, and on the 12th of April General Ampudia, then in command, notified General Taylor to break up his camp within twenty-four hours and to retire beyond the Nueces River, and in the event of his failure to comply with these demands announced that arms, and arms alone, must decide the question. But no open act of hostility was committed until the 24th of April. On that day General Arista, who had succeeded to the command of the Mexican forces, communicated to General Taylor that "he considered hostilities commenced and should prosecute them." A party of dragoons of 63 men and officers were on the same day dispatched from the American camp up the Rio del Norte, on its left bank, to ascertain whether the Mexican troops had crossed or were preparing to cross the river, "became engaged with a large body of these troops, and after a short affair, in which some 16 were killed and wounded, appear to have been surrounded and compelled to surrender."

The grievous wrongs perpetrated by Mexico upon our citizens throughout a long period of years remain unredressed, and solemn treaties pledging this redress have been disregarded. A government either unable or unwilling to enforce the execution of such treaties fails to perform one of its plainest duties. . . . The cup of forbearance had been exhausted even before the recent information from the frontier of the Del Norte. But now, after reiterated menace, Mexico has passed the boundary of the United States, has invaded our territory and shed American blood upon the American soil. She has proclaimed that hostilities have commenced, and that the two nations are at war.

As war exists, and, notwithstanding all our efforts to avoid it, exists by the act of Mexico itself, we are called upon by every consideration of duty and patriotism to vindicate with decision the honor, the rights, and the interests of our country. . . .

In further vindication of our rights and defense of our territory, I invoke the proper action of Congress to recognize the existence of the war, and to place at the disposition of the Executive the means of prosecuting the war with vigor, and thus hastening the restoration of peace. . . .

APPENDIX III

McKinley's War Message

EVEN THOUGH, IN THE SPRING OF 1898, there were still those who thought war with Spain could be avoided, President William McKinley sent a war message to Congress on April 11, 1898.

To the Congress of the United States:

Obedient to that precept of the Constitution which commands the President to give from time to time to the Congress information of the state of the Union and to recommend to their consideration such measures as he shall judge necessary and expedient, it becomes my duty to now address your body with regard to the grave crisis that has arisen in the relations of the United States to Spain by reason of the warfare that for more than three years has raged in the neighboring island of Cuba. . . .

The present revolution is but the successor of other similar insurrections which have occurred in Cuba against the dominion of Spain, extending over a period of nearly half a century, each of which during its progress has subjected the United States to great effort and expense in enforcing its neutrality laws, caused enormous losses to American trade and commerce, caused irritation, annoyance, and disturbance among our citizens, and, by the exercise of cruel, barbarous, and uncivilized practices of warfare, shocked the sensibilities and offended the humane sympathies of our people. . . .

Our trade has suffered, the capital invested by our citizens in Cuba has been largely lost, and the temper and forbearance of our people have been so sorely tried as to beget a perilous unrest among our own citizens. . . .

The war in Cuba is of such a nature that, short of subjugation or extermination, a final military victory for either side seems impracticable. The alternative lies in the physical exhaustion of the one or the other party, or perhaps of both—a condition which in effect ended the ten years' war by the truce of Zanjon. The prospect of such a protraction and conclusion of the present strife is a contingency hardly to be contemplated with equanimity by the civilized world, and least of all by the United States, affected and injured as we are, deeply and intimately, by its very existence.

Realizing this, it appeared to be my duty, in a spirit of true friendliness, no less to Spain than to the Cubans, who have so much to lose by the prolongation of the struggle, to seek to bring about an immediate termination of the war. To this end I submitted on the 27th ultimo, as a result of much representation and correspondence, through the United States minister at Madrid, propositions to the Spanish Government looking to an armistice until October 1 for the negotiation of peace with the good offices of the President.

In addition I asked the immediate revocation of the order of reconcentration, so as to permit the people to return to their farms and the needy to be relieved with provisions and supplies from the United States, cooperating with the Spanish authorities, so as to afford full relief. . . .

With this last overture in the direction of immediate peace, and its disappointing reception by Spain, the Executive is brought to the end of his effort.

In my annual message of December last I said:

> Of the untried measures there remain only: recognition of the insurgents as belligerents; recognition of the independence of Cuba; neutral intervention to end the war by imposing a rational compromise between the contestants, and intervention in favor of one or the other party. I speak not of forcible annexation, for that can not be thought of. That, by our code of morality, would be criminal aggression. . . .

The forcible intervention of the United States as a neutral to stop the war, according to the large dictates of humanity and following many historical precedents where neighboring states have interfered to check the hopeless sacrifices of life by internecine conflicts beyond their borders, is justifiable on rational grounds. It involves, however, hostile constraint upon both parties to the contest, as well to enforce a truce as to guide the eventual settlement.

The grounds for such intervention may be briefly summarized as follows:

First. In the cause of humanity and to put an end to the barbarities, bloodshed, starvation, and horrible miseries now existing there, and which the parties to the conflict are either unable or unwilling to stop or mitigate. It is no answer to say this is all in another country, belonging to another nation, and is therefore none of our business. It is specially our duty, for it is right at our door.

Second. We owe it to our citizens in Cuba to afford them that protection and indemnity for life and property which no government there can or will afford, and to that end to terminate the conditions that deprive them of legal protection.

Third. The right to intervene may be justified by the very serious injury to the commerce, trade, and business of our people and by the wanton destruction of property and devastation of the island.

Fourth, and which is of the utmost importance. The present condition of affairs in Cuba is a constant menace to our peace and entails upon this Government an enormous expense. With such a conflict waged for years in an island so near to us and with which our people have such trade and business relations; when the lives and liberty of our citizens are in constant danger and their property destroyed and themselves ruined; where our trading vessels are liable to seizure and are seized at our very door by war ships of a foreign nation; the expeditions of filibustering that we are powerless to prevent altogether, and the irritating questions and entanglements thus arising—all these and others that I need not mention, with the resulting strained relations, are a constant menace to our peace and compel us to keep on a semi-war footing with a nation with which we are at peace.

These elements of danger and disorder already pointed out have been strikingly illustrated by a tragic event which has deeply and justly moved the American people. I have already transmitted to Congress the report of the naval court of inquiry on the destruction of the battleship *Maine* in the harbor of Havana during the night of the 15th of February. The destruction of that noble vessel has filled the national heart with inexpressible horror. Two hundred and fifty-eight brave sailors and marines and two officers of our Navy, reposing in the fancied security of a friendly harbor, have been hurled to death, grief and want brought to their homes and sorrow to the nation.

The naval court of inquiry, which, it is needless to say, commands the unqualified confidence of the Government, was unanimous in its conclusion that the destruction of the *Maine* was caused by an exterior explosion—that of a submarine mine. It did not assume to place the responsibility. That remains to be fixed.

In any event, the destruction of the *Maine,* by whatever exterior cause, is a patent and impressive proof of a state of things in Cuba that is intolerable. That condition is thus shown to be such that the Spanish Government can not assure safety and security to a vessel of the American Navy in the harbor of Havana on a mission of peace, and rightfully there. . . .

The long trial has proved that the object for which Spain has waged war can not be attained. The fire of insurrection may flame or may smolder with varying seasons, but it has not been and it is plain that it can not be extinguished by present methods. The only hope of relief and repose from a condition which can no longer be endured is the enforced pacification of Cuba. In the name of humanity, in the name of civilization, in behalf of endangered American interests which give us the right and the duty to speak and to act, the war in Cuba must stop.

In view of these facts and of these considerations I ask the Congress to authorize and empower the President to take measures to secure a full and final termination of the hostilities between the Government of Spain and the people of Cuba, and to secure in the island the establishment of a stable government, capable of maintaining order and observing its international obligations, insuring peace and tranquillity and the security of its citizens as well as our own, and to use the military and naval forces of the United States as may be necessary for these purposes.

And in the interest of humanity and to aid in preserving

the lives of the starving people of the land I recommend that the distribution of food and supplies be continued and that an appropriation be made out of the public Treasury to supplement the charity of our citizens.

The issue is now with the Congress. It is a solemn responsibility. I have exhausted every effort to relieve the intolerable condition of affairs which is at our doors. Prepared to execute every obligation imposed upon me by the Constitution and the law, I await your action.

Yesterday, and since the preparation of the foregoing message, official information was received by me that the latest decree of the Queen Regent of Spain directs General Blanco, in order to prepare and facilitate peace, to proclaim a suspension of hostilities, the duration and details of which have not yet been communicated to me.

This fact, with every other pertinent consideration, will, I am sure, have your just and careful attention in the solemn deliberations upon which you are about to enter. If this measure attains a successful result, then our aspirations as a Christian, peace-loving people will be realized. If it fails, it will be only another justification for our contemplated action.

APPENDIX IV

The Roosevelt Corollary

IN HIS ANNUAL MESSAGE to Congress, on December 6, 1904, President Theodore Roosevelt included a section that came to be known as the Roosevelt Corollary to the Monroe Doctrine. With it he changed the Monroe Doctrine from one of non-intervention by European powers to one of intervention by the United States.

. . . It is not true that the United States feels any land hunger or entertains any projects as regards the other nations of the Western Hemisphere save such as are for their welfare. All that this country desires is to see the neighboring countries stable, orderly, and prosperous. Any country whose people conduct themselves well can count upon our hearty friendship. If a nation shows that it knows how to act with reasonable efficiency and decency in social and political matters, if it keeps order and pays its obligations, it need fear no interference from the United States. Chronic wrongdoing, or an impotence which results in a general loosening of the ties of civilized society, may in America, as elsewhere, ultimately require intervention by some civilized nation, and in the Western Hemisphere the adherence of the United States to the Monroe Doctrine may force the United States, however reluctantly, in flagrant cases of such wrongdoing or impotence, to the exercise of an international police power. If every country washed by the Caribbean Sea would show the progress in stable and just civilization which with the aid of the Platt amendment Cuba has shown since our troops left the island, and which so many of the republics in both Americas are constantly and brilliantly showing, all question of interference by this Nation with their affairs would be at an end.

Our interests and those of our southern neighbors are in reality identical. They have great natural riches, and if within their borders the reign of law and justice obtains, prosperity is sure to come to them. While they thus obey the primary laws of civilized society they may rest assured that they will be treated by us in a spirit of cordial and helpful sympathy. We would interfere with them only in the last resort, and then only if it became evident that their inability or unwillingness to do justice at home and abroad had violated the rights of the United States or had invited foreign aggression to the detriment of the entire body of American nations. It is a mere truism to say that every nation, whether in America or anywhere else, which desires to maintain its freedom, its independence, must ultimately realize that the right of such independence can not be separated from the responsibility of making good use of it.

In asserting the Monroe Doctrine, in taking such steps as we have taken in regard to Cuba, Venezuela, and Panama, and in endeavoring to circumscribe the theater of war in the Far East, and to secure the open door in China, we have acted in our own interest as well as in the interest of humanity at large. There are, however, cases in which, while our own interests are not greatly involved, strong appeal is made to our sympathies. Ordinarily it is very much wiser and more useful for us to concern ourselves with striving for our own moral and material betterment here at home than to concern ourselves with trying to better the condition of things in other nations. We have plenty of sins of our own to war against, and under ordinary circumstances we can do more for the general uplifting of humanity by striving with heart and soul to put a stop to civic corruption, to brutal lawlessness and violent race prejudices here at home than by passing resolutions about wrongdoing elsewhere. Nevertheless there are occasional crimes committed on so vast a scale and of such peculiar horror as to make us doubt whether it is not our manifest duty to endeavor at least to show our disapproval of the deed and our sympathy with those who have suffered by it. The cases must be extreme in which such a course is justifiable. There must be no effort made to remove the mote from our brother's eye if we refuse to remove the beam from our own. But in extreme cases action may be justifiable and proper. What form the action shall take must depend upon the circumstances of the case; that is, upon the degree of the atrocity and upon our power to remedy it. The cases in which we could interfere by force of arms as we interfered to put a stop to the intolerable conditions in Cuba are necessarily very few.

APPENDIX V

The Platt Amendment

AFTER THE END OF THE Spanish-American War the United States wanted to be able to intervene in Cuba if the government thought it necessary. To preserve that right the United States had it embedded not only in the Cuban Constitution but in a treaty between the two nations so Cuba could not unilaterally revoke that right. The language was that of the Platt Amendment to the army appropriation bill. Although largely written by Secretary of War Elihu Root, it was named after the Senator who sponsored it, Orville H. Platt of Connecticut. It was adopted on March 2, 1901.

I. That the government of Cuba shall never enter into any treaty or other compact with any foreign power or powers which will impair or tend to impair the independence of Cuba, nor in any manner authorize or permit any foreign power or powers to obtain by colonization or for military or naval purposes or otherwise, lodgment in or control over any portion of said island.

II. That said government shall not assume or contract any public debt, to pay the interest upon which, and to make reasonable sinking-fund provision for the ultimate discharge of which, the ordinary revenues of the island, after defraying the current expenses of government, shall be inadequate.

III. That the government of Cuba consents that the United States may exercise the right to intervene for the preservation of Cuban independence, the maintenance of a government adequate for the protection of life, property, and individual liberty, and for discharging the obligations with respect to Cuba imposed by the treaty of Paris on the United States, now to be assumed and undertaken by the government of Cuba.

IV. That all Acts of the United States in Cuba during its military occupancy thereof are ratified and validated, and all lawful rights acquired thereunder shall be maintained and protected.

V. That the government of Cuba will execute, and as far as necessary extend, the plans already devised or other plans to be mutually agreed upon, for the sanitation of the cities of the island, to the end that a recurrence of epidemic and infectious diseases may be prevented thereby assuring protection to the people and commerce of Cuba, as well as to the commerce of the southern ports of the United States and the people residing therein.

VI. That the Isle of Pines shall be omitted from the proposed constitutional boundaries of Cuba, the title thereto being left to future adjustment by treaty.

VII. That to enable the United States to maintain the independence of Cuba, and to protect the people thereof, as well as for its own defense, the government of Cuba will sell or lease to the United States lands necessary for coaling or naval stations at certain specified points to be agreed upon with the President of the United States.

APPENDIX VI

Wilson Statement on Latin America

ONLY A WEEK AFTER his inauguration, President Woodrow Wilson, on March 11, 1913, made a statement of policy that he had sent to Latin-American diplomats.

One of the chief objects of my administration will be to cultivate the friendship and deserve the confidence of our sister republics of Central and South America, and to promote in every proper and honorable way the interests which are common to the peoples of the two continents. I earnestly desire the most cordial understanding and co-operation between the peoples and leaders of America and, therefore, deem it my duty to make this brief statement.

Cooperation is possible only when supported at every turn by the orderly processes of just government based upon law, not upon arbitrary or irregular force. We hold, as I am sure all thoughtful leaders of republican government everywhere hold, that just government always rests upon the consent of the governed, and that there can be no freedom without order based upon law and upon the public conscience and approval. We shall look to make these principles the basis of mutual intercourse, respect, and help-fulness between our sister republics and ourselves. We shall lend our influence of every kind to the realization of these principles in fact and practice, knowing that disorder, personal intrigues, and defiance of constitutional rights weaken and discredit government and injure none so much as the people who are unfortunate enough to have their common life and their common affairs so tainted and disturbed. We can have no sympathy with those who seek to seize the power of government to advance their own personal interests or ambition. We are the friends of peace, but we know that there can be no lasting or stable peace in such circumstances. As friends, therefore, we shall prefer those who act in the interests of peace and honor, who protect private rights, and respect the restraints of constitutional provision. Mutual respect seems to us the indispensable foundation of friendship between states, as between individuals.

The United States has nothing to seek in Central or South America except the lasting interests of the peoples of the two continents, the security of governments intended for the people and for no special group or interest, and the development of personal and trade relationships between the two continents which shall redound to the profit and advantage of both and interfere with the rights and liberties of neither.

From these principles may be read so much of the future policy of this Government as it is necessary now to forecast, and in the spirit of these principles, I may, I hope, be permitted with as much confidence as earnestness to extend to the Governments of all the Republics of America the hand of genuine disinterested friendship, and to pledge my own name and the honor of my colleagues to every enterprise of peace and amity that a fortunate future may disclose.

APPENDIX VII

Eisenhower's Message on Lebanon

AFTER THE EISENHOWER ADMINISTRATION had held informal talks with Congressional leaders and after troops had already been sent to Lebanon, President Dwight D. Eisenhower sent this message to Congress late in the day on July 15, 1958.

To the Congress of the United States,

On July 14, 1958, I received an urgent request from the President of the Republic of Lebanon that some United States Forces be stationed in Lebanon. President Chamoun stated that without an immediate showing of United States support, the government of Lebanon would be unable to survive. This request by President Chamoun was made with the concurrence of all the members of the Lebanese cabinet. I have replied that we would do this and a contingent of United States Marines has now arrived in Lebanon. This initial dispatch of troops will be augmented as required. U.S. forces will be withdrawn as rapidly as circumstances permit.

Simultaneously, I requested that an urgent meeting of the United Nations Security Council be held on July 15, 1958. At that meeting, the Permanent Representative of the United States reported to the Council the action which this Government has taken. He also expressed the hope that the United Nations could soon take further effective measures to meet more fully the situation in Lebanon. We will continue to support the United Nations to this end.

United States forces are being sent to Lebanon to protect American lives and by their presence to assist the Government of Lebanon in the preservation of Lebanon's territorial integrity and independence, which have been deemed vital to United States national interests and world peace.

About two months ago a violent insurrection broke out in Lebanon, particularly along the border with Syria which, with Egypt, forms the United Arab Republic. This revolt was encouraged and strongly backed by the official Cairo, Damascus, and Soviet radios which broadcast to Lebanon in the Arabic language. The insurrection was further supported by sizable amounts of arms, ammunition, and money and by personnel infiltrated from Syria to fight against the lawful authorities. The avowed purpose of these activities was to overthrow the legally constituted Government of Lebanon and to install by violence a government which would subordinate the independence of Lebanon to the policies of the United Arab Republic.

Lebanon referred this situation to the United Nations Security Council. In view of the international implications of what was occurring in Lebanon, the Security Council on June 11, 1958 decided to send observers into Lebanon for the purpose of insuring that further outside assistance to the insurrection would cease. The Secretary General of the United Nations subsequently undertook a mission to the area to reinforce the work of the observers.

It was our belief that the efforts of the Secretary General and of the United Nations observers were helpful in reducing further aid in terms of personnel and military equipment from across the frontiers of Lebanon. There was a basis for hope that the situation might be moving toward a peaceful solution, consonant with the continuing integrity of Lebanon, and that the aspect of indirect aggression from without was being brought under control.

The situation was radically changed, however, on July 14, when there was a violent outbreak in Baghdad, in nearby Iraq. Elements in Iraq strongly sympathetic to the United Arab Republic seem to have murdered or driven from office individuals comprising the lawful government of that country. We do not yet know in detail to what extent they have succeeded. We do have reliable information that important Iraqi leaders have been murdered.

We share with the Government of Lebanon the view that these events in Iraq demonstrate a ruthlessness of aggressive purpose which tiny Lebanon cannot combat without further evidence of support from other friendly nations.

After the most detailed consideration, I have concluded that, given the developments in Iraq, the measures thus far taken by the United Nations Security Council are not sufficient to preserve the independence and integrity of Lebanon. I have considered, furthermore, the question of our responsibility to protect and safeguard American citizens in Lebanon of whom there are about 2,500. Pending the taking of adequate measures by the United Nations, the United States will be acting pursuant to what the United Nations Charter recognizes is an inherent right—the right of all nations to work together and to seek help when necessary to preserve their independence.

It is clear that the events which have been occurring in Lebanon represent indirect aggression from without, and that such aggression endangers the independence and integrity of Lebanon.

It is recognized that the step now being taken may have

serious consequences. I have, however, come to the considered and sober conclusion that despite the risks involved this action is required to support the principles of justice and international law upon which peace and a stable international order depend.

Our Government has acted in response to an appeal for help from a small and peaceful nation which has long had ties of closest friendship with the United States. Readiness to help a friend in need is an admirable characteristic of the American people, and I am, in this message, informing the Congress of the reasons why I believe that the United States could not in honor stand idly by in this hour of Lebanon's grave peril.

As we act at the request of a friendly government to help it preserve its independence and to preserve law and order which will protect American lives, we are acting to reaffirm and strengthen principles upon which the safety and security of the United States depend.

APPENDIX VIII

President Johnson on the Dominican Intervention

IN JUSTIFYING THE AMERICAN intervention in the Dominican Republic, President Lyndon B. Johnson made two public statements on television, the first on April 28 and the second on May 2, 1965.

April 28:

I've just concluded a meeting with the leaders of the Congress. I reported to them on the serious situation in the Dominican Republic. I reported the decision that this Government considers necessary in this situation in order to protect American lives.

The members of the leadership expressed their support of these decisions.

The United States Government has been informed by military authorities in the Dominican Republic that American lives are in danger. These authorities are no longer able to guarantee their safety and they reported that the assistance of military personnel is now needed for that purpose.

I've ordered the Secretary of Defense to put the necessary American troops ashore in order to give protection to hundreds of Americans who are still in the Dominican Republic and to escort them safely back to this country.

This same assistance will be available to the nationals of other countries, some of whom have already asked for our help.

Pursuant to my instructions, 400 Marines have already

landed. General Wheeler, the chairman of the Joint Chiefs of Staff, has just reported to me that there have been no incidents.

We have appealed repeatedly in recent days for a cease-fire between the contending forces in the Dominican Republic in the interest of all Dominicans and foreigners alike.

I repeat this urgent appeal again tonight.

The Council of the OAS has been advised of the situation by the Dominican Ambassador and the Council will be kept fully informed.

May 2:

Good evening ladies and gentlemen. I have just come from a meeting with the leaders of both parties in the Congress, which was held in the Cabinet Room of the White House.

I briefed them on the facts of the situation in the Dominican Republic. I want to make those same facts known to all the American people and to all the world.

There are times in the affairs of nations when great principles are tested in an ordeal of conflict and danger. This is such a time for American nations. At stake are the lives of thousands, the liberty of the nation, and the principles and the values of all the American republics and that is why the hopes and the concern of this entire hemisphere are on this Sabbath Sunday focused on the Dominican Republic.

In the darkness of conflict and violence, revolution and confusion, it is not easy to find clear and uncloudy truths.

But certain things are clear. They require equally clear

action. To understand, I think it is necessary to begin with the events of eight or nine days ago.

Last week our observers warned of an approaching political storm in the Dominican Republic. I immediately asked our Ambassador to return to Washington at once so that we might discuss the situation and might plan a course of conduct.

But events soon outran our hopes for peace. And Saturday, April 24, eight days ago while Ambassador Bennett was conferring with the highest officials of our government, revolution erupted in the Dominican Republic. Elements of the military forces of that country overthrew their government.

However, the rebels themselves were divided. Some wanted to restore former President Juan Bosch. Others opposed his restoration. President Bosch, elected after the fall of Trujillo and his assassination, had been driven from office by an earlier revolution in the Dominican Republic. And those who opposed Mr. Bosch's return formed a military committee in an effort to control that country. The others took to the streets and began to lead a revolt on behalf of President Bosch.

Control and effective government dissolved in conflict and confusion. Meanwhile, the United States was making a constant effort to restore peace.

From Saturday afternoon onward our embassy urged a cease-fire, and I and all the officials of the American Government worked with every weapon at our command to achieve it.

On Tuesday, the situation of turmoil was presented to the peace committee of the Organization of American States.

On Wednesday the entire Council of the Organization of American States received a full report from the Dominican Ambassador.

Meanwhile, all this time, from Saturday to Wednesday, the danger was mounting. Even though we were deeply saddened by bloodshed and violence in a close and friendly neighbor we had no desire to interfere in the affairs of a sister republic. On Wednesday afternoon there was no longer any choice for the man who is your President. I was sitting in my little office reviewing the world situation with Secretary Rusk and Secretary McNamara and Mr. McGeorge Bundy.

At shortly after 3 o'clock I received a cable from our Ambasssador and he said that things were in danger. He had been informed that the chief of police and the governmental authorities could no longer protect us. We immediately started the necessary conference calls to be prepared.

At 5:14, almost two hours later, we received a cable that was labeled "critic," a word that is reserved for only the most urgent and immediate matters of national security.

The cable reported that Dominican law enforcement and military officials had informed our embassy that the situation was completely out of control, and that the police and the government could no longer give any guarantee concerning the safety of Americans or of any foreign nationals.

Ambassador Bennett, who is one of our most experienced foreign service officers, went on in that cable to say that only an immediate landing of American forces could safeguard and protect the lives of thousands of Americans and thousands of other citizens of some thirty other countries.

I thought that we could not—and we did not—hesitate.

Our forces, American forces, were ordered in immediately to protect American lives. They have done that. They have attacked no one, and although some of our servicemen gave their lives, not a single American civilian and the civilians of any other nation, as a result of this protection, lost their lives.

There may be those in our own country who say that such action was good but we should have waited or we should have delayed or we should have consulted further or we should have called a meeting.

But from the very beginning the United States at my instructions had worked for a cease-fire, beginning the Saturday the revolution took place.

The matter was before the OAS peace committee on Tuesday at our suggestion. It was before the full Council on Wednesday and when I made my announcement to the American people that evening, I announced then I was notifying the Council.

And when that cable arrived, when our entire country team in the Dominican Republic, made up of nine men, one from the Army, Navy and Air Force, our Ambassador, our aid man, and others, said to your President unanimously, "Mr. President, if you do not send forces immediately, men and women, Americans and those of other lands, will die in the streets—" well, I knew there was no time to talk, to consult, or to delay, for in this situation delay itself would be decision, decision to risk and to lose the lives of thousands of Americans and thousands of innocent people from all lands.

I want you to know that it is not a light or an easy matter to send our American boys to another country, but

1 do not think that the American people expect their President to hesitate or to vacillate in the face of danger, just because the decision is hard, when life is in peril.

Meanwhile, the revolutionary movement took a tragic turn. Communist leaders, many of them trained in Cuba, seeing a chance to increase disorder, to gain a foothold, joined the revolution. They took increasing control.

And what began as a popular democratic revolution committed to democracy and social justice very shortly moved and was taken over and really seized and placed into the hands of a band of Communist conspirators.

Many of the original leaders of the rebellion, the followers of President Bosch, took refuge in foreign embassies, because they had been superseded by other evil forces.

And the Secretary General of the rebel government, Martinez Francisco, appealed for a cease-fire, but he was ignored. The revolution was now in other and dangerous hands.

And when these new and ominous developments emerged, the OAS met again, and it met at the request of the United States.

I am glad to say they responded wisely and decisively. A five-nation OAS team is now in the Dominican Republic acting to achieve a cease-fire to insure the safety of innocent people, to restore normal conditions, and to open a path to democratic process. That is the situation now.

I plead therefore with every person and every country in this hemisphere that would choose to do so to contact their Ambassador in the Dominican Republic directly and to get first-hand evidence of the horrors and the hardship, the violence, and the terror, and the international conspiracy from which United States servicemen have rescued the people of more than 30 nations from that war-torn island.

Earlier today I ordered two additional battalions, 2,000 extra men, to proceed immediately to the Dominican Republic.

In the meeting I just concluded with the Congressional leaders, following that meeting, I directed the Secretary of Defense and the Chairman of the Joint Chiefs of Staff to issue instructions to land an additional 4,500 men at the earliest possible moment.

The distribution of food to people who have not eaten for days, the need of medical supplies and attention for the sick and the wounded, the health requirements to avoid an epidemic, because there are hundreds who have been dead for days that are now on the streets, and the further protection of the security of each individual that is caught on that island require the attention of the additional forces which I have ordered to proceed to the Dominican Republic.

In addition, our servicemen have already, since they landed on Wednesday night, evacuated 3,000 persons from 30 countries in the world from this little island.

But more than 5,000 people, 1,500 of whom are foreign nationals, are tonight awaiting evacuation as I speak.

[In the three following paragraphs the President repeated earlier material because of a mishap with a television prompting device.]

We just must get on with that job immediately. The evidence that we have of the revolutionary movement indicates that it took a very tragic turn. Communist leaders, many of them trained in Cuba, seeing a chance to increase disorder, and to gain a foothold, joined the revolution. They took increasing control. What began as a popular democratic revolution that was committed to democracy and social justice moved into the hands of a band of Communist conspirators.

Many of the original leaders of the rebellion, the followers of President Bosch, took refuge in foreign embassies, and they are there tonight.

The American nations cannot, must not, and will not permit the establishment of another Communist government in the Western Hemisphere. This was the unanimous view of all the American nations when in January, 1962, they declared, and I quote, "the principles of Communism are incompatible with the principles of the inter-American system." This is what our beloved President John F. Kennedy meant when less than a week before his death he told us, we in this hemisphere must also use every resource at our command to prevent the establishment of another Cuba in this hemisphere.

This is and this will be the common action and the common purpose of the democratic forces of the hemisphere. For the danger is also a common danger and the principles are common principles. So we have acted to summon the resources of this entire hemisphere to this task. We have sent on my instructions the night before last special emissaries such as Ambassador Morosco of Puerto Rico, our very able Ambassador Averell Harriman and others to Latin America to explain the situation, to tell them the truth and to warn them that joint action is necessary.

We are in contact with such distinguished Latin-American

statesmen as Rómulo Betancourt and José Figueres. We are seeking their counsel and their advice.

We have also maintained communication with President Bosch who has chosen to remain in Puerto Rico. We have been consulting with the Organization of American States and our distinguished Ambassador, than whom there is no better, Ambassador Bunker, has been reporting to them at great length all the actions of this government, and we have been acting in conformity with their decisions.

We know that many who are now in revolt do not seek a Communist tyranny. We think it's tragic indeed that their high motives have been misused by a small band of conspirators, who receive their directions from abroad.

To those who fight only for liberty and justice and progress, I want to join with the Organization of American States in saying, in appealing to you tonight to lay down your arms and to assure you that there is nothing to fear.

The road is open to you to share in building a Dominican democracy and we in America are ready and anxious and willing to help you.

Your courage and your dedication are top qualities which your country and all the hemisphere need for the future.

You are needed to help shape that future and neither we nor any other nation in this hemisphere can or should take it upon itself to ever interfere with the affairs of your country, or any other country.

We believe that change comes, and we're glad that it does, and it should come through peaceful process.

But revolution in any country is a matter for that country to deal with. It becomes a matter calling for hemisphere action only, repeat only, when the object is the establishment of a communistic dictatorship.

Let me make clear tonight that we support no single man or any single group of men in the Dominican Republic. Our goal is a simple one. We are there to save the lives of our citizens and to save the lives of all people.

Our goal in keeping the principles of the American system is to help prevent another Communist state in this hemisphere, and we would like to do this without bloodshed or without large-scale fighting.

The form and the nature of a free Dominican Government, I assure you, is solely a matter for the Dominican people, but we do know what kind of government we hope to see in the Dominican Republic. For that is carefully spelled in the treaties and agreements which make up the fabric of the entire inter-American system.

It is expressed time and time again in the words of our statesmen and the values and hopes which bind us all together.

We hope to see a government freely chosen by the will of all the people. We hope to see a government dedicated to social justice for every single citizen. We hope to see a government working every hour of every day to feeding the hungry, to educating the ignorant, to healing the sick, a government whose only concern is the progress, the elevation and the welfare of all the people.

For more than three decades the people of that tragic little island suffered under the weight of one of the most brutal and despotic dictatorships in the history of the Americas.

We enthusiastically supported condemnation of that Government by the Organization of American States. We joined in applying sanctions and when Trujillo was assassinated by his fellow citizens, we immediately acted to protect freedom and to prevent a new tyranny.

And since that time we have taken the resources from all our people, at some sacrifice to many, and we have helped them with food and with other resources. With the Peace Corps volunteers, with the aid of technicians, we have helped them in the effort to build a new order of progress.

And how sad it is tonight that the people so long oppressed should once again be the targets of the forces of tyranny. Their long misery must weigh heavily on the heart of every citizen of this hemisphere.

So I think it's our mutual responsibility to help the people of the Dominican Republic toward the day when they can freely choose the path of liberty and justice and progress. This is required of us by the agreements that we are party to and that we have signed. This is required of us by the values which bind us together.

Simon Bolivar once wrote from exile, "the veil has been torn asunder, we have already seen the light and it is not our desire to be thrust back into the darkness."

Well, after decades of night the Dominican people have seen a more hopeful light. And I know that the nations of this hemisphere will not let them be thrust back into the darkness.

And before I leave you, my fellow Americans, I want to say this personal word.

I know that no American serviceman wants to kill anyone. And I know that no American President wants to give an order which brings shooting and casualties and death.

But I want you to know and I want the world to know, that as long as I am President of this country we are going to defend ourselves. We will defend our soldiers against attackers. We will honor our treaties. We will keep our commitments. We will defend our nation against all those who seek to destroy not only the United States but every free country of this hemisphere.

We do not want to bury anyone, as I have said so many times before. But we do not intend to be buried.

Thank you, and God bless you. Good night.

BIBLIOGRAPHIC AND REFERENCE NOTES

Author's Preface

1. For fuller treatment of the Korean and Vietnam Wars, see *Korea: Land of the 38th Parallel* by Frank Gosfield and Bernhardt J. Hurwood (1969) and *The Story of Vietnam* by Hal Dareff (1966), both Parents' Magazine Press, New York.

The Mexican War

A good, concise account of the Mexican War is given by Charles L. DuFour in *The Mexican War,* Hawthorn Books, New York, 1968. It contains much original material, a good index, and a comprehensive bibliography. A masterpiece of both history and literature is Bernard DeVoto's *The Year of Decision: 1846,* Houghton Mifflin (Sentry 11), Boston, 1961 (original hardcover edition published 1942). This extraordinary book deals not only with the Mexican War but with the whole American movement westward to the Pacific. A good brief summary of the various reasons given for the Mexican War is *The Mexican War,* edited by Ramon E. Ruiz, Holt, Rinehart & Winston, New York, 1963. The war seen from south of the border is recorded in *Mexico During the War with the United States* by José Fernando Ramirez, edited by Walter V. Scholes and translated by Elliot B. Scherr, University of Missouri, Columbia, Missouri, 1950.

Chapter One

1. DeVoto, p. 13

Chapter Two

1. *Zachary Taylor, Soldier of the Republic* by Holman Hamilton. Bobbs Merrill, Indianapolis, 1941, p. 166.

2. *Fifty Years in Camp and Field; Diary of Major-General Ethan Allen Hitchcock,* edited by W. A. Croffut. Putnam, New York, 1909), p. 212.

259

3. DeVoto, p. 194
4. DeVoto, p. 70
5. DeVoto, p. 72

Chapter Three

1. DeVoto, p. 252

That "Splendid Little War"

For most of the vivid, first-hand reports I have relied on
Frank Freidel's *The Splendid Little War,* Little, Brown, Boston,
1958. This book is handsomely illustrated with photographs and
drawings of the period. *The Imperial Years* by Foster Rhea Dulles,
Thomas Y. Crowell (Apollo Edition), New York, 1956, dis-
cusses the entire period. Focused solely on the war is *America's
Road to Empire: The War with Spain and Overseas Expansion* by
H. Wayne Morgan, Wiley, New York, 1965. Perhaps the best-
known book on the subject is Walter Millis's *The Martial Spirit,*
Houghton Mifflin, Boston, 1931. Useful in putting the Spanish-
American War in the context of United States–Latin-American
relations is *The Latin American Policy of the United States,* by
Samuel Flagg Bemis, Norton, New York, 1967. Also useful is
Hubert Herring's *A History of Latin America,* Knopf, New York,
1961.

Chapter Five

1. Dulles, p. 32
2. Dulles, p. 33
3. Dulles, p. 47
4. Morgan, p. 7

Chapter Six

1. Morgan, p. 54
2. Freidel, p. 15

Chapter Seven

1. As quoted in Freidel, p. 61
2. Freidel, p. 173
3. Morgan, p. 96

Dollar Diplomacy

The standard work on this chaotic period is *Intervention and Dollar Diplomacy in the Caribbean 1900–1921*, by Dana G. Munro, Princeton University Press, Princeton, N. J., 1964. This is a work of enduring value, on which the author has relied heavily. Another fine work is Dexter Perkins' *The United States and the Caribbean*, Harvard University Press, Cambridge, Mass., 1966, an updating of his famous earlier work. Again useful are Bemis' *The Latin American Policy of the United States* and Herring's *A History of Latin America*, both cited in the previous section.

Chapter Eight

1. Roosevelt, *Letters*, The Roosevelt Papers, Library of Congress, Vol. VI, p. 1491
2. Bemis, p. 388

Chapter Nine

1. Roosevelt, *Letters*, Vol. III, p. 399. To G. W. Hinman
2. Roosevelt, *Letters*, Vol. IV, p. 801. To Elihu Root
3. Roosevelt, *Letters*, Vol. IV, p. 821. To Elihu Root
4. Bemis, p. 157
5. Bemis, p. 155
6. Munro, p. 13

Chapter Ten

1. Munro, p. 26
2. Perkins, p. 94
3. *Our Cuban Colony* by Leland Jenks. Vanguard Press, New York, 1928.

Chapter Eleven

1. Munro, p. 162
2. Munro, p. 163
3. Munro, p. 187
4. For complete text, see *Foreign Relations*, 1912, pp. 1043–44.
5. Bemis, p. 164
6. Munro, p. 216
7. A good brief account of Sandino's resistance is given by the

famous correspondent Carleton Beals in the 100th anniversary
issue of *The Nation,* September 20, 1965.
8. Herring, p. 467

Chapter Twelve
1. Bemis, p. 172
2. Bemis, p. 173
3. Bemis, p. 183

Chapter Thirteen
1. Madison Smith to William Jennings Bryan, Feb. 21, 1914
2. Munro, p. 373
3. Herring, p. 433

Chapter Fourteen
1. Munro, p. 306
2. Munro, p. 317
3. Herring, p. 441
4. Herring, p. 443

Chapter Fifteen
1. The Additional Protocol Relative to Non-Intervention:
Article I. The High Contracting Parties declare inadmissible
the intervention of any one of them, directly or indirectly,
and for whatever reason, in the internal or external affairs
of any other of the Parties.
The violation of the provisions of this Article shall give rise
to mutual consultation, with the object of exchanging views
and seeking methods of peaceful adjustment.
Article II. It is agreed that every question concerning the
interpretation of the present Additional Protocol, which it
has not been possible to settle through diplomatic channels,
shall be submitted to the procedure of conciliation provided
for in the agreements in force, or to arbitration, or to
judicial settlement.
2. Introduction to Perkins by Sumner Welles.

Intervention in Lebanon

Comparatively little has been written about the Lebanon intervention, but a good brief account is given by Richard J. Barnet, on pages 132–152 of his provocative *Intervention and Revolution.* World (An NAL Book), Cleveland, 1968. The author has also relied on contemporary accounts in the New York *Times* and on United Nations documents. The author's own book, *America and the Cold War,* by Richard J. Walton, Seabury, New York, 1969, contains, on pages 110–111 and 116–118, a brief account of the Suez Crisis and the simultaneous Hungarian crisis. A good discussion of the Eisenhower Doctrine is given in *The Revolution in American Foreign Policy,* by William G. Carleton, Random House, New York, 1967, pp. 328ff.

Chapter Sixteen
1. Carleton, p. 331
2. UN Document S/4007, May 23, 1958
3. UN Document S/4023, June 11, 1958
4. UN Document S/4040 and Add. 1, July 1, 1958
5. New York *Times,* August 13, 1958
6. *Foreign Policy Bulletin,* August 15, 1958

Again the Dominican Republic

Clearly the best account, on which the author has relied heavily, is that of Tad Szulc, the New York *Times* correspondent on the scene during most of the crucial weeks. His *Dominican Diary,* Delacorte Press, New York, 1965 and Dell, New York, 1966, gives a detailed, day-by-day report. Barnet's *Intervention and Revolution* gives a good brief account of the Dominican intervention on pages 153–180. Also useful is the account of another correspondent on the scene, Dan Kurzman, *Revolt of the Damned,* Putnam, New York, 1965. John Bartlow Martin tells his own story in *Overtaken by Events,* Doubleday, New York, 1966. Almost as crucial as the events in the Dominican Republic were those at the United Nations, which was the focus of the world-wide criticism of the United States intervention. This is discussed by the author in his *The Remnants of Power: The Tragic Last Years of Adlai Stevenson,* Coward-McCann, New York, 1968.

Chapter Seventeen
1. Barnet, p. 159
2. Martin, p. 129
3. Barnet, p. 161
4. Szulc, p. 25
5. Quoted by John Bartlow Martin in *Overtaken by Events,* p. 601
6. Szulc, p. 53

Chapter Eighteen
1. Szulc, p. 82
2. Szulc, p. 82
3. Szulc, p. 307

INDEX

ADAMS, HENRY, 54
Adams, John Quincy, 7
Aguinaldo, Emilio, 89–92
Alamo, 8–9
Alaska, and United States, 56
Alger, Russell, 76
Almonte, Juan N., 11
America, see United States
Ampudia, Pedro de, 26, 28, 29, 41
Arabs, 173, 174, 177, 184; see also Israel and Middle East
Argentina, 137, 157, 167, 207
Arias, Desiderio, 155, 157–160, 162
Arista, Mariano, 3, 17, 18, 19, 20
Arnold, Marty, 211
Asia, Seward on, 56
Aswan High Dam, 175, 176
Atkins, John Black, quote from, 80
Auguste, Tancrède, 141
Austin, Stephen F., 8
Atocha, A. J., 25

BACON, ROBERT, 113
Báez, Ramón, 158
Baghdad Pact, see METO
Bailly-Blanchard, Arthur, 143
Balaguer, Joaquín, 190, 191, 215
Baltimore, 69, 71–75
Batista, Maximiliano Americo Ruiz, 197
Bayard, Thomas F., 60
Beals, Carleton, 129–131
Bemis, Samuel Flagg, on Roosevelt's actions, 100, 103–104; on Nicaragua, 127; on Latin-American policy, 135–136; on Wilson's Mexican policy, 138–139
Bennett, W. Tapley, Jr., 196–197, 199, 202, 203, 205, 208
Benoit, Pedro Bartolomé, 204, 205
Benton, Thomas Hart, 34, 37, 39
Betancourt, Rómulo, 189–190

Birney, James G., 10
Blount, James H., 57
Bonnelly, Rafael, 192, 193
Bordas Valdez, José, 155, 156, 157
Borno, Louis, 149
Bosch, Juan, 192–199, 200, 210, 211, 214–215
Boston, 57, 72
Bowen, Herbert W., 101
Bowie, Jim, 8
Brazil, as mediator, 137, 157
Britain, see Great Britain
Bryan, William J., 155, 157, 159
Bryant, William Cullen, 38
Buchanan, James, 12, 45
Bull, Odd, 179
Bunau-Varilla, Philippe, 99
Bundy, McGeorge, 211–214
Bunker, Ellsworth, 211
Burr, Aaron, 7
Butler, Smedley, 124

CAAMAÑO DEÑO, FRANCISCO, 203, 208, 210, 213
Cabral, Donald Reid, 195–197, 199, 208
Cabrera, Manuel Estrada, 117, 120
Cáceres, Ramón, 152, 153
Calderón, Colonel, 208
Calhoun, John C., 5
California, U. S. and, 4, 12, 13, 15, 25, 30, 32–37, 38, 47, 50
Canada, U. S. and, 4, 12, 54, 59
Canal Zone, 99–100
Cannon, Lee Roy, 119, 121
Caperton, W. B., 144–147, 161
Caribbean, conditions in, 95–97; U. S. and, 95, 97, 101, 103–108, 109, 116, 118; see also countries of
Carleton, J. H., 42
Carnegie, Andrew, 53, 117
Carranza, Venustiano, 138
Carson, Kit, 35, 36
Castilla, 73, 75
Castro, Cipriano, 101
Castro, Fidel, 190, 200
Castro, José, 33
Central America, Federal Republic of,